D1486365

National Identity,
Nationalism and
Constitutional Change

Also by Frank Bechhofer

LIVING IN SCOTLAND: Social and Economic Change since 1980 (*with Lindsay Paterson and David McCrone*)

SOCIAL AND POLITICAL ECONOMY OF THE HOUSEHOLD (*ed. with Michael Anderson and Jonathan Gershuny*)

THE AFFLUENT WORKER: Industrial Attitudes and Behaviour (*with John Goldthorpe, David Lockwood and Jennifer Platt*)

THE AFFLUENT WORKER: Political Attitudes and Behaviour (*with John Goldthorpe, David Lockwood and Jennifer Platt*)

THE AFFLUENT WORKER IN THE CLASS STRUCTURE (*with John Goldthorpe, David Lockwood and Jennifer Platt*)

THE PETITE BOURGEOISIE: Comparative Studies of the Uneasy Stratum (*ed. with Brian Elliott*)

Also by David McCrone

LIVING IN SCOTLAND: Social and Economic Change since 1980 (*with Lindsay Paterson and Frank Bechhofer*)

NEW SCOTLAND, NEW SOCIETY? (*ed. with John Curtice, Alison Park and Lindsay Paterson*)

POLITICS AND SOCIETY IN SCOTLAND (*with Alice Brown and Lindsay Paterson*)

SCOTLAND – THE BRAND: The Making of Scottish Heritage (*with Angela Morris and Richard Kiely*)

THE SOCIOLOGY OF NATIONALISM: Tomorrow's Ancestors

UNDERSTANDING SCOTLAND: The Sociology of a Nation

National Identity, Nationalism and Constitutional Change

Edited by

Frank Bechhofer
Emeritus Professor of Social Research
University of Edinburgh, UK

and

David McCrone
Professor of Sociology
University of Edinburgh, UK

First published 2009 by
PALGRAVE MACMILLAN

Palgrave Macmillan in the UK is an imprint of Macmillan Publishers Limited,
registered in England, company number 785998, of Houndmills, Basingstoke,
Hampshire RG21 6XS.

Palgrave Macmillan in the US is a division of St Martin's Press LLC,
175 Fifth Avenue, New York, NY 10010.

Palgrave Macmillan is the global academic imprint of the above companies
and has companies and representatives throughout the world.

Palgrave® and Macmillan® are registered trademarks in the United States,
the United Kingdom, Europe and other countries.

ISBN-13: 978-0-230-22411-7   hardback
ISBN-10: 0-230-22411-3   hardback

This book is printed on paper suitable for recycling and made from fully
managed and sustained forest sources. Logging, pulping and manufacturing
processes are expected to conform to the environmental regulations of the
country of origin.

A catalogue record for this book is available from the British Library.

A catalog record for this book is available from the Library of Congress.

10 9 8 7 6 5 4 3 2 1
18 17 16 15 14 13 12 11 10 09

Printed and bound in Great Britain by
CPI Antony Rowe, Chippenham and Eastbourne

Contents

Figures

Tables

Acknowledgements

The editors are grateful to The Leverhulme Trust, and in particular to its Chief Executive, Sir Richard Brook and his trustees, for their financial support for the programme of research on which this book is based. We are also grateful to all our colleagues who worked on the programme, and especially to those contributing to this book. Last but not least, we are grateful to Moyra Forrest for the index and help with copy editing, and Margaret MacPherson who saw the book through to its production.

Notes on Contributors

Frank Bechhofer is emeritus professor at the University of Edinburgh where he was professor of social research until 1997. He is a Fellow of the Royal Society of Edinburgh. For more than a decade, he has carried out research with David McCrone on national identity and nationalism.

Ross Bond is a lecturer in sociology at the University of Edinburgh. He has published a range of work concerned with national identities, addressing the social factors which influence national 'belonging' and the significance of national identities for political attitudes, economic development and higher education.

John Curtice is professor of politics at Strathclyde University and a research consultant to the National Centre for Social Research. He has written widely on how the public across the United Kingdom has reacted to the advent of devolution in Scotland and Wales.

Kate Harrison obtained her Ph.D. in psychology from the University of St. Andrews. She was a research fellow investigating the nature and impact of Scottish national identity. She works as a UK Government statistician, running the Health Information Branch of Defence Analytical Services and Advice.

Jonathan Hearn is a senior lecturer in sociology, and also teaches the MSc in nationalism studies at the University of Edinburgh. Trained as an anthropologist, he has an interdisciplinary interest in understanding power and culture, and has specialised in the study of nationalism, identity, social change, civil society, moral discourse and Scotland.

Anthony Heath is professor of sociology at the University of Oxford, a Fellow of Nuffield College and co-director of the Centre for Research into Elections and Social Trends (CREST). He was elected a Fellow of the British Academy in 1992. His research interests cover social stratification, ethnicity, electoral behaviour and national identity.

Nick Hopkins, a social psychologist at the University of Dundee, is interested in the construction of group identities. He is particularly interested in how such constructions may be significant in the organisation of group behaviour.

David McCrone is professor of sociology and co-director of the Institute of Governance at the University of Edinburgh. He is a Fellow of the Royal Society of Edinburgh and a Fellow of the British Academy. He coordinated the research programme on constitutional change and national identity funded by The Leverhulme Trust on which this book is based.

Lindsay Paterson is professor of educational policy at Edinburgh University, and has written widely on Scottish education, politics and society. His recent work has paid particular attention to the connections among education, civic values and political leadership, relating these to changing conceptions of culture, democracy and the state.

Pille Petersoo studied the sociology of nationalism at the University of Edinburgh. In 2005 she was awarded Ph.D. for her thesis on 'The discursive construction of national identities in the media: Scotland and its others'. She is currently a senior research fellow at Tallinn University in Estonia.

Stephen Reicher is a professor and head of the School of Psychology at the University of St. Andrews. He has long been interested in the relationship between social identity and collective behaviour and has studied various topics related to this general issue, including crowd behaviour, intergroup hostility, leadership and national identity.

Michael Rosie is a senior lecturer in sociology at the University of Edinburgh. He specialises in the sociology of Scotland and in the mobilisation of national and religious identities. His book *The sectarian myth in Scotland: Of bitter memory and bigotry* was published by Palgrave Macmillan in 2004.

1
National Identity, Nationalism and Constitutional Change

Frank Bechhofer and David McCrone

Introduction

Why write a book about national identity, and especially one about national identity in the context of constitutional change? National identity is one of the most basic social identities; it is also, in Michael Billig's term, banal. Most people in Western societies at least, hardly give it a second thought, not because it is unimportant, but because, quite literally, it comes with the territory. Being a 'citizen' makes you French, Spanish, Canadian, while some in these societies see their 'national identity' differently, as Breton, Catalan or Quebecois. But who are the British? We live in a state, the United Kingdom of Great Britain and Northern Ireland to give it its full title, which makes us 'British'. That is what it says on our passports.

What is the difference, if any, between being English, Scottish, Welsh on the one hand, and being British on the other? The easy answer is that people can be both, that being British is a sort of umbrella identity sitting loosely upon the older territorial identities of England, Scotland and Wales. Simply put, you can be both English and British, Scottish and British, Welsh and British; these may be seen by academics and the person in the street alike as nested identities, complementary, not contradictory, although in practice people sometimes see them as alternatives depending on context. However, over the last 20 years, there has been a steady decline in the number of people signing up to the view that such identities are nested. In our studies of national identity going back almost two decades, we have found that substantial numbers of citizens of this realm no longer think of themselves as British. Notably in Scotland and in Wales, and increasingly in England, more and more people give priority to what we might call for shorthand their 'national' identity over their 'state' one. In one part of the United Kingdom, Northern Ireland, issues of Britishness have a particular political meaning which relate to history and patterns of settlement which have no counterpart elsewhere in the British state. Not only do the people of the 'mainland' feel less need to proclaim that they are British, but they are subject to an even more fundamental puzzle.

One of the most striking features of the new century to date has been the rise of political parties in Scotland and Wales dedicated to loosening or even ending the ties that historically bound this island together. Nationalist parties are in power in devolved Scotland and Wales, as a minority government in the former and a junior coalition partner in the latter. Further, a party – Sinn Féin – dedicated to ending the union in Northern Ireland is also in coalition with its erstwhile unionist nemesis. What price the United Kingdom in *those* contexts?

That, however, is to see national identity as straightforwardly 'political'. As we shall see in this book, how ordinary people construe and articulate their national identity does not easily predict their politics, neither which party they vote for, nor their constitutional preference. People who deny that they are British do not, necessarily, vote for the nationalist parties dedicated to ending the British Union, nor themselves want that Union to end. Even the growing number of people in England who say they are not British are not, for the time being anyway, clamouring for 'an English parliament for an English people'. So what is going on? Are people hopelessly confused, or are things far more complex than they seem? We think the latter.

National identity is one of those concepts which seem to evoke different responses. On the one hand, there is the view that, quite frankly, there is little to say, for everyone has a national identity whether they like it or not. It is, in fact, conferred by the state in the form of nationality or citizenship; it is an add-on of being a citizen, not a distinct concept varying from person to person. We may debate how long it has been that way, but it certainly seems to be a central part of the apparatus of the modern state. Ernest Gellner pointed out that we are all nationals now, and that nationalism is the taken-for-granted ideology which binds us to the state, or, as he would have it, the nation. People fight and die for the nation – *pro patria mori* – with alarming willingness; *dulce et decorum est*, however, tongue in cheek. Why, Benedict Anderson asked, are people willing to die for their nation, but rarely for their social class? Those who would not die for their nation are remarkably few, and it is not because they have somehow been tricked into so doing. As Gellner observed, the size, scale and complexity of modern societies are such as to demand loyalty and identification with the state, through the medium of the nation. National identification becomes the *sine qua non* of citizenship. Because, as Gianfranco Poggi has pointed out, the modern state is a 'made historical reality', a 'purposively constructed, functionally specific machine' (Poggi, 1978: 95, 101), it needs to mobilise commitment through a national ideology; in other words, it is continuously faced with legitimising itself to its citizens, and it does so by and large because it stands for the nation; it is its constitutional expression.

From this theoretical perspective, national identity is taken as 'natural', as essential, but it is also seen as actively constructed by the state. Its taken-for-granted quality may serve the state well, but it has to be continually manufactured and sustained. It is not a once-and-for-all process. To some – but not Gellner – national identity is something of a con trick, worked by the state and its institutions to make the citizenry malleable and willing to do its bidding. This is the view that nationalism is a form of secular religion, and national identity our 'church' membership card. We belong whether we like it or not, and most of us like it. Hardly any of us question it.

This has led some writers to be sceptical of national identity, seeing it as a form of what Marxists call 'false consciousness', somehow not quite right as identities go, and certainly less 'real' than social class, gender, ethnicity, because from these certain clear-cut life chances derive. In a sustained attack on the national identity concept, Brubaker and Cooper (2000) argue that national identity is far too loose to have much analytical value. In their view, it can mean identification and categorisation, self-understanding and social location, as well as commonality, connectedness and groupness. As a concept it is too vague, internally inconsistent and unspecific.

We do not share this pessimism. We think it is time to recover national identity as an analytical concept. We do not find it helpful simply to treat it as a 'top-down' idea, as some kind of ideological cement in modern, complex societies, open to construction and manipulation by the state. Put simply, modern societies can no longer be described as 'nation-states' in which the political realm, the state, wraps itself in the cultural concept of the nation, such that the two become coterminous. We have grown so used to treating state and nation as synonyms that we forget that they belong to different realms, the political and cultural respectively. States may have several nations within them. They are multination-states. It is one of the criticisms of Gellner's work that if he is correct that the modern state has the power and capacity to manage nationalism as a secular ideology, it doesn't do it at all well. Across the Western world at least, the so-called nation-state suffers from what Benedict Anderson called 'the crisis of the hyphen', a growing inability to make the political and the cultural planes connect. The Israeli sociologist Yael Tamir commented: 'The era of the homogeneous and viable nation-states is over (or rather the era of the illusion that homogeneous and viable nation-states are possible is over, since such states never existed) and the national vision must be redefined' (1993:3). In fact, the nation-state strictly defined was always more of a political aspiration than a sociological reality, based on a claim that the cultural sphere – the nation – and the political realm – the state – coincided. As Daniel Bell aptly comments, the nation-state is 'too big for the small problems of life, and too small for the big problems of life' (quoted in McGrew, 1992:87).

National identity matters. In fact, it seems to matter more as time goes on, and not only because added fixes of 'nationalism' are required to hold the citizenry closer to the state precisely at the moment at which it can deliver less and less in a 'globalised' world. One of its most obvious manifestations is the emergence, or re-assertion, of substate nationalisms, of being Scottish, Welsh, Flemish, Quebecois, rather than British, Belgian or Canadian. These are interesting to us, not because we necessarily believe in their virtue – that is for electorates to decide upon – but because they provide imagined alternatives to the dominant national ideologies of the state itself. Why does that matter? Because it helps to make explicit what is usually taken for granted. From our perspective as social researchers, the existence of alternative and contested forms of national identity makes the varying accounts of their national identity, which groups of people give in different contexts, very revealing. As people struggle to grasp such tools of the social scientific trade as national identity, the alternatives they offer make their 'imagined' identity accessible to the outside observer. They frequently envisage their national identity by comparing themselves, sometimes implicitly, sometimes explicitly, with 'others'. This may be to assert similarity but they often express their national identity by contrasting it to that of others, by delineating who (or what) they are not.

Getting at national identity

In our previous work on national identity, we found the atypical and unusual a valuable analytical device. It took a novelist rather than a social scientist to put his finger on the issue. The Scottish writer Willie McIlvanney once observed, back in 1999 just before the first Scottish parliament was elected: 'Having a national identity is like having an old insurance policy. You know you've got one somewhere but you're not sure where it is. And if you're honest, you would have to admit you're pretty vague about what the small print means' (*The Herald*, 6 March 1999). What he seems to have been getting at is that most people will say they have a national identity, but they are usually unclear about precisely what it signifies. Such clarity dawns sporadically in specific contexts or while interacting with specific people. On the other hand, we can point to some groups where it is much more salient; because they are somehow peripheral to mainstream concerns or their claims to be 'national' are rejected by the majority or they are accused of not being 'loyal'.

When we, the editors, began our research on national identity in the early 1990s, we chose to study two 'elite' groups, one of Scottish landowners, and the other of arts managers who were in charge of Scottish national institutions in music, drama and the arts more generally. Clearly we did so not because they were in any way representative of the population at large, but because at the time many of them were accused in the media of not being fit and proper persons to be in charge of such 'national' icons, land and the arts. They were judged not to be fit because, the accusers said, they were not 'Scottish', but born in England in particular, and could not be properly trusted to speak for, or even properly understand, the nation.

The point of our focus on these groups was not because we went along with the accusations in any way, but because they presented us with two contrasting, ready-made and identifiable groups who were far more likely to have had to consider who they were and what they were doing. To return to McIlvanney's analogy, they were far more likely than most to know what the 'small print' said and to have evolved accounts of who they were. And so it proved. Virtually all had thought about national identity, their own and that of the institution in their charge, and were able to give quite sophisticated accounts. Much, for example, hinged around the significance or otherwise of birthplace, which we know from our surveys tends to be the taken-for-granted criterion used by the population at large. You are a Scot or English or whatever, because you were born in Scotland, England and so on. However, as many people told us, none of us choose where we are born; that's for our parents to decide. Choosing where you want to live, and investing time, knowledge and skill, and even money in order to contribute to the country of your choosing, seemed to many far more significant indicators of commitment, and hence 'national identity'. In other words, it had more to do with a process of identification, than a static sense of national identity over which you had little or no control.

'To identify' – the active verb – was deemed much more important than 'identity' – the noun, and signified a process of action and choice. Criteria other than birthplace could be put in the pot: your ancestry or parentage – the bloodline, if you like; what you were 'taken for' by others – accent and dress being two of the more obvious factors affecting this. In other words, if you spoke with what was thought to be a 'national' accent, or if you dressed in a 'national' way, then you had far more chance of being taken as 'one of us' rather than 'one of them', whatever your birthplace or parentage.

A couple of years later, we moved on from contestable people to contestable places. The literature on nationalism has many examples relating to borders and frontiers, where, by and large, those occupying – sometimes literally, as occupiers – debatable lands tend to be much more aware of who they are and who they are not. In the case of the former Yugoslavia, living on the border could be dangerous, and a 'frontier mentality' developed whereby those who lived there were more 'national' than the nationals. In these islands, on the other hand, there is only one serious, and contested, land border – between Northern Ireland and the Republic. One might make a case for saying that, historically at least, those from the 'mainland' who were settled in the north from the seventeenth century became vociferously more British than the people they left behind, overlaid as they were by religious, cultural and political differences.

How, we wondered, did people living in historically debatable land do identity? Even if a border was no longer contested, did simply living on a salient and at one time shifting border impact on people's sense of identity? Between England and Scotland lies Berwick-upon-Tweed, within the current jurisdiction of England but a town which had changed hands 14 times between Scotland and England up to the sixteenth century. We found that the people of Berwick related easily to issues of territorial identity, and most, within the old town of Berwick, or 'within the walls' as they still said, solved the problem of national identity by emphasising their Berwickness. There is in fact a ditty which captures this nicely: 'They talk about Scotland and England indeed; There's Scotland, and England and Berwick-upon-Tweed'. We found that claiming local identity was considerably more important than national, but that, if pressed, at the time more claimed to be English than Scottish. More than ten years on, the local media revisited the issue and ran their own opinion poll, this time showing that a majority of those answering thought Berwick should be in Scotland. Why? Had the good people of Berwick suddenly uncovered Scottish ancestors? The answer seems more mundane and the result of a process which was already evident in nascent form at the time of our study but had been accelerated by constitutional change. Ten years of a Scottish parliament had reinforced awareness that they lived on the border dividing two nations and, importantly, made the material differences between the Scottish and English jurisdictions more pronounced, with better quality educational, social and welfare services to the north. Berwick found itself a periphery on a periphery: the county of Northumberland was distant from London, and Berwick was peripheral to the more populous city of Newcastle where local power was located. The fact that the county of Berwickshire was in Scotland but the town of Berwick in England became an anomaly with growing political significance, especially as Scotland's nationalist government went out of its way to make welcoming noises.

What, one might properly ask, does studying contestable people or contestable places have to do with studying constitutional change as we then went on to do? The short answer is that such change seemed to us to present an opportunity, a context within which we could more effectively get at issues of national identity. To what extent, in other words, does constitutional change, notably creating a Scottish parliament, make people feel more Scottish (or possibly less); or was constitutional change driven by a prior increase in national feeling in Scotland? These are important issues which are dealt with in this book, although, as we have already indicated, our reason for creating the programme[1] had much more to do with the potential devolution had for raising the *salience* of national identity rather than changing or determining it. In other words, it set the context within which a study of national identity became timely; it gave the opportunity to get people to look out their national identity 'insurance policy' and possibly even examine the small print for us. Identity politics were on the agenda, and as Mercer pointed out: 'identity only becomes an issue when it is in crisis, when something assumed to be fixed, coherent and stable is displaced by the experience of doubt and uncertainty' (1990:43). We are not claiming that identity became 'an issue', that there was some identity crisis in Scotland or in England, but we were attracted to the context of heightened identity salience which devolution provided.

Researching national identity

How did we then go about creating the programme? Identity, including national identity, is not the preserve of any single social science discipline; it is plainly a political, sociological, cultural and psychological phenomenon, and more. Inevitably, and usefully, sociologists, social anthropologists, social psychologists and political scientists bring different perspectives to bear. Accordingly, our team was drawn deliberately from different disciplines, using a variety of methods and approaches. We were attracted to the possibilities of a combination of research perspectives and the triangulation of research methods – surveys, in-depth interviews, done singly or repeated at intervals to see whether people's opinions had changed, ethnographic studies of organisations, as well as case studies and laboratory experimentation such that key stimuli could be controlled and varied, and results measured more precisely. Not all the perspectives and associated findings are represented in this book, but we have tried as far as possible to give a flavour of their richness and variety.

We made no attempt to get all the researchers signed up to the same set of assumptions and approaches, for in many ways that would have defeated the purpose of our search for diversity. The editors were, however, the prime movers in this research programme, and to a large but not exclusive extent gave the programme its underlying rationale. This is worth spelling out more explicitly. In our previous work, we were attracted by the performative and presentational aspect of identity, and symbolic interactionism, especially as manifested in the distinctive and groundbreaking work of Erving Goffman was an early influence. Goffman took the view that identity was a tactical construction designed to maximise player advantage. We are less concerned with identity as a tactical issue but have developed further the idea from Goffman that it involves claims, the receipt of claims and the attribution of identity characteristics to others on the basis of what the audience is able to perceive. One of the obvious implications of this approach is that people have more control over and 'play' more with aspects of identity than a top–down approach might imply. Our research on landed and arts elites, for example, suggested that actors have considerable capacity to construct and negotiate national identities. Thus, presenting oneself as Scottish, English, British or whatever is a matter of meaning and mobilisation involving actors and audiences, as well as an ability to read signs of identity. In other words, there is a complex matrix involving how actors define themselves, how they attribute identity to others and how they think others attribute identity to them. This moves us away considerably from the view that national identity is handed down from on high as tablets of stone. Rather, it confers much more negotiating and mobilising power on the actors themselves. This is not to imply that individuals freely and without constraint can make it up for themselves as they go along. It was Stuart Hall (1992) who pointed out that identities are constituted *within*, not outside, representations. He comments: 'we only know what it is to be "English" because of the way "Englishness" has come to be represented, as a set of meanings, by English national culture' (1992:292). What we have here is a good example of the interplay of social structure and social action, the former emphasising the constraints on individuals in the interests of social order; the latter emphasising the capacity of social actors to shape the world around them – society as the creation of its members, as it were. The concept of identity, therefore, can be seen as the hinge between structure and action. People are neither extemporising actors on a stage, making it up as they go along, nor are they puppets dancing to the hidden strings of state and institutional power.

We have also found useful Anthony Cohen's concept of 'personal nationalism' which asserts the primacy of the actor as a 'thinking self' (1994:167). Our concern with the small-scale, personalised and negotiated nature of national identity drew us to Billig's 'banal nationalism', which argues that, for example, national flags 'melt into the background as "our" particular world is experienced as *the* world' (Billig, 1995:50). This seemed to us close to Ernest Renan's famous dictum that national identity involves a 'daily plebiscite', each individual asserting in action their national identity in a matter-of-fact, hence, daily, way. In the second chapter in this book, Steve Reicher, Nick Hopkins and Kate Harrison point to the capacities, the power, of national identities to shape how we see the world, and our capacity to act within it. They argue that identity definitions, far from being set in stone, may be redefined and reinvented.

This focus on the individual, the personal, means that our prime concerns are with how people 'do' identity, who they think they are, who they think others are, what kinds of people are thought to be 'like us' and 'not like us'. National identity also involves quite basic social, political and economic issues such as the legitimacy of public policies, matters of social inclusion and exclusion, prejudice and discrimination, whether we judge the actions of organisations to be in the 'national' interest, that is, the interest of the collective 'we', and whether we are willing or not to move away from 'us' and live among 'them'. In other words, we see identity as helping to organise social action in different ways. First, the *content* of identity affects the types of action which are seen as legitimate or illegitimate, the type of policies and projects which are endorsed or rejected, and the types of goals pursued. Second, the *boundaries* of identity will affect who is accepted as part of the community, and who is excluded as 'the other'. Third, the way identity is visualised affects which place one thinks of as 'home' and which place one sees as 'foreign'. We chose to examine these aspects of national identity through the prism of devolution as it developed across the Scottish–English divide in the first five or six years after the decision to create the Parliament. Constitutional change afforded the key critical context in which the nature of the claims to identities, and the way they are negotiated, are likely to change. Once more, the novelist Willie McIlvanney articulates it best: 'Identity, personal or national, isn't merely something you have like a passport. It is also something you discover daily like a strange country. Its core isn't something solid, like a mountain. It is something molten, like magna' (*The Herald*, 13 March 1999).

In the first place, then, we were strongly committed to finding out how individuals 'did' national identity, how such identities were carried, altered and used by people themselves. We did this in a number of ways. First of all, we tried to assess the general level of public opinion in both Scotland and England concerning how constitutional change was received, and how issues of territorial identity were negotiated around it. This meant establishing through surveys, as benchmarks, what people in the two countries thought. We have drawn on these surveys largely but not exclusively to answer questions such as are people in England becoming more or less English, as opposed to British? This matters hugely, because 85 per cent of the UK population lives in England. If they are shifting away from saying they are British to saying they are English, one wonders how great that withdrawal of identification can be without calling into question the survival of the British state.

A prior and more fundamental issue, however, is whether people in England make any distinction between what we have called state identity and national identity. It could be, for example, that calling oneself English as opposed to British is simply a change of label for what the English see as the same thing. Running alongside these territorial issues are 'ethnic' ones, for England's ethnic minority populations have to bring identity labels such as 'British' and 'English' into line with their own ethnic identities. These also reflect back onto the indigenous white population's own conception of themselves and others, which raises issues as to whether such claims are legitimate or not. The 'English Question', whether there indeed has been a rise in Englishness, either along with, or at the expense of Britishness, is addressed in this book by John Curtice and Anthony Heath, whose chapter on trends in national identity in England uses data from the British Social Attitudes series. Drawing upon different measures of national identity they explore whether there has been an increase in English national identity, and whether such a shift has social and political implications which give rise to specific political claims. While these two authors were not formally part of the research programme, they draw upon survey data specifically collected for the programme, as well as other British Social Attitudes data since the late 1990s. Ross Bond takes the relationship, if there is one, between national identities and political attitudes a stage further. His chapter has two main themes: first, that if nationalism is in essence political in nature, we might expect a close connection between the way people think of themselves in national terms and their views on how the country should be governed. We are dealing here not simply with which political party people support and identify with, but also their constitutional aspirations and beliefs, as well as how willing (or not) people are to trust the government of their choice. Bond's second set of issues concerns how much solidarity there is post-devolution across Scotland and England. If, for example, the peoples of the two countries have similar views about the best way of governing the other country, think both countries benefit in economic and social terms from Union, and have similar social and political values, then there is a *prima facie* case for saying that the state will survive. If, on the other hand, they diverge on how the state should be governed, considering there are grievances because one country or the other gets more than its fair share, as well as having different sets of values, then this would seem to be a much greater challenge to state cohesiveness.

The focus on the individual level was not confined to carrying out large-scale surveys. These are good at establishing benchmarks of public opinion, but less good at getting at what people mean by their responses. For that, we need more intensive interviews which allow people to explain in their own time and in their own ways what national identity means. Cross-sectional surveys also have their limitations because they are discrete surveys of different people, unlike the more powerful but extremely expensive longitudinal surveys which are of the same people surveyed at more than one time-point. There is also the issue of migrants who were born in one country and migrated to another. How do they manage issues of identity? Do they keep hold of, even intensify, their identity of birth and upbringing when they migrate, or do they seek to take on the new identity of their country of destination? Or, indeed, do they seek to find ways of accommodating both, by appealing to supranational identities, by saying, for example, that they are British, an identity which they assume is shared by the hosts? In their chapter 'Being Scottish', the editors, Bechhofer and

McCrone, use both quantitative survey material and qualitative interviews to make sense of what 'being Scottish' means both to people born
and living in Scotland and also to those who have migrated to England. Is
it in fact that important, and if so, to whom? Do people 'do Scottish' in
particular situations? Can people born in England and now resident
in Scotland become Scottish, and what is the impact of race and ethnicity?
Are some people going to find their claims to be Scottish more readily
accepted than others?

Thinking you won't be accepted if you go and live somewhere else
can be a barrier to mobility, and in their chapter, Steve Reicher, Nick
Hopkins and Kate Harrison report on social psychological studies in
which participants are encouraged to think of themselves in different
ways. In their experiments the salience of identities, notably Scottish
and English, is measurably increased or decreased. These experiments
allowed them to explore what happens when they vary the information
they give to participants about identity, and to assess how likely they
are to accept or reject claims from different people for inclusion. Such
techniques permit the exploration of people's assumptions about inclusion and exclusion with a degree of subtlety which may cast doubts on
some of the things people say in more overtly challenging situations.
Their studies reveal how identities shape perception and action, including who is seen as a member of the national community and who is not,
and on what basis. In other words, identity is less a matter of attitude
and more a matter of action, if and when circumstances arise.

There is however more to identity than what individuals think and
do. If we only focus on this aspect of identity, we miss important
dimensions, as well as run foul of the charge that if we only ask people
about identity, and they tell us about it, how can we be sure that it
really matters as people go about their daily lives? That is the value of
doing ethnographic research which is arguably a much more naturalistic research method than surveys and preferable in that regard even to
qualitative interviews. Can we be sure, for example, that in work and
organisational settings, matters of national identity will matter very
much? How does national identity work, if at all, as people go about
their daily business? Jonathan Hearn's chapter explores the nature, salience and consequences of national identity in the organisational setting
of a bank, in this case, the Bank of Scotland, which quite fortuitously
embarked on a merger with Halifax to form HBOS at the time of the
study. The bank found itself becoming the vehicle for Scottish national
identity at a time of major organisational and cultural change. As a
major economic player, the bank became the carrier of national identity

values for many of its staff, and as such teaches us vital lessons in how changes in the modern capitalist economy impact upon issues of identity. In situations where 'rationalisation' and amalgamation occur in the banking and commercial sectors, how does the language of nationality and locality get used and mobilised, if at all? The point about studies such as these is that they illuminate in a naturalistic setting just how relevant or irrelevant national identity can become. In other words, organisations themselves are carriers of national identity, or sites where issues and conflicts of such identity are played out.

There is a related question: from where do individuals get their sense of identity? Stuart Hall's comment that identities are constituted within representations is relevant here. Just as there are private organisations, such as the bank, which might come to be carriers of identity, at least for some members of its staff, so public institutions are bearers of identity, *a priori* perhaps to a greater degree. In this book, we explore two such institutions: universities and the media. Lindsay Paterson explores the role of universities in Scotland, although they also have this role in England and Wales, in educating leaders of civil society. Indeed, a key component of governance in the United Kingdom in the twentieth century has been the informal division of power between the central state and the institutions of civil society. The relative autonomy of civil society in Scotland and Wales is one of the key reasons why there is a sense of distinct national identities, for a long time nested within but independent of British identity. Put simply, people in Scotland in particular long thought of themselves as Scottish because they were brought up and educated by Scottish institutions, governed and judged by a distinct legal system and, in the case of Presbyterians, worshipped in a Scottish way through a Scottish national church. The question then becomes not what has made Scots feel Scottish, but why they seem to have downgraded their sense of being British. Education systems, and in particular universities, have been central to nationalist movements not only in these islands (including Ireland) but in the rest of Europe. Paterson argues that the relationship between formally 'British' universities and nationalism is unusual in this respect. Each country, England, Scotland and Wales, developed distinctive features of university education which had a central role in forming the professional classes. This quasi-autonomy helped to shape the 'national' agendas in each country, and with it heightened the role of civic leadership, especially when universities came directly under the auspices of a devolved government at the end of the twentieth century. National identity is carried by education systems which instruct people in how to be 'national', partially forging the link between identity and culture, as well as shaping the relationship between universalistic values embedded in education, and those deemed to be attached to a particular nation.

If education systems, and universities in particular, are important institutional carriers of national identities, then the same can be said for the broadcasting and print media. News media in particular are assumed to reproduce 'national' culture, reporting 'home' events to a 'domestic' audience. The media help to frame what it means to be 'national' by reporting, or not, events in a particular way and using key descriptors. In their chapter 'Drifting Apart?', Michael Rosie and Pille Petersoo focus on how news is 'framed' and the degree to which it flags a national readership or audience. They examine the content of the news and its national 'habits', as well as the production of news agendas and contents. What seems to be happening post-devolution, they argue, is that news agendas within the United Kingdom are fragmenting. Thus, Scots can read and watch and listen to news about Scotland, but receive less information about Welsh, English and Northern Irish current affairs through their media. The same seems true for people in England. One might ask: if there is no unified public media space, can the United Kingdom cohere in any meaningful way? Public institutions like the universities and the media have the power to refract social and political processes through a 'national' prism, and in an increasingly diverse United Kingdom, have the capacity not simply to reflect national identity but to amplify it. The key point is that public institutions themselves are crucially involved in the process of producing and negotiating national identity, and refract these back to the population as a whole.

In conclusion

We live in times of heightened awareness of 'national identity' in the United Kingdom. Politicians and the media judge it to be of such social and political consequence that they give speeches, write lengthy articles and pronounce *ex cathedra*, and generally in the absence of hard data, on the future of being British, Scottish or English in the light of social and political change. The tercentenary in 2007 of the union between Scotland and England provided commentators with a suitable peg on which to hang debates about whether the United Kingdom in its present form will continue. The decade between 1997 and 2007 in particular was a period of major social and political change in the United Kingdom, with pressure in Scotland as well as Wales to devolve political control away from Westminster and towards the two national capitals of Edinburgh and Cardiff. The ramifications and implications of these changes are still being worked through the system, and no one can say where they might end. The general assumption is that the rise in nationalism in its broadest sense is fuelled by changing national identities. It is widely accepted that devolution was driven by people in Scotland and Wales thinking of themselves in 'national' terms (i.e. as Scottish or Welsh) rather than in 'state' terms, that is, as British. There is also the possibility that setting up a Scottish parliament, albeit one within the United Kingdom, has itself in turn made people feel more Scottish.

This book, then, reports on some of the key findings of the major and unique research programme funded by The Leverhulme Trust just at the point at which devolution in Scotland (and Wales) became a fact of political life. The programme continued until the middle of the first decade of the new century, thus covering the first crucial years of devolution on the British mainland. The book focuses on some of the key issues of our day: how people in Scotland and England 'do' national identity; whether devolution has had much impact on how they see themselves in national terms; the relationship between national identities and the rise of nationalism; whether any of these changes challenge the British state by undermining what it means to be British. It also examines how devolution is related to changes in education and the media, and how changes in the economy have impacted on national identity.

The book has two related aims. It seeks to make a significant contribution to understanding the impact of major constitutional change in these islands. Whether or not the United Kingdom will continue in anything like its current form is an open question; no one can be sure where any of these changes will lead. It seems to us just as plausible to say that the United Kingdom will continue in an amended form, as it is to say that it will cease to exist. No one can say what shape it will be in, say, in ten years', never mind 50 years' time. The aim of the book, however, is not simply to make a contribution to a current political debate. It also seeks to make much better sense of 'national identity' as a concept. Richard Jenkins (1996) commented that the study of national identity is 'perhaps the best device that I know for bringing together "public issues" and "private troubles", and encouraging us to use one to make sense of the other'. We acknowledge this allusion to C. Wright Mills as being one of the central tasks for social scientists, and intend that our work on national identity makes a critical and informed contribution to one of the most important issues of our times.

Note

1. The research programme 'Constitutional Change and National Identity' was funded by The Leverhulme Trust from 1999 to 2005, involving studies of national identity by an interdisciplinary group of social scientists using a variety of research methods. Full details and findings are available at http://www.institute-of-governance.org/forum/Leverhulme/TOC.html#ident.

Bibliography

Anderson, B. (1996) *Imagined communities: Reflections on the origin and spread of nationalism*. Revised edn. London: Verso.

Billig, M. (1995) *Banal nationalism*. London: Sage.

Brubaker, R. and Cooper, F. (2000) Beyond 'Identity'. *Theory and Society*, **29**, 1–47.

Cohen, A. P. (1994) *Self consciousness: An alternative anthropology of identity*. London: Routledge.

Gellner, E. (1983) *Nations and nationalism*. Oxford: Blackwell.

Goffman, E. (1973) *The presentation of self in everyday life*. New York: Overview Press.

Hall, S. (1992) The question of cultural identity. In S. Hall, D. Held and T. McGrew (eds) *Modernity and its futures*. Cambridge: Polity Press.

Jenkins, R. (1996) *Social identity*. London: Routledge.

McGrew, A. (1992) A Global Society? In S. Hall, D. Held and T. McGrew (eds) *Modernity and its futures*. Cambridge: Polity Press.

Mercer, K. (1990) Welcome to the jungle: Identity and diversity in post-modern politics. In J. Rutherford (ed.) *Identity: Community, culture and difference*. London: Lawrence and Wishart.

Mills, C. Wright (1959) *The sociological imagination*. Oxford University Press.

Poggi, G. (1978) *The development of the modern state*. London: Hutchinson.

Renan, E. (1882) What is a nation? Reprinted in H. K. Bhabha (ed.) (1990) *Nation and narration*. London: Routledge.

Tamir, Y. (1993) *Liberal nationalism*. Princeton: Princeton University Press.

2
Identity Matters: On the Importance of Scottish Identity for Scottish Society

Stephen Reicher, Nick Hopkins and Kate Harrison

Introduction: Burns, bread and butter

Not long ago, we attended the launch event for a new raft of educational qualifications aimed at police officers and police staff. The core of the presentation was a necessarily dry outline of the various pathways by which different staff could acquire different levels of qualification from diplomas to degrees to doctorates. This was not stuff to quicken the pulse.

However, the event began very differently. A lone drummer stood in silhouette behind a screen at the front of the lecture theatre. His beat was joined by the sound of pipes. The sound rose to an almost deafening crescendo as six pipers in full Highland dress marched into the room and stood playing in the aisles that cut through the audience. After they left, to prolonged applause, the meeting was addressed by the Scottish Minister for Justice, Kenny McAskill. He spoke in some detail of Scottish football and of expatriate Scottish communities in the United States. He told us how the Mexican word for an American, gringo, was a corruption of the marching tune 'green grow the rushes oh' sung by the Scots–Irish troops at the Alamo. He talked with pride of Burns and of the Burns statues that can be found in so many US cities – he even confided his plan to write a book on Burns statues when he retires from politics. But above all, he spoke of Scottish values. Of positive Scottish values: 'what we are rather than what we are not'. And at the core of these values was a belief in education. This value, he insisted, was exemplified by the topic of the day. And so, the minister concluded, he was proud to support the new Scottish policing qualifications.

The question for us is how we should see the relationship between the two parts of the meeting. Do pipes and kilts and Rabbie Burns have anything to do with pathways to Scottish Qualifications at levels 5–11? Is all the tartanry just so much froth on the cold hard business of the day? Or is the detailed educational machinery the reflection and realisation of a distinctively Scottish view of the world. In more general terms, did Scottishness make the difference? Does identity *matter*?

It should be clear from the tone of this book as a whole that we think that the answer to this question is an emphatic 'yes', and in this chapter we shall seek both to justify our confidence and also to explain the various ways in which identity impacts upon what people do and the sorts of worlds we live in. However we need to start by acknowledging that there are many people and many academics – probably the majority – who would disagree. Indeed, the dominant approach in the social sciences regards people as rational actors who approach the world as a balance sheet of profit and loss and who always choose those options which maximise their profit. When all the smoke and the mist and the noise drifts away, people ultimately act in terms of self-interest. In more popular terms, you can talk all you like of other things, but in the end, it's the economy, stupid! To be more parochial, the impact of a devolved parliament in Edinburgh is to be measured in its effects on the economy, the structure of the labour market and the institutional arrangements which regulate such things. Equally, matters like Holyrood elections and independence referendums will be decided on 'bread and butter' issues like what happens to wages and jobs and house prices and not whether there is a St Andrew's Day holiday or a Scottish entry to the Eurovision song contest.

Of course, going back to ancient Greece, it has long been argued that people may not always live up to the demanding standards of rational calculation. In particular the uneducated or those gathered together in the mass may lack (or lose) their capacity for judgement and become prey to demagogues who wave the flag in front of them, flatter their prejudices and arouse their passions. In such circumstances people may do extreme things in the name of the nation or some other collectivity (their religion, their team or whatever). When sufficiently inflamed, people can act against their self-interests. They can be roused to kill and even to sacrifice themselves for their country. *Dulce et decorum est pro patria mori* (it is sweet and honourable to die for one's country) to quote the old lie.

Putting these two perspectives together, it seems that we are left with an unenviable choice between either denying the impact of identity on human behaviour or else seeing identities (collective identities in particular) as a source of emotion and error. Identity might sometimes be of importance, but it shouldn't be, and one should seek to minimise its impact.

In this chapter, we will outline a very different position. It is not only that we deny both that identity is irrelevant *and* that it substitutes passion for reason. We reject the very dichotomy which underpins these views. That is, we don't see rationality and emotionality as opposites such that the more one has of the one, the less one will have of the other. Indeed, we see the two as interdependent and as mutually implicated in goal-directed human behaviour. To be rather less cryptic about it, if we are to decide what to do in the world, we need both to have a sense of what the world is like along with what impact our decisions will have on it and also to have a sense of what matters in the world along with what sort of outcomes we value. Without both *knowing* and *feeling*, we would either have an idea of where we are but no idea of where we want to go, or else a sense of where we want to end up but no sense of how to get there. In either case, we couldn't behave in a meaningful way.

To take the argument one step further, identity is the psychological process which brings these two elements together and makes behaviour meaningful. To adopt an identity (say, 'I am Scottish') is to tell me where I stand in the world: I live in a world of nations, with a specific relation to the English, the Irish, the Americans and so on. It is also to tell me what matters in this world: both through a concern with the fate of my country and with the values deriving from my Scottishness. It is with reference to my identity that I can evaluate good and bad, success and failure – and hence that I feel happy or angry, exhilarated or deflated. To put it slightly differently, identity is neither rational nor emotional. It does something more important, namely to provide the grounds for our rationality and emotionality.

We shall presently show how this operates in the case of Scottish identity – and hence explore the importance of Scottishness for Scottish society. But, first, we need to say a little more about the nature of identity and identity processes.

Social identity and social action

Identity is everywhere in our society. It is hard to pick up a newspaper or listen to the television without encountering the ceaseless interrogation of who we are. The situation is similar in the academic world where the term identity cuts across multiple disciplines from psychology and sociology to politics and anthropology. Recently the prime funder in this area, the Economic and Social Research Council, organised its largest ever programme of research on 'Identities and Social Action'. Our own work was funded as part of a grant of over a million pounds from The Leverhulme Trust to study the impact of devolution on Scottish identity. So if identity is worth so much money, what on earth is it?

On the whole, we tend to think of our identity in the singular as if we have but one identity. And yet, if one asks anyone to answer the question 'who am I?', one will get many answers. What is more, while some of those answers might refer to our personal characteristics ('I am tall'; 'I have blue eyes'; 'I am shy'), others will refer to our group memberships ('I am a Catholic'; 'I am a woman'; 'I am Scottish'). In other words, as social psychological research has shown, identity (see Tajfel, 1978; Turner, Hogg, Oakes, Reicher and Wetherell, 1987) is not a thing but a system and that system operates at different levels of abstraction.

Notably, we have a *personal identity* which defines what makes us unique as individuals compared to other individuals ('I' vs. 'you') and a *social identity* which defines what makes our group unique compared to other groups ('we' vs. 'they'). We all belong to a range of groups, so different social identities will be operative (or 'salient' to use the technical term) in different contexts: at Church, religious identity will be salient; at an international game against the auld enemy, Scottish identity will be salient, and so on).

The recognition that we have multiple selves means that, whenever anyone refers to 'the self', we must always ask 'what self'. The same for any 'self' related term: self-esteem, self-efficacy, self-regard or whatever. For instance our esteem for ourselves as individuals may be different from our esteem for ourselves as Scottish and will also derive from different sources. We might feel quite miserable as regards our personal self at the same time as a victory at Twickenham or Wembley makes us feel good about our Scottishness. Perhaps the most radical implications of this relate to the term 'self-interest'. Often, when rationality is defined in terms of acting in terms of one's interest, the 'self' part of the term is hidden. But it needs to be made explicit so we can, as we must, ask 'what self'. And once we do, it becomes clear that our interest as an individual, or as a Scot, will differ. We will return to this issue, but for now we simply want to underscore the point that if rationality is a function of interest, and if the nature of interest depends upon the nature of the self, then selfhood necessarily defines the terms of rational action.

In all these matters of self and identity, psychology (as well as a plethora of self-help books and magazine articles) has tended to concentrate on the personal level of analysis. From economists who presuppose that the self of 'self-interest' is the lone individual, to the countless magazine articles and 'self-help' books which obsess over our personal relationships with others at work or in the bedroom, self means 'I', not 'we'. However it is the latter – our social identity – which determines how we relate to others in the broader society, how we act together with others in ways that sometimes create social conflicts, sometimes serve to create or change our social world. It is our social identities, in other words, that are relevant to societal and political realities. It is therefore social identity which shall concern us here, and it is the nature of social identity processes which we need to elaborate.

The starting point for social identity research is that the shift from individual to group behaviour is underpinned by a psychological shift from personal to social identity. That is, we start to act together to the extent that we think of ourselves as members of a common social category. To put it more strongly still, social identification is the *psychological* mechanism that makes group behaviour possible (Turner, 1982). We stress 'psychological' because, of course, there is a host of structural and ideological factors which influence whether we do think of ourselves in terms of group identity (Scottish identification, for instance, derives from a historical legacy and present reality of distinctively Scottish institutions and a distinctively Scottish set of cultural resources), but equally the impact of these factors depends upon whether they affect our collective self-definitions.

Next, once a social identity is salient, it becomes a prism through which we view ourselves and others in the world. The fact that we view others in terms of their group membership – that is, the fact that we stereotype outgroups – is hardly news. But the fact that we also self-stereotype ourselves is rather more interesting and also more far-reaching in its consequences. As a group member, that is, we define ourselves in terms of the values, norms and beliefs that define our group. What is more, we conform to these collective understandings. That means that, insofar as we have multiple identities that are relevant at different times and places, the nature of our behaviour will likewise change. In the lecture theatre I conform to academic values of objectivity, of being dispassionate and conveying the evidence. At the political rally, by contrast, my behaviour is underpinned by values of loyalty, of passion and of partisanship. I am most unlikely to declare 'well, looked at objectively, the rival candidate really does have more consistent policies than ours'.

But it is important to note that identities are not like a set of rigid rules or scripts which we follow like robots. They are more akin to frameworks that guide our interpretation of the world. To be Scottish or a socialist or a woman is to say what counts in the world, what we should be bothered about and what doesn't really matter. This is illustrated in a study we did a number of years ago (Levine and Reicher, 1996) where we took female Physical Education (PE) students and then made salient either their gender identity or their subject identity. We then asked them to evaluate different medical conditions and say how serious they are. When defining themselves as women, they were much more concerned with disfigurements like facial scarring since that would threaten the gendered concern with appearance. However, when thinking of themselves as PE teacher trainees, their concern was with disorders that made them excessively vulnerable to knocks and collisions since that would threaten the professional concern with physicality.

There is one more general consequence of social identification which we need to explain before addressing issues concerned specifically with Scottish identity. That is, when a set of people assume a common social identity, they don't only take on a shared set of values to guide their behaviour. The relations between group members are also transformed in such a way as to allow them to work together effectively in order to realise their aims.

To illustrate this contention (see Reicher and Haslam, 2009 for a review of the literature) let us start with a rather basic example. We simply divided people into two groups on entirely trivial grounds (allegedly, whether they overestimated or underestimated the number of dots in a complex pattern – although to be absolutely sure there were no differences between groups, we actually divided them randomly). People were then told that they were to have a conversation with another person and all they were told about this person was whether they were in the same group (the ingroup) or the other group (the outgroup) as themselves. They were asked to prepare the chairs for this conversation so as to be comfortable. We then measured the distance between the chairs and found that, with an ingroup member, they are placed about 20 per cent closer (Novelli, Drury and Reicher, 2009). This provides a stark illustration of the fact that we feel more comfortable with ingroup members, we are more willing to be intimate with them and we are prepared to be close to them not only physically but also psychologically. The research shows, for instance, that we are more likely to trust and respect others when we see them as sharing our social identity.

This 'transformation into intimacy' among group members is not only a matter of sentiment. It can take important tangible forms. And to illustrate this, let us use another simple but stark example. In this study we took Manchester United football fans (Levine, Prosser, Evans and Reicher, 2005). In a first variant, we stressed their club identity before asking them to go and do a task in another building. As they walked there, they saw someone run along, fall over, and seemingly hurt their knee. This person was either wearing a Manchester United shirt, a Liverpool shirt or an ordinary red T-shirt. In this situation where the Manchester United shirt was worn (that is, the 'victim' was a fellow ingroup member) almost every participant gave help. Where the other shirts were worn (the 'victim' was an outgroup member) help was almost never given. The message to take from this study is that ingroup members tend to be concerned for each other's fate and to give each other concrete support. In this way, they form an effective co-acting unit.

However there is another message to take as well. For, in a second variant of the same study, we repeated the procedure described above, but with one critical change. This time, we didn't stress the club identity of our Manchester United fans. Instead we stressed their identity as football fans. This time we found that they helped the 'victim' wearing either a Manchester United or a Liverpool shirt, but not the person wearing a non-football red shirt. Thus, people still direct their help to the ingroup member, but when the ingroup is more extended, our helping is directed more widely. Consequently, the way we define our ingroups and who belongs to them is crucial in terms of who is aided or ignored, included in the collective embrace or excluded from it.

If this seems a rather grand conclusion to draw from such a limited study, consider another more consequential example (see Reicher, Wolpert, Cassidy, Levine and Hopkins, 2006; for original documents, see also Todorov, 2001). Of all the countries under Axis control during the Second World War, only one, Bulgaria, successfully mobilised against attempts to deport its Jewish population to the death camps. Not a single Jew from the lands of old Bulgaria was taken away. When we looked at the arguments used to oppose the deportation, it was striking that the word 'Jew' was rarely used. Instead, the stress was laid on the fact that this was an attack on Bulgarian people. And when the word 'Jew' appeared, it was to stress just how Bulgarian these people were: 'Bulgaria's Jews … speak and think in Bulgarian … They sing Bulgarian songs and tell Bulgarian stories. Their private selves are modelled on ours … our sufferings are their sufferings, our joys their joys too' (cited in Todorov, 2001, p. 65).

In this case, solidarity was not a matter of substituting one (broader) identity for another (narrower) one, but rather a matter of extending the boundaries of the same (national) identity. There is a crucial lesson here, one that is critical to whether (and to whom) we are a 'walk on by' society or a society that welcomes and defends the marginal and weak. That is, the way we define the nature of our groups, and who is included or excluded by this definition, can literally be a matter of life and death.

So, to summarise the argument thus far, social identities tell us who we are and our place in the world, they tell us what matters to us and what we aspire to, they help people to coordinate their efforts in achieving their aspirations. Hence social identity is a source of social power which allows people to become agents who can make their own history rather than adapt to a history made by others. This makes social identities of critical psychological importance to the individual (we have, for instance, shown how having a strong social identity allows people better to cope with the world and is a source of well-being – see Haslam and Reicher, 2006). At the same time, social identities are of critical political importance for they define whether and in what way people will mobilise together to (re)shape society. In a phrase, social identities are *world-making things*. This makes the question of exactly how identities are defined in any given situation (both what category is salient, who is included or excluded from the category, and what values norms and beliefs are associated with the category) a matter of the greatest importance. But it is a matter that we shall postpone for now and return to later in our discussion of Scottish identity and why it matters for Scottish society.

The importance of Scottish identity

Identity and mobility

We have spent some time arguing why social identity matters in general terms. It follows from this that Scottish identity probably matters as well. But now let's look at some more direct evidence. In order to get the discussion under way, we will combine two themes that have already arisen in the course of this chapter. The one concerns the relationship between economic concerns and identity matters. It will be recalled that we do not see 'economy' as more important than 'identity'. Indeed we don't see 'economy' as counterposed to 'identity'. Rather we see identity as an underlying factor that feeds into economic behaviour. We will be looking at an aspect of this relationship, one which is slightly different to the claim that identities supply the values which determine how we calculate profit and loss, one which relates to our second theme – the relationship between identity and spatial behaviour.

We have looked at one small facet of this relationship – the fact that we prefer greater proximity with ingroup members. But there is growing interest in the rich and varied ways in which who we are relates to where we are and where we are allowed to go (Hopkins and Dixon, 2006). Indeed the notion of what sort of people fit in what sort of places is one of the major ways in which social relations (and social inequalities) in our society are maintained. The question of whether black people disfigure leafy suburbs is one of the means whereby racial division is maintained in post-Apartheid South Africa. The question of what sort of people render public spaces unsightly (drunks and tramps not wanted in beautiful ancient city squares) is one of the means by which democratic participation is regulated in our own society. But this link is not only a matter of how we are regulated by others, it is also a means by which we regulate our own behaviour: where we choose to visit and, as we will examine, where we choose to live and work.

This issue of labour mobility (another way of phrasing our interest) is, of course, critical to the well-being of a market economy. For the system to work as it is meant to, people have to be willing to move to where jobs are available and to be sensitive to inducements such as higher wages. A constitutional change, such as the establishment of a devolved parliament in 1999, may affect mobility by introducing different labour market regulations in different parts of the Union. However we also need to consider if it might have another effect – namely, if devolution impacts on Scottish identity, will it also affect the willingness of Scots to work in different parts of the United Kingdom? If it does, it is strong evidence that identity is much more than the froth on the devolution (and the independence) debate.

We investigated the relationship between Scottish identity and labour mobility choices using a combination of experimental and interview techniques. To start with the experiments (Reicher, Hopkins and Harrison, 2006), our basic set up involved giving young Scottish people a list of four locations, two in Scotland (Dumfries and Livingston) and two in England (Carlisle and Crewe), and then asking them a number of questions about each of them: how much they would be accepted by others if they moved there, how well they would fit in, the extent to which they would lose their identity by moving and, crucially, how much they would want to go there. In one set of studies, we kept the salience of national identity constant (using only people who identified highly as Scots) and manipulated the national salience of the towns of destination.

As can be seen from Figure 2.1, this was done by presenting a map of the British Isles either with or without the division between England

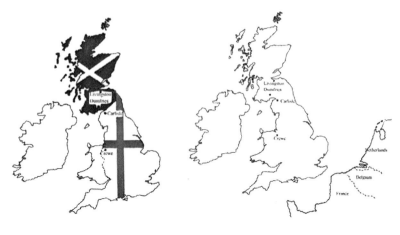

Condition 1: Borders salient   Condition 2: Borders not salient

Figure 2.1 Manipulation of national boundary salience in labour mobility experiments.

and Scotland imposed upon it (and hence with or without a reminder of which country each of the four towns was located in).

The results of these studies indicated that, when the borders were made salient, the preference for moving to Scottish locations over English locations was significantly greater. However, this was only true when considering a long-term move rather than a short-term placement. This is hardly surprising. For a limited period, going somewhere different may be interesting, exciting and even exotic (although it might be stretching things a bit to attach the term 'exotic' to Carlisle and Crewe). But when it comes to a choice of where one settles down and raises a family, difference acquires an entirely different meaning. It begins, at least potentially, to disrupt one's sense of belonging and feeling at home. Hence highlighting the difference by accentuating the national boundary begins to make one wonder if one could forge a successful life in 'foreign' towns. This interpretation is supported by the finding that, when considering a long-term move, making the border salient decreases one's sense that one will 'fit in' to English towns and this, in turn, renders them less attractive as locations. For those conversant with statistical language, 'fitting in' fully mediates the relationship between border salience and Scottish town preference.

In further studies, we have begun to look at the consequences of making different identities salient for our participants. So, this time, we again take young Scots but, instead of changing the salience of the border, we stress either their national identity (as Scots) or their generational identity (as young people). Drawing on our earlier discussion that difference can have several meanings, we suggest that different groups may value difference in different ways. Thus, while it might be more problematic in national terms, youth will put a far greater premium on new experiences and alternative lifestyles. Hence, we would predict that the preference for Scottish towns should be less when youth identity is made salient than when national identity is made salient – and this is what is emerging from our preliminary findings. Although, interestingly, it is not that 'youth' leads our participants to value Carlisle and Crewe more (again, it hardly needs saying that these are not usually the dream destinations for those in search of thrills and new experiences), but rather that they value Dumfries and Livingston less. These too are towns of limited appeal for young people, and when their Scottishness is no longer valued, there is not that much left.

There are two general points to be taken from these experiments. The one is that Scottish identity does indeed seem to impact on mobility decisions, because there is more to living than working and earning. The second, and possibly the more important, however, is that there is no automatic or fixed relationship between being Scottish and wanting to be in Scotland rather than, say, England. It entirely depends upon, first, whether people think of themselves in terms of their Scottish identity and, second, whether they think of locations in terms of whether they are in Scotland – and these things are not set in stone.

For all the criticisms that can be made of psychological experimentation (and there are many), one big advantage over other methods is that they show that the way we see ourselves (social identities) and the world (social representations) are variables rather than givens. They are open to manipulation – or rather (since, in ordinary language, the word 'manipulation' is replete with negative and totalitarian associations), they can be easily changed. Our conclusion, then, is not absolute ('Scots avoid England') but conditional to the extent that Scottish identity and national borders are made salient, then mobility to England will be restricted. The importance of that lies in its practicality. It doesn't present us with a fait accompli but rather tells us how to operate if we want to achieve certain outcomes such as promoting or restricting mobility. Experiments, that is, are valuable to the extent that they don't just describe how the world is, but instead elucidate processes that tell us what the world can be.

However, while experiments might be very valuable for examining the consequences of manipulating particular constructs (such as identity salience), they are not particularly good when it comes either to examining how things like identity are negotiated and constructed, whether they are actually relevant in real world contexts, and what they actually mean to people. This is where the interviews come in, for, even if they cannot demonstrate the systematic impact of identity, they do allow us to see whether identity considerations do come into play when people consider mobility issues. They also allow us to explore the various ways in which identity considerations feed into mobility decisions and, in particular, the way in which identity serves to shape the meaning of going to different places. Each method therefore has its strengths and weaknesses and neither is better nor worse than the other in any general sense. Each is more or less appropriate depending on the questions one is asking. However by combining the two, we are able to use the strength of each to cover the weakness of the other – a methodological strategy known as 'triangulation'.

We interviewed around 100 young Scots who were about to leave school and who therefore were faced with an important decision about where they would go and work. We explored a series of issues such as their sense of identity, particularly Scottish identity, their sense of meaningful boundaries within the United Kingdom, where they would feel at home, how they would feel about being in different parts of the UK and what actual mobility decisions they were planning to make. This, of course, yielded a wealth of information from which we only have space to draw out three points (Hopkins, Reicher and Harrison, 2006).

First, identity was a key topic around which issues of relocation were discussed. Moreover, when people talked about themselves as Scots, it certainly raised issues of how they would fit into English settings. They were concerned about such things as 'sticking out' because of their Scottish accents, being unsure of how others would react to them, and simply feeling ill at ease because of an uncertainty of how to do all the little things that one can take for granted in Scotland. As one young woman put it when talking of London (although she later made clear that her feelings referred to *English* city life in general), 'I never know what to say when I'm on a bus, or, like, do you ask the guy in the taxi before you get in? Or when you're in? Or just things like that remind you that you're not used to city life'.

Above all, though, the relationship between Scotland and England was conceptualised in class terms, with England as the 'posh' side. Those who thought about their Scottishness therefore worried that they would face not just problems of difference, but also problems of discrimination. In the words of one interviewee, 'if I went to an English place I might sound common'.

Second, Scottishness was not the only way that people viewed themselves, and difference was not always seen as a problem. Home is all very well, but it can be claustrophobic – especially where one's concern is less with staying Scottish than with developing into adulthood. A girl from Dumfries insisted that 'I want new people and I don't want a place that is going to be so similar in culture and attitude and personality to Dumfries. I want a change'. She continued, 'Life experience, you don't get life experience in Dumfries because it is so small. It is not so cosmopolitan. You don't – most people are so similar – you don't get a lot of really rebellious people or people who are extremes of anything'. For similar reasons, she didn't want to go to Glasgow University because all her friends were going, she would be surrounded by friends and would be locked into an old identity rather than being able to develop a new self.

Third, then, there is an added dimension to the richness of identity processes. People don't just shift identities from one context to another; they also shift in terms of whether they want to preserve or play with identity. We must beware of treating the self as an environmentalist treats an endangered species. Sometimes people want the freedom to be who they like when they like. They don't want to be trapped into a single identity and be forced to live up to it. And that leads to extra complexities in the relationship between mobility and identity. On the one hand, as we have just seen, young Scots want to leave Scotland in order to escape the networks that tie them down to their past selves. But on the other hand, in going to England, they might just find that they have leapt from the frying pan into the fire. Consider the following interchange from one of our group interviews:

Interviewee: I'd rather be a Scottish person in a Scottish university with lots of other Scottish people than a Scottish person in a university full of English people and hardly any other Scots.
Interviewer: Why is that? Because you'd feel you'd stand out?
Interviewee: Yeah. You'd be known as 'that Scottish girl' because there probably wouldn't be that many others there.

In other words, people may at times wish to stay in Scotland, not because they feel Scottish but precisely in order to avoid their Scottishness. We should not be surprised at such paradoxes and such complexities, for identity is a multifaceted thing that cannot be mapped onto behaviour in any simple way (this is the topic of our final section). But nor should we regard it as diluting our general message here. That is, in a host of ways – more than we imagined when we undertook our research – basic behaviours of fundamental importance to the state of the economy and society are inescapably bound up with questions of who we think we are and who we want to be.

Identity and society

Much of our discussion of mobility was focussed on relations between Scotland and England. Let us stick with this theme for a while, for it is clearly at the heart of contemporary debate about both the effects and the morality of national identity and nationalism. Every time an international competition comes along in which England is participating, Scottish politicians and the Scottish media (the English media as well) agonise about whom Scots should be supporting. Indeed, Kenny McAskill's insistence that Scots should look to what they are rather than what they are not (which we cited at the start of this chapter) can, in part, be seen as a veiled attempt to get beyond the obsession with endlessly comparing Scotland to England – and gaining satisfaction if 'we' are not quite as bad as 'they' are.

Our work suggests that people are quite right to be concerned with this comparison. For Scottish identity, as indeed for any social identity, who we are depends upon who we compare ourselves to (what we will refer to as the 'comparative context' – see Haslam and Turner, 1992). A number of years ago, we asked Scots to describe what it means to be Scottish after either describing the Greeks or describing the English (Hopkins, Regan and Abell, 1997). In comparison to the Greeks, Scots portrayed themselves as rather serious and hard-working, but the collective self-image that emerged in comparison to the English was much more friendly and laid-back. The importance of this, as should be clear by now, is that collective values shape collective action. To compare Scotland to England, according to this logic, is not only to affect what Scots are but also what they do.

More recently, then, we have begun to explore whether and how this might be true. We started by looking at the impact of comparisons upon the types of social issue that are taken seriously in Scotland – and, more particularly, how seriously Scots take the issue of racism (this at a time

Condition 1: North European comparison   Condition 2: English comparison

Figure 2.2   Manipulation of comparison countries in studies on the importance of racism in Scotland.

when the then Scottish Executive was running a prominent campaign to persuade people that Scotland is 'no place for racism'). We used what will by now be a fairly familiar method. Scots were told either that we were doing a study in Scotland and England, or else that we were doing the study in Scotland and other North European countries and this was underscored by putting different maps on the front of their response booklet in which people had then to say how serious a problem they considered racism to be in Scotland and how much priority there should be on efforts to tackle racism (see Figure 2.2).

Given that northern European (specifically, Scandinavian) countries have a reputation for tolerance, while England has a reputation for racial tension, we predicted that Scots would see racism in Scotland as a bigger problem in comparison to the former and a smaller problem in comparison to the latter – and that is what we found. When measured against the English, the attitude seems to be '*they* have got a problem, don't say *we* have got a problem' – an attitude which undermines the good work of the Executive by suggesting that there really is nothing to worry about. Or, to invoke biblical authority, we ignore whatever is in our own eye when we can invoke a larger beam in the eye of the other.

In another study, we altered the logic a little, looking at how the desire to challenge negative views that the English are seen to hold about the Scots may drive prosocial action (Hopkins, Reicher, Harrison, Cassidy, Bull and Levine, 2007). Thus, our Scottish participants were told either that the English thought them to be mean or else that the English thought them to be a soft touch. In an ostensibly unrelated incident, they were then given the opportunity to give to charity. In one variant the charity helped victims of violence in Scotland, in another, the charity helped victims of violence in Wales. What we found was that, when accused of meanness, Scottish people were prepared to donate more time, effort and money to charity, particularly the Welsh (outgroup) charity. This finding squares with the argument that helping in this situation is a statement designed to challenge English insults. If one helps one's own, that could still be explained away as just being introverted and clannish. But helping people from another country is hard to see as anything but generosity and hence is a far more effective way of disproving an accusation of being 'mean'.

The significance of this study is that it begins to turn round the relationship between the comparative context and identity. If the 'Greek' study and the 'racism' study show how our relationship to the English impacts on identity and on social action, this 'helping' study shows how identity concerns (notably, giving our group a positive standing) leads to actions designed to reconfigure our relationship to the English. Now let us take this argument a step further and address what is perhaps the most important issue in Scottish political life – the constitutional relationship to England. For over three hundred years now, this issue has been in almost constant debate, and the debate shows no signs of ending anytime soon. Should we remain part of the United Kingdom? Should we have a devolved parliament with greater powers? Should we opt for independence? The political debate is endless, but what determines what ordinary Scots think? They, after all, will be those who will now make the choice.

We argue that Scottish identity is critical to determining the fate of the Union, but not in a simplistic way. It has long been recognised that there is no direct relationship between identifying oneself as Scottish, voting for the Scottish National Party (SNP) or supporting an independent Scotland (e.g. Brown, McCrone, Paterson and Surridge, 1999). We have similar findings (Sindic and Reicher, in press). Our study shows that what counts is how people conceive of the impact of being in the Union (or of being independent) upon the ability to follow a Scottish way of life – that is to say, one based on Scottish values and beliefs. Where people consider that Scottishness can be better realised within the Union ('as an entrepreneurial people, we thrive as part of a larger market') they are against independence. Where they consider that it cannot and that Scottish identity is practically undermined in the Union ('individualist English values will always predominate over Scottish communal values in framing British policies') they will favour independence.

Here we return to a general point that we made about human action in general and identity processes in particular. Human beings do not act mechanically. We are not like extraordinarily sophisticated calculating machines, differing only from existing machines in complexity. We differ in kind. We are creatures who are constantly involved in making sense of our world and in interpreting what it means to us (Taylor, 1985). Identity, we have suggested throughout, is a necessary part of that enterprise. So it would be paradoxical and contradictory to suggest that identity itself supplies mechanical rules of behaviour – albeit different rules for different identities. The argument we have just made presents a very different vision of the relationship between Scottish identity and political behaviour. That is, Scottishness does not substitute for sense making, but rather provides the framework that is necessary for it to occur. We are able to evaluate independence by asking what effects it will have and how those relate to what (as Scots) we hold dear. The response depends upon precisely how we construe both the events themselves and also how we construe what Scottishness means – is it about entrepreneurship, about community or about other things besides?

This, in turn, takes us to a critical discussion that we have put off for a long time and can delay no longer. We have argued in general terms that identity definitions have important consequences for the individual and for society. We have shown a number of ways in which identity is of importance for the Scottish nation – to the extent of even affecting whether we have a separate Scottish nation. So how is identity defined? What is this intangible thing, Scottishness, which seems to have such tangible effects on our lives?

Defining Scottishness

On the whole, debates about the definition of identity tend to be couched in terms of identifying the criteria and the characteristics which best capture what it means to be Scottish or English or whatever. When it comes to defining true Scottishness, who is right: those who emphasise the rugged individualism of the entrepreneur or those who emphasise the caring and sharing of the community? And when it comes to defining the true Scot, should the emphasis be put on ancestry and birth, upbringing and accent or commitment and future plans? As soon as one enters the debate, it is hard to avoid getting into a terrible tangle. For instance, in 1999 when Scotland played England at football, the Wembley authorities decided to reserve just 5,000 tickets for Scottish fans. But how would they decide who was Scottish and how could they prevent Scots posing as English in order to get extra tickets. The debate was never sublime, but as it progressed it got more and more ridiculous. To cite one small extract from a long article in the *Guardian* newspaper: 'A Wembley spokesman said that if anyone rang the hotline with a Scottish name but had an English accent and lived at an English address then they would be sold a ticket. However, a caller with a Scottish name and English accent with an address in Scotland would not be sold a ticket'.[1]

Of course one can ask people what they think makes someone Scottish and also what defines Scottish identity. We, along with many of the other authors in this book have done precisely this. In particular, we have been interested in a rather attractive and inclusive vision that has been articulated by a number of prominent Scottish figures, notably by the current First Minister, Alex Salmond, in a speech to the Scottish National Party Conference in 1995: 'we see diversity as a strength not a weakness of Scotland and our ambition is to see the cause of Scotland argued with English, French, Irish, Indian, Pakistani, Chinese and every other accent in the rich tapestry of what we should be proud to call, in the words of Willie McIlvanney "the mongrel nation" of Scotland'. The implication is that anyone can be Scottish as long as they are prepared to argue Scotland's cause. Nationhood is therefore inclusive, a matter of commitment and of chosen destiny (what is sometimes referred to as a 'civic' definition) rather than something exclusive, over which one has no control, a matter of parentage and descent (an 'ethnic' definition).

To cut a very long story short, Scots don't reject such claims to Scottishness through commitment out of hand, but they are suspicious of them, especially when people want not only to be accepted in Scottish society but also to represent Scotland. In particular, they are concerned that anyone who can give up another national identity in order to be a Scot might equally give up their Scottishness and move on in the future. In a sense, such people threaten the very principle of nationhood and hence place their own as well as their national identity in question.

One might argue that people might not be entirely honest in what they say – although if anything, people are concerned to avoid accusations of racism and prejudice and therefore one might expect them to over- rather than underplay their preference for civic over ethnic definitions of nationhood (Wetherell and Potter, 1992). So, in order to address this concern, we ran some studies using a rather more indirect approach. These studies involved asking people to watch someone making a speech which involved some elements which clearly chimed with shared norms (e.g. valuing the land and environment) and some elements which clearly violated such norms (e.g. giving farmers control over access to the land). First, though, the speaker would emphasise his Scottishness and love of Scotland, but, in different conditions, that claim was based either on descent (ethnic variant) or on commitment (civic variant).

Based on the well-known finding that people will agree with ingroup members more than outgroup members until they deviate from group norms, at which point ingroup members will be rejected more than outgroup members (Marques, Yzerbyt and Leyens, 1988), we reasoned that the more someone is seen as an ingroup member, the greater will be the discrepancy in agreement with the speaker between the normative and counter-normative phases of the speech. In order to measure agreement, we used the type of 'audience response' technology that political parties often use in order to gauge opinion. People watch the speech holding a little dial in their hand which they can turn to give a real-time measure of their response. The responses are fed into a computer which can then provide a graph of the results and analyse the differences between the two variants of the study. These results support the argument that ethnic claims to Scottishness retain more purchase than civic claims. A Scot by descent is more likely to plummet in popular support when violating group norms than a Scot by commitment. It might seem a paradoxical affirmation to accept someone as a group member through rejecting their arguments. However we expect more of ingroup members: anger has greater significance than indifference.

So it seems that the arguments of Salmond and others remain more an aspiration than a reality. But that is not to say that we should ignore their words or their aspirations, for in many ways they tell us something far more interesting and important about identity than all our interviews and all our experiments. They also tell us something fundamental about the nature of political influence and how leadership works.

In order to understand these various implications, consider why these politicians talk of an inclusive Scottish nation. In part, it doubtless has to do with genuine principle. For all our contemporary cynicism about politics, there is ample evidence that our representatives themselves need to believe in the legitimacy of their policies and principles in order to convince us, the electorate, of the same (Barker, 2001). Nonetheless, all the principles in the world will amount to little if one does not have the office to implement them. Hence politicians also have to couch their policies in ways that appeal best to the widest possible proportion of electors. That is where a definition of national identity that (at least potentially) includes the entire population is so useful. It allows one to constitute one's entire intended audience as a single group, to pose one's policies as representing the interests of the entire group and to pose oneself as representative of the whole group.

Here is the key point. Precisely because identities constitute collectivities and shape how they act – as we put it above, because they are world-making things – those who wish to shape the world (politicians, activists, leaders of all stripes) will have an interest in harnessing identity to their projects. They will seek to define 'who belongs' and 'who we are' in such a way as to make their proposals the concrete manifestation of the shared identity. In a phrase, effective leaders need to be effective *entrepreneurs of identity*. (For a more detailed exposition of this argument and for more examples of our ensuing points, see Reicher and Hopkins, 2001.)

The first implication of this argument is that the category one uses needs to be matched to the audience one seeks to address – and since all politicians seeking office are appealing to the same audience, it is likely that they will appeal to the support of same category. More immediately, all politicians seeking support from the entire population of Scotland are likely to constitute themselves as Scots speaking to their audience as Scots. That is something we have found consistently in nearly two decades of studying political rhetoric in speeches, public meetings and private interviews.

All politicians from all major parties defer to no one in their Scottishness. Whether unionist, devolutionist or separatist they speak for the nation unto the nation. Irrespective of policy, they are all nationalists. In terms of using Scottishness, and defining Scottishness inclusively, the distinction is not between parties or ideologies, but rather between those who pursue electoral vs. non-electoral strategies. The latter don't need to mobilise the majority for their votes but can be content to mobilise a minority for direct action. Hence they can be content to employ more restrictive categories, whether they be narrow ethnic definitions of nationhood on the right or narrow class definitions of the people on the left.

Where the elected politicians do differ, however, is in the meanings and values they associate with Scottish identity. Because they are trying to mobilise the same people to support different proposals, so they ascribe different content to the same categories. In each case, though, the attempt is to establish consonance between proposal and identity: 'it is our policies which reflect what we Scots truly value and believe in'. So we find the SNP extolling the qualities of independence which define the Scot from the time of Bannockburn to this day. We find Labour politicians quoting Burns' 'A man's a man for a' that' in order to insist that equality and a belief in public services mark the Scottish character. We find Conservatives insisting that the self-help of small communities and the self-made entrepreneurial 'lad o pairts' constitute the 'real' Scotland. Indeed one prominent Tory complained to us that for all that the Scots hated Thatcher – perhaps, he reflected, because they don't like to be told what to do by a woman – they failed to see that they are really natural Thatcherites.

So, to return again to a question we posed earlier, which of these characterisations is right? What is the true Scot? Does Scottish identity make Scotland naturally SNP, Labour or Tory? To ask these questions is precisely to fall into the politicians' trap and to misunderstand the true nature of social identity. If identity were simply a description of the present, then it might make sense to ask questions about which description is more or less correct. After all, there is but a single present reality. But if, as we are arguing, identities are tools designed to produce the future, and different versions of identity are oriented to producing different futures, then the question of accuracy no longer makes sense.

'Which is more effective'? Yes, that is a fair question. 'Which is more practical'? That too makes sense. Even 'which is more plausible?' is a reasonable query, since our vision of what we might be is often rooted in shared understandings of what we have been. But 'which is more accurate?' that is to confuse what we want Scotland to be with what it is. It is to take the politicians' vision as a self-evident reality. It is therefore to lose a clear-sighted choice over what we might want our own future to be.

Conclusion: Understanding the importance of identity

In a misogynistic fit, the Roman poet and spurned lover Catullus once wrote of women's words as written on running water and passing clouds. In a sense, the same could be said about the words of identity.

They are ephemeral, constantly changing, constantly drawing upon and yet rewriting history. This might seem like a paradoxical point to have arrived at, since we have spent so much of the earlier part of this chapter insisting on the very concrete consequences of identity, from governing our physical distribution in space to governing the policies and issues which shape our society.

However, this apparent paradox is nothing of the sort. The ephemeral content and the substantive consequences of identity actually go hand in hand with each other. Indeed, if the meaning of an identity were fixed, then it would be a far more limited and hence a far less useful tool for producing the future. In his description of the Bismarck myth, Frankel (2004) gives a beautiful illustration of this. Bismarck's achievements in unifying Germany made him a powerful symbol for symbolising the nature of German identity. But as long as he was alive, his symbolic value was limited, for he might always speak up and contest the uses to which his name was being put. Once dead, however, Bismarck became far more useful to the entire spectrum of those who sought to speak for the German nation. For now, the limits upon the ways his name could be used were gone. In the same way, the symbols of Scottish identity – Bruce, Bannockburn, Burns and others – are all safely dead and hence open to unlimited use. The king and the battle can be made to entrench either Scottish independence or rugged self-sufficiency. The poet can be quoted to make the Scots lovers of state socialism or haters of state bureaucracy. We have as many pasts as we have futures.

So, for all the length of what has gone before, our conclusion can now be brief. Yes, identity matters and Scottish identity matters to all aspects of Scottish life – economic, political, social and cultural. And no, the minister's words about Scotland's educational values are not froth but essential to making Scotland an educated society.

The good news is that the actual substance of this identity (and hence the shape of our economic, political, social and cultural life) is not fixed but is rather open to discussion. The bad news is that we all too often fall for the lie that identity is fixed and hence allow ourselves to be excluded from this discussion.

What we make of our identity is of inestimable importance. It is at the core of our democracy. If war is too important to be left to the generals, identity is certainly too important to be left to the politicians. It is an ever-evolving debate in which we must all remain constantly involved.

Note

1 Accessed on 18th July 2008 from http://www.guardian.co.uk/football/1999/oct/16/newsstory.sport13

Bibliography

Barker, R. (2001) *Legitimating identities*. Cambridge: Cambridge University Press.

Brown, A., McCrone, D., Paterson, L. and Surridge, P. (1999) *The Scottish electorate: The 1997 general election and beyond*. London: Macmillan.

Frankel, R. (2004) *Bismarck's shadow*. Poole: Berg.

Haslam, S. A. and Reicher, S. D. (2006) Stressing the group: Social identity and the unfolding dynamics of stress. *Journal of Applied Psychology*, **91**, 1037–52.

Haslam, S. A. and Turner, J. C. (1992) Context dependent variation in social stereotyping 2: The relationship between frame of reference, self-categorization and accentuation. *European Journal of Social Psychology*, **22**, 251–77.

Hopkins, N. P. and Dixon, J. (2006) Space, place and identity: Issues for political psychology. *Political Psychology*, **27**, 173–86.

Hopkins, N. P., Regan, M. and Abell. J. (1997) On the context dependence of national stereotypes: Some Scottish data. *British Journal of Social Psychology*, **36**, 553–64.

Hopkins, N. P., Reicher, S. D. and Harrison, K. (2006) Young people's deliberations on geographic mobility: Identity and cross-border relocation. *Political Psychology*, **27**, 227–45

Hopkins, N. P., Reicher, S. D., Harrison, K., Cassidy, C., Bull, R. and Levine, M. (2007) Helping to improve the group stereotype: On the strategic dimension of prosocial behaviour. *Personality and Social Psychology Bulletin*, **33**, 776–88.

Levine, M., Prosser, A., Evans, D. and Reicher, S. D. (2005) Identity and emergency intervention: How social group membership and inclusiveness of group boundaries shapes helping behaviour. *Personality and Social Psychology Bulletin*, **31**, 443–53.

Levine, M. and Reicher, S. D. (1996) Making sense of symptoms: Self-categorisation and the meaning of illness and injury. *British Journal of Social Psychology*, **35**, 245–56.

Marques, J., Yzerbyt, V. and Leyens, J. P. (1988) The black sheep effect: Extremity of judgement towards ingroup members as a function of group identification. *European Journal of Social Psychology*, **18**, 1–16.

Novelli, D. L., Drury, J. and Reicher, S. D. (2009) Come together: Two studies concerning the impact of group relations on personal space. Unpublished manuscript. University of Sussex

Reicher, S. D. and Haslam, S. A. (2009) Beyond help: A social psychology of collective solidarity and social cohesion. In M. Snyder and S. Sturmer (eds) *The psychology of helping*. Oxford: Blackwell.

Reicher, S. D. and Hopkins, N. P. (2001) *Self and nation*. London: Sage.

Reicher, S. D., Hopkins, N. P. and Harrison, K. (2006) Social identity and spatial behaviour: The relationship between national category salience, the sense of home and labour mobility across national boundaries. *Political Psychology*, **27**, 247–64.

Sindic, D. and Reicher, S. D. (in press) Our way of life is worth defending: Testing a model of attitudes towards superordinate group membership through a study of Scots attitudes towards Britain. *European Journal of Social Psychology*.

Tajfel, H. (1978) *Differentiation between social groups*. London: Academic Press.

Taylor, C. (1985) *Philosophical papers: Human agency and language. Part 1*. Cambridge: Cambridge University Press.

Todorov, T. (2001) *The fragility of goodness*. London: Weidenfeld and Nicolson.

Turner, J. C. (1982) Towards a cognitive redefinition of the social group. In H. Tajfel (ed.) *Social identity and intergroup relations*. Cambridge: Cambridge University Press.

Turner, J. C., Hogg, M. A., Oakes, P. J., Reicher, S. D. and Wetherell, M. (1987) *Rediscovering the social group*. Oxford: Blackwell.

Wetherell, M. and Potter, J. (1992) *Mapping the language of racism*. London: Harvester Wheatsheaf.

3
England Awakes? Trends in National Identity in England

John Curtice and Anthony Heath

Do you feel English or British?

Both of course! What's the difference?

Such an imaginary exchange captures a commonly held view about national identity in England (Kumar, 2003). As members of by far the predominant part of the Union, people in England can easily come to regard England and Britain as synonymous with each other. The remainder of the United Kingdom impinges little on their everyday lives or consciences. As a result they can happily and freely describe themselves as English on one occasion, British on another – and mean little or nothing by the difference. It is perhaps little wonder that national identity in England has been described as 'fuzzy' (Cohen, 1995).

But perhaps this picture is outdated (Gamble, 2003). After all, in recent years, England has had to endure the sight of Scotland and Wales being granted separate national political institutions – and then use those institutions to pursue different public policies. Scotland, for example, scrapped upfront tuition fees for university students and introduced 'free' personal care for older people. Wales got rid of prescription charges. More recently, in both countries, power has been secured by nationalist parties strongly committed to advancing the interests of their particular part of the UK. If people in England were not previously aware of the distinction between Britain and England, then arguably they ought to be now. So maybe more people have come in recent years to say they are English and/or fewer people are happy to consider themselves British. Perhaps too which term people use has come to have political significance, with those who prefer to say they are English now being more likely to feel that, like Scotland and Wales, England should have its own distinct political institutions as well.

There is also a second potentially powerful force that could mean that British and English are no longer interchangeable identities. Thanks to post-war immigration, and in particular immigration from the 'New' Commonwealth, England has become a relatively diverse society in terms of its ethnic composition. Indeed its capital, London, is now often described as one of the most diverse cities in the world. Moreover until the 1960s, immigrants from the Commonwealth were regarded as 'British subjects' and so automatically had full citizenship rights (Goldsmith, 2008); being 'British' has thus long had an association with a worldwide former empire that being English has never had. But at the same time policymakers have had to develop ways of encouraging the indigenous population to accept its new neighbours and of enabling the country's new residents to feel part of the wider society they have joined. One method has been to promote Britishness as a 'multi-cultural' identity that acknowledges and embraces a wide range of symbols and cultures (Meer and Modood, forthcoming). As well as being associated with, for example, pubs, Dickens and Shakespeare, Britishness is also said to embrace the Asian corner shop, Salman Rushdie and Zadie Smith.

True, concerns (fuelled by rioting and subsequently acts of terrorism associated with Muslims) about the possible adverse social consequences of cultural diversity have meant that more recently the policy emphasis has been on 'Britishness' rather than 'multi-culturalism' (Cantle, 2001; Joppke, 2004). Nevertheless it is still Britishness, not Englishness, that is being promoted in, for example, admission ceremonies for new citizens. Britishness is being portrayed as the one identity to which all residents in Britain have the right as well as an obligation to acknowledge (Goldsmith, 2008).

In short, British national identity, which after all has always been a multinational 'state' identity, has been portrayed as a civic identity, an identity to which all those permanently resident in Britain can lay claim, irrespective of place of birth, ethnic origin or religion (Brubaker, 1992; Bryant, 1997; Tilley et al., 2004). The same is not true of Englishness, which, in consequence, may appeal more to those who hold a more exclusive ethnic conception of what it means to be part of English society. Only those born in the country or perhaps even only those whose parents were, are acknowledged as fellow citizens. So perhaps two important differences between the two identities have emerged. Members of the country's ethnic minority population may be willing to describe themselves as British but reluctant to consider themselves English. And among the population in general perhaps those who prefer to claim they are English rather than British are more inclined to feel that birth and ethnic origin are important determinants of identity and are more likely to hold prejudicial attitudes towards ethnic minorities or indeed 'others' in general.

In this chapter we consider the apparent impact of the devolution and diversity debates on the pattern of national identity in England. We address three main questions in particular. First, is there any evidence that adherence to English national identity has increased in recent years, and that in so doing it has displaced Britishness? Second, has the advent of devolution in Scotland and Wales awakened a demand for devolution for England and especially so among those who adhere to an English identity? Finally, is adherence to an English rather than a British national identity a marker of a more ethnic conception of who is regarded as a fellow citizen?

Our evidence comes from the *British Social Attitudes* survey conducted by the National Centre for Social Research (Park et al., 2008). In recent years this high quality annual survey has provided the platform for a number of research projects on attitudes to national identity and devolution, including projects funded by The Leverhulme Trust. In consequence it provides an unusually rich source of evidence of relevance to the questions we wish to address. Although the survey interviews respondents in Scotland and Wales as well as in England, all the analysis presented here is based only on respondents living in England.

English, British or both

Our first task, then, is to examine whether people currently resident in England describe themselves as English, British or both. In Table 3.1, we show the answers that have been obtained over the last decade or so

Table 3.1   Trends in free choice national identity (England, 1996–2007)

% by column	1996	1997	1998	1999	2000	2001	2002	2003	2004	2005	2006	2007
English	52	54	55	65	59	63	57	59	55	60	67	57
British	71	76	70	71	67	67	73	70	69	70	68	68
Both*	29	36	34	44	35	39	37	38	33	38	45	34
N	1019	3150	2695	2718	2887	2761	2897	3709	2684	3643	3666	3517

* 'Both' refers to those stating they are 'both British and English'.
Percentages do not add up to 100 because respondents could give more than one answer.
Answers other than 'British' or 'English' not shown.
Sources: British Social Attitudes 1996, 1998–2007; 1997: British Election Study.

when people have been presented with a list of national identities and asked to state 'which, if any, describes how you think of yourself'. This list of identities contains all of the national identities commonly associated with one or more parts of Great Britain or Ireland, together with 'European'. But most people chose 'English' or 'British' – or as the question allowed them to do, both. So it is on the incidence of these three answers over the last ten years or so on which Table 3.1 concentrates.

The results are quite striking. First, we acquire some affirmation of our opening remark that many people in England freely choose both English and British identities. In most years just over a third, sometimes rather more, have opted to say that both identities best described themselves. Perhaps for many people the two identities do indeed constitute a distinction without a difference? Second, there are some signs that English national identity may have become more popular in recent years. Up to and including 1998, the proportion saying they are English was never above 55 per cent. Since then it has never fallen below that level. Third, however, this slight increase in the incidence of English identity has not been accompanied by any marked decline in willingness to acknowledge a British identity. Apart from an unusually high proportion saying they were British in 1997, the incidence of British identity has exhibited little more than trendless fluctuation.[1] Moreover, it has continued to be the case that more people opt to say they are British than claim to be English.

Nevertheless, the apparent slight increase in English identity is intriguing, not least because it coincides with the creation of the devolved institutions in Scotland and Wales in 1999. Meanwhile the data in Table 3.1 do not give us any idea of the relative importance of the two identities to those who acknowledge both. Perhaps in saying they are British, our survey respondents are simply recognising the official legal label of their citizenship, whereas in saying they are English, they are indicating where their affective loyalties lie. If, as a result, the latter matters more to them then perhaps we will find that when people are asked to choose just one identity, it is English identity that is (increasingly) the more common.

Table 3.2 shows the incidence of the two national identities when people are asked to choose just one identity rather than left to pick as many as they want from the list that was presented to them. It suggests that, despite our reservations, English national identity still seems to play second fiddle to British identity among people resident in England in general. Nevertheless, the impression that English national identity may have become somewhat more common since the advent of

Table 3.2 Trends in forced choice national identity (England, 1992–2007)

% by column	1992	1996	1997	1998	1999	2000	2001	2002	2003	2004	2005	2006	2007
English	31	34	33	37	44	41	43	37	38	38	40	47	39
British	63	57	55	51	44	47	44	51	48	51	48	39	48
N		2125	1019	3150	2695	2718	2887	2761	2897	3709	2684	3643	3666	3517

Percentages do not add up to 100 because answers other than 'British' or 'English' not shown.
Sources: British Election Studies 1992, 1997; British Social Attitudes 1996, 1998–2007.

devolution is reinforced. Between 1997 and 1999 the proportion saying that English was their sole or most important identity increased from a third to 44 per cent.[2] Although thereafter the proportion fell back somewhat, it has never again fallen as low as it was between 1992 and 1997. Equally, the proportion saying they are British has never returned to the level recorded during that period.

So it seems that the advent of devolution in Scotland and Wales may have helped to awaken feelings of English identity among some people in England. But what if we adopt a rather different approach to tapping people's sense of identity, one that explicitly acknowledges the possibility that many people may feel both English and British? In an adaptation of the so-called Moreno scale (Moreno, 2006), survey respondents have been asked to choose one of five possible descriptions of themselves. Two of these descriptions are exclusive in character – 'English, not British' and 'British, not English'. The remainder, however, give people the chance to express a multiple identity in a relatively nuanced manner. They may say they are equally English and British, or they can say that while they reckon they are both, they feel one more than the other.

Presented with this explicit opportunity to express some form of multiple identity, a clear majority do so (see Table 3.3). In most years the figure has been just under two-thirds, though on the most recent reading it has fallen a little to 59 per cent. The two identities of British and English are indeed intertwined with each other for most people, but perhaps a little less so than they once were. Meanwhile, the proportion saying they are wholly English or 'more English than British' rose from 24 per cent in 1997 to 31 per cent in 1999 and has been at or above that higher level ever since. So this line of questioning too suggests that adherence to an English national identity became rather stronger at around the time that devolved institutions were established in the rest of the UK. Interestingly, too, when national identity is asked about

Table 3.3   Trends in Moreno national identity (England, 1997–2007)

% by column	1997	1999	2000	2001	2003	2007
English, not British	7	17	18	17	17	19
More English than British	17	14	14	13	19	14
Equally English and British	45	37	34	42	31	31
More British than English	14	11	14	9	13	14
British, not English	9	14	12	11	10	12
N	3150	2718	1928	2761	1917	859

Sources: British Election Study 1997; British Social Attitudes 1999–2007.

in this way, English identity seems to matter to more people than does British identity. For example, in 2007, 33 per cent said they were wholly or mostly English, while only 26 per cent said they were wholly or mostly British. This may, perhaps, be a sign that those who do acknowledge an English identity feel that identity relatively strongly.

So we have uncovered some sign that, when people are invited to choose between it and being British, the incidence of English national identity may have increased around the time that devolution was introduced. But perhaps there are more profound, longer-term forces at work? Perhaps feeling British is an identity linked with past glories, with the Empire and the successful defence of the country in the Second World War? While such glories may still resonate with older people, they may have little appeal or meaning for younger generations. In addition the youngest generation will have entered the electorate at a time when separate political institutions were already in existence in Scotland and Wales, and thus might have particular reason to be aware of the difference between being English and being British.

Indeed some feelings that might be thought to be linked to identity have been shown to be less common among younger people. Heath and Roberts (2008) have shown that those in younger age groups are less likely to say they belong strongly to Britain. Meanwhile Tilley and Heath (2007) have demonstrated that the proportion saying they are very proud to be British has fallen since the 1980s, as less proud younger generations have replaced their older counterparts. However, we cannot be sure that younger people have not always been less likely to feel a sense of belonging, which may after all only come after a period of residential, employment and family stability, something that by definition can only have been experienced by older people. Meanwhile 'pride' may not be the same thing as 'identity'. Identity is a statement of individual attachment to a particular social group or 'imagined community' (Anderson, 1983); 'pride' can reflect perceptions of the standing or achievements of that group. People may acknowledge a British identity yet still be aware that possible sources of pride such as the standing and influence of Britain in the world have diminished during the post-war period (Parekh, 2000).

Table 3.4 shows, when asked to choose just one identity, the proportion in each age group saying they are English, and the proportion claiming to be British. It suggests that in contrast to measures of belonging and pride, the willingness of younger people to acknowledge a British identity is not markedly lower than that of older people. True, in 1997 only 49 per cent of those aged 18–24 said that they were British, at least five percentage points below the proportion in any other age group. But in 2007 it is the oldest age group, that is those aged 65 and over, who are least likely to say they are British. Conversely, there is not any consistent evidence that English national identity is more likely to be acknowledged by younger people. Meanwhile a similar analysis of the Moreno scale also fails to show that younger people are less likely to say they are wholly or mostly British.

Of course it may be the case that younger people are less likely to feel strongly English or British. Both may be traditional forms of identity that, thanks to processes of individualisation, younger people no longer feel obliged to embrace as their parents once did (Bauman, 2000). But if that were the case then we would expect to see more younger people refuse to say they are either. Of this, however, there is no sign in our data (see also Heath et al., 2007).

Table 3.4 Forced choice national identity by age (1997 and 2007)

% for each age group by year	1997			2007		
	English	**British**	**N**	**English**	**British**	**N**
18–24	36	49	287	39	46	237
25–34	26	59	671	32	42	554
35–44	33	55	667	37	50	704
45–54	34	54	502	36	52	590
55–64	34	57	393	38	54	566
65+	38	56	612	51	41	863

Sources: British Election Study 1997; British Social Attitudes 2007.

So we have uncovered some evidence that English identity has become relatively more important than British identity among people in England. Moreover it appears that we can date this development to the period when devolved institutions were created in Scotland and Wales – though there is no sign of this process continuing thereafter, let alone any evidence of English identity being more popular among younger generations. But does this mean that England has also developed an interest in having its own devolved institutions, and especially so among those who feel a sense of English identity?

An English parliament for the English?

Advocates of devolution for England do not agree on what form that devolution should take (Hazell, 2006). Some believe that a system of regional devolution should be introduced. The last Conservative government established a system of government offices in each of nine regions of the country. Thereafter Labour introduced in each region an unelected 'regional chamber' that, inter alia, scrutinised the work of regional development agencies that were responsible for promoting the economy of their region. Labour's intention was that eventually each unelected regional chamber would become an elected assembly that had responsibilities for planning and housing as well as the local economy. However, an initial attempt to introduce an elected assembly in the North East of England was overwhelmingly defeated by the voters of that region in a referendum held in November 2004. That defeat effectively killed Labour's plans for regional devolution, and indeed the existing unelected chambers are to be abolished in 2010.

Others, however, take the view that England should have its own national institutions that mimic those created in Scotland and Wales. Although not supported by any mainstream political party, the idea is promoted by the pressure group, the Campaign for an English Parliament, while the English Democrats party advocates the cause at the ballot box. Insofar as an English parliament is intended to provide a symbol of English national identity and meet nationalist sentiment for English self-government, it is this latter option that we might anticipate should be particularly popular among those who say they are English.

Table 3.5 shows how popular the option of regional assemblies and an English parliament have been since 1999 when respondents are asked to choose between one of these forms of the devolution plus the status quo whereby England is governed by the UK Government and Parliament. It shows that when faced with these alternatives consistently a half or

Table 3.5 Constitutional preferences for England (1999–2007)

With all the changes going on in the way different parts of Great Britain are run, which of the following do you think would be best for England?

% by column	1999	2000	2001	2002	2003	2004	2005	2006	2007
England should be governed as it is now, with laws made by the UK Parliament	62	54	57	56	50	53	54	54	57
Each region of England to have its own assembly that runs services like health*	15	18	23	20	26	21	20	18	14
England as whole to have its own new parliament with law-making powers	18	19	16	17	18	21	18	21	17
N	2718	1928	2761	2897	3709	2684	1794	928	859

* In 2004–6, the second option read 'that makes decisions about the region's economy, planning and housing'. The 2003 survey carried both versions of this option and demonstrated that the difference in wording did not make a material difference to the pattern of response. Throughout this chapter, notably Table 3.6, the figures quoted for 2003 are those for the two versions combined.

Source: British Social Attitudes 1999–2007.

more of people in England favour the status quo. Of the two alternatives, regional devolution became the more popular in the period prior to the 2004 referendum in the North East, but that popularity has subsequently fallen away again. This, however, has not resulted in a boost in support for an English parliament, which, at 17 per cent, is on the most recent reading still no greater than it was in 1999. There is no apparent sign here that the creation of national political institutions in Scotland and Wales has persuaded people in England that they should have their own separate political institutions too.

But how strong is the link between support for an English parliament and adhering to an English national identity? If such a parliament is an expression of English nationalist sentiment, then we should find that those who say they are English are markedly more likely to favour creating such an institution than are those who say they are British. Table 3.6 shows for a number of years between 1999 and 2007 the constitutional preferences of those who, when asked to choose, say they are English and compares those preferences with the views of those who say they are British.

There is some link between national identity and support for an English parliament, but it can hardly be described as a strong one. In each of the years 1999, 2003 and 2006, those who said they were English were only seven or eight percentage points more likely to favour an English parliament than were those who stated they were British. Conversely, those who said they were British were a little more likely to favour the constitutional status quo. But on this evidence one could hardly conclude that such support for an English parliament as does exist is based on English nationalist sentiment. Meanwhile we should bear in mind that as many as half or so of those who say they are English support the constitutional status quo.

Nevertheless, we should also note that the association between national identity and constitutional preference was rather stronger when the last reading was obtained in 2007.[3] On that occasion those who said they were English were no less than sixteen percentage points more likely than those who claimed to be British to express support for an English parliament. As a result support for a parliament among English identifiers reached its highest level yet. Perhaps there is a sign here that English identity is beginning to demand political expression?

First though, perhaps, we should check that the picture we have portrayed of the link between national identity and constitutional preference is not disturbed if we measure national identity using the Moreno scale. After all, there is perhaps little reason why those who feel both English and British in some combination should be particularly keen on

Table 3.6 Constitutional preferences for England by forced choice national identity (1999–2007)

With all the changes going on in the way different parts of Great Britain are run, which of the following do you think would be best for England?

% by column	1999		2003		2006		2007	
	English	British	English	British	English	British	English	British
England should be governed as it is now, with laws made by the UK Parliament	60	67	49	52	54	59	50	69
Each region of England to have its own assembly that runs services like health*	15	14	24	27	16	18	16	12
England as whole to have its own new parliament with law-making powers	21	14	23	16	25	17	27	11
N	1186	1208	1785	1447	362	431	408	346

* See note to Table 3.5.
Source: British Social Attitudes 1999–2007.

an English parliament. If English national sentiment does exist, then we would seem most likely to find it among those who not only say they are English, but also explicitly deny they are British.

As Table 3.7 overleaf shows this group is certainly the one most likely to favour the idea of an English parliament. But its views are not consistently outstandingly different from those who say they are some mixture of British and English. It seems that support for an English parliament does indeed have relatively little to do with national identity.

We might wonder whether English national identity is linked more strongly to a preference that England should actually become a fully independent country than it is to support for a devolved English parliament. But this does not seem to be the case either. When in 2007 the British Social Attitudes survey asked for the first time which would be 'better for England', just 16 per cent said 'for England to become an independent country, separate from the rest of the United Kingdom', while no less than 77 per cent favoured 'for England to remain part of the United Kingdom, along with Scotland, Wales and Northern Ireland'. Of those who, when asked to chose just one identity, said they were English, 22 per cent backed English independence, compared with 11 per cent of those who said they were British – much the same gap as in the case of support for a devolved parliament (see Table 3.6). Equally, with just 29 per cent of those who say they are 'English, not British' supporting English independence, the strength of the link between independence and Moreno national identity is much the same as it is between attitudes towards a devolved parliament and Moreno.

There are at least two important reasons why relatively few of those who say they are English wish to see that national identity expressed in distinct political institutions. First, they do not feel antipathy to symbols of Britishness; rather they are just as likely to embrace them as those who say they are British. In 2007, for example, 39 per cent of those who said they were English said it was 'very important' to keep the monarchy, more than matching the equivalent figure of 38 per cent among those who said they were British. Second, English identifiers are not particularly inclined to the view that the UK Government fails to look after the best long-term interests of England. In 2007 46 per cent of those who stated they were English said that they trusted the UK Government to work in England's long-term interests 'just about always' or 'most of the time', only a little below the equivalent figure of 54 per cent among those who say they are British. In short, those who adhere to an English identity feel little differently from those who claim to be British about either the symbolic institutions of the British

Table 3.7 Constitutional preferences for England by Moreno national identity (1999 and 2007)

% by column	English, not British		English more than British		Equally English and British		British more than English		British, not English	
	1999	2007	1999	2007	1999	2007	1999	2007	1999	2007
England should be governed as it is now, with laws made by the UK Parliament	59	54	63	52	61	61	71	66	65	61
Each region of England to have its own assembly that runs services like health*	14	11	16	17	17	15	13	12	14	19
England as whole to have its own new parliament with law-making powers	23	28	19	23	18	14	11	20	17	9
N	491	165	389	129	999	267	298	116	354	102

* See note to Table 3.5.
Sources: British Social Attitudes 1999 and 2007.

state or the way in which instrumentally that state serves the people of England.

Constitutional grievances

England may not want devolution for itself, but that does not necessarily mean it is entirely comfortable with the constitutional status quo. One well-known anomaly, the West Lothian question, arises from the fact that Scotland has its own Parliament with law making powers whereas all laws for England continue to be made in a UK Parliament that includes Scottish MPs (Dalyell, 1977). MPs from Scotland have the right to vote on laws affecting such matters as health and education in England, but MPs from England cannot vote on laws about these devolved matters for Scotland. We might wonder whether this has increasingly become a cause for grievance in England – and especially so among those who feel English. After all, the fact that people who feel English largely do not feel antipathy towards the symbols and institutions of the British state does not necessarily mean that they feel the same way about Scotland in particular. Even if Britain is not regarded as 'other', Scotland might still well be.

Much the same might be true of another apparent anomaly that predates devolution but which has become more prominent in media commentary since the creation of the devolved institutions in Scotland and Wales. Public spending per head has long been consistently higher in Scotland and Wales than it is in England (HM Treasury, 2008; McLean, 2005; McLean et al., 2008; Scottish Government, 2008). It is often argued, not least in popular commentary (see, for example, Heathcoat-Amory, 2007; Heffer, 2007; Stirling, 2007) that this difference cannot be justified (for example, on the grounds that Wales and Scotland have greater needs). Perhaps such an apparent discrepancy might have been acceptable to people in England when decisions about spending in England, Scotland and Wales were all being made by the same government. But now that Scotland and Wales have the freedom to decide for themselves how to spend their money – and have apparently used that freedom to introduce benefits such as free personal care and free prescriptions that are denied to those living in England – the public mood might well have changed.

The West Lothian question certainly does seem to be a potential source of irritation to people in England. As Table 3.8 shows, consistently around three in five agree that Scottish MPs should no longer be allowed to vote on laws that only affect England. Moreover, the proportion that

Table 3.8   Attitudes towards the 'West Lothian' question (2000–07)
Scottish MPs should no longer be allowed to vote on English legislation

% by column	2000	2001	2003	2007
Strongly agree	18	19	22	25
Agree	45	38	38	36
Neither agree nor disagree	19	18	18	17
Disagree	8	12	10	9
Strongly disagree	1	2	1	1
N	1695	2341	1530	739

Source: British Social Attitudes.

'strongly agree' with that proposition has slowly increased, suggesting perhaps that the irritation has become a little stronger in the wake of a number of examples that have occurred of English legislation being passed thanks to the votes of non-English MPs (for further details see Russell and Lodge, 2006). Even so it remains the case that far more people simply say that they just 'agree' rather than that they 'strongly agree'; the issue may thus not be one that arouses strong resentment.

Moreover, such resentment as does exist does not seem to be particularly strong among those who say they are English. Of this group in 2000, 22 per cent said they 'strongly agree' that Scottish MPs should not be allowed to vote on English laws, only a little higher than the equivalent figure, 17 per cent, among those who state they are British. In 2007 the difference between the two groups is bigger – 33 per cent of those who say they are English strongly agree that Scottish MPs should not vote on English laws, 21 per cent of those who reckon they are British – but the increase in the difference between the two groups is not statistically significant.[4] That so many people who say they are British regard the situation as an anomaly suggests that it is its apparent illogicality that explains people's responses rather than nationalist resentment of an advantage enjoyed by Scotland.[5]

Meanwhile, Table 3.9 suggests that resentment about Scotland's share of public spending is relatively muted. When people have been asked in recent years whether Scotland secures more or less than its fair share of public spending, typically only around one in five say that the answer is more than its fair share. However, in the most recent survey in 2007 this figure rose to 32 per cent, suggesting that the claims in recent years that Scotland is too generously funded may have begun to make a mark on public opinion.

Table 3.9   Perceptions of Scotland's share of public spending (2000–07)
Compared with other parts of the UK, Scotland's share of government spending is ...

% by column	2000	2001	2002	2003	2007
Much more than fair	8	9	9	9	16
Little more than fair	13	15	15	13	16
Pretty much fair	42	44	44	45	38
Little less than fair	10	8	8	8	6
Much less than fair	1	1	1	1	1
N	1928	2761	2897	1927	859

Source: British Social Attitudes.

Table 3.10   Perceptions of Scotland's share of spending by forced choice national identity (2000–07)
Compared with other parts of the UK, Scotland's share of government spending is ...

	2000		2003		2007	
% by column	English	British	English	British	English	British
More than fair	23	22	26	19	37	29
Pretty much fair	42	43	45	46	35	43
Less than fair	11	10	8	8	8	6
N	877	822	898	760	408	346

Source: British Social Attitudes.

Still that view remains no more than a minority one. Moreover, it is not clear that the change in opinion is an expression of increased nationalist sentiment. As Table 3.10 shows, in 2007 those who stated they were English were only 8 percentage points more likely than those who felt British to say that Scotland receives more than its fair share. More importantly, the increase between 2003 and 2007 in support for that view among those who say they are English is at eleven percentage points, more or less the same as the ten-point increase among those who say they are British (see Table 3.10).

Given the debate about devolution, we might wonder too whether English national identity is expressed in the ballot box. After all, the Conservative manifesto in both the 2001 and 2005 general elections proposed that Scottish MPs should not be able to vote on English laws. More generally, as a party with only one MP in Scotland, we might anticipate that the Conservatives have come to be regarded as primarily an English party that those who feel English would be particularly inclined to support. Yet in 2007 the proportion of English identifiers who said they identified with the Conservative party was, at 30 per cent, just four percentage points higher than the equivalent figure among British identifiers. Equally, support for the Conservatives among those who in response to the Moreno question said they were 'English, not British' was just four percentage points higher than it was among those said they were 'British, not English'.

The West Lothian question appears to be an irritant to many people in England. There are also signs of growing resentment about the level of public spending enjoyed by Scotland. But it seems that neither pattern represents an outbreak of nationalist sentiment among those who adhere to an English identity. For the most part it seems that English identity plays relatively little role in the politics of England.

An exclusive identity?

But this of course is to leave aside the role of English identity in attitudes towards questions of ethnicity, questions that occasionally can play a powerful role on the political stage. We suggested at the beginning of this chapter that thanks to its association with a more diverse society, British national identity may have a less exclusive character than English identity. As a result those who belong to an ethnic minority may be reluctant to claim an English identity, while those who do adhere to that identity may have a more restrictive view about who has the right to claim a particular national identity.

Table 3.11 considers the first of these possibilities. In our surveys respondents were shown a list of possible ethnic identities that they might adopt, such as 'White: of European origin', 'Black: of Caribbean

Table 3.11   Forced choice national identity by ethnic origin (1997–2007)

	1997	1999	2003	2007
White	%	%	%	%
English	35	47	42	44
British	55	44	47	47
N	2423	2551	3363	3181
Non-white	%	%	%	%
English	5	15	7	5
British	58	50	54	58
N	704	126	305	301

Note: The 1997 survey included a booster sample of ethnic minority respondents.
Sources: British Election Study 1997; British Social Attitudes 1999–2007.

origin' and 'Asian: of Indian origin', and asked to which group they felt they belonged. In the table we show the forced choice identity chosen, first of all, by those who said they were White (of either European or other origin) and secondly, by those who said they were Black, Asian or mixed (of any origin). The contrast between the two halves of the table is striking. Since 1999, at least among those who say they are 'white' the proportion saying they are English has been little different from the proportion claiming to be British. But among those who claim any other ethnic identity only a relatively small minority say they are English, while over half state they are British. Moreover, although there appears to have been an increase in the proportion of 'non-white' people saying they are English in 1999, over the longer term the increase in the proportion saying they are English appears to have been confined entirely to that section of the population that says it is 'white'. At 5 per cent the proportion of 'non-white' people in our most recent survey who stated they were English is no higher than it was ten years earlier.

So it seems that Englishness is not something with which many of those from an ethnic minority background feel much empathy. Indeed, many people from a 'non-white' background appear explicitly to reject the idea of being English at all; in response to the Moreno question no less than 38 per cent of this group say they are 'British, not English', compared with just 8 per cent of those who state they are 'white'. Evidently the association of Britishness with a more diverse society has had its impact on the identity that those who belong to England's minority groups feel able to adopt.

But does this also mean that those who say they are English rather than British are more likely to hold an ethnic rather than a civic conception of nationality? There are a number of ways we can address this question. The most direct is to examine whether those who say they are English are less likely to accept the right of those who move to England to call themselves British or English. But we might anticipate too that those who say they are English are less tolerant towards those whom they regard as different, such as those who belong to a different racial or ethnic group. Indeed we might also expect a more nationalist approach to how Britain should conduct itself in the world, such as in its relations with Europe.

In fact all of these approaches suggest that those who say they are English do indeed hold a more exclusive, more ethnic perspective on whom they are willing to regard as part of the same society as themselves. The 2006 *British Social Attitudes* survey asked its respondents whether 'People from outside the United Kingdom who move permanently to England to live and work here are entitled to describe themselves as

British if they want to'. Among those who said they were English, just 34 per cent agreed with this statement; among those who said they were British as many as 44 per cent did so. Much the same difference emerged when respondents were asked whether someone who moved to England could call themselves English. Just 27 per cent of those who would call themselves English agree that they could, whereas 38 per cent of those who regard themselves as British do so. It is, of course, also striking that both groups are less likely to feel that someone who moves to England from outside the UK has the right to call themselves English rather than British; this would appear to be an implicit recognition that English is considered to be a more exclusive identity.

Meanwhile, Table 3.12 demonstrates that those who in response to the Moreno question say they are English and not British are consistently less likely than those who give any other response to claim that they are not prejudiced against people of other races. They are also consistently more inclined to believe that Britain should leave the European Union. For example, in 1997, just 15 per cent of those who said they were British wanted to leave the EU, whereas as many as 25 per cent of those who said they were English did so. When the question was last asked in 2006, much the same difference still existed; 12 per cent of those who said they were British wanted to leave compared with 20 per cent of those who regarded themselves as English.

In general, liberal attitudes towards those of a different race or towards Britain's role in the world are usually more common among those who have been in receipt of some kind of university education (Evans, 2000; Park and Surridge, 2003). Thus, given the tendency for those who say they are English to be less likely to hold such views, it should perhaps come as little surprise that graduates are least keen on calling themselves

Table 3.12 Self-rated prejudice against people of other races by Moreno national identity (1999–2007)

	English, not British	N	More English than British	N	Equally English and British	N	More British than English	N	British, not English	N
1999	62	491	67	389	72	999	69	298	79	354
2003	56	325	66	373	71	596	71	256	73	192
2007	54	165	68	129	68	267	69	116	68	102

Note: Figures give percentage for each national identity category saying they are not prejudiced against people of other races.
Source: British Social Attitudes.

English. In our 2007 survey, just 28 per cent of those in receipt of a university degree said they were English, compared with as many as 44 per cent of those without any qualifications. Not, however, that graduates are particularly likely to call themselves British; the proportion that do so, 46 per cent, is much the same as the equivalent proportion, 45 per cent, among those without any qualifications. Rather, graduates are more likely to adopt identities that are not associated with one or more parts of Great Britain or Ireland – including, not least, European.

The differences we have uncovered here between the attitudes of those who say they are English and those who consider themselves British are not large. However, for the most part they are somewhat larger and more consistent than the differences between the two groups in respect of attitudes towards devolution. They do suggest that the outlook of those who say they are English towards those who might be regarded as 'other' is rather more exclusive than those who consider themselves to be British. There also seems to be some recognition among the public in England that 'English' is an identity that is less easily available to immigrants. The distinction between being English and being British does have some difference attached to it after all.

Conclusion

It seems that the advent of devolution in Scotland and Wales has had some impact on the sense of identity of those living in England. While they remain as willing as ever to acknowledge they are British, their sense of Englishness appears to have been stronger and more important since 1999. To that degree at least, England has seemingly become more aware of its own distinctive national identity.

Yet it is far from clear that this development has significant implications for the maintenance of the United Kingdom. Feeling English rather than British makes surprisingly little difference to people's attitudes towards how England should be governed. While those who feel English more than they do British are somewhat more inclined to support the idea of an English parliament than those for whom the reverse is true, the difference of outlook between the two groups is relatively small. Much the same is true of attitudes towards the position of Scotland and Wales within the United Kingdom. Such resentment as does exist in England about the 'advantages' enjoyed by the country's near neighbours seems to have relatively little to do with feeling English rather than British.

On the other hand, we have uncovered one stark difference between the two identities. Few of those who belong to one of England's ethnic minority groups feel able or are willing to state they are English. In contrast they evidently feel no particular difficulty at all in claiming to be British. Further, the increased incidence of English identity since 1999 has been wholly confined to the country's 'white' population. Meanwhile those who prioritise an English rather than a British identity are somewhat more likely to hold an exclusive attitude towards those who might be regarded as 'other'.

In short, it seems that English national identity is, as we anticipated, associated in the public mind with a less inclusive outlook on the world. The historical association of Britishness with a multicultural empire, together with its more recent promotion as a civic multicultural identity, has helped ensure that it appears better suited than English identity to provide a basis for community cohesion. Here, it seems, there is an important difference between British and English national identity.

There are of course two possible responses to this evidence. One would be to regard it as an affirmation of the current tendency to promote Britishness as the one identity that can help bind society together. It is evidently a civic identity to which all can aspire and which encourages acceptance of a multicultural society. At the same time it is more evidently consistent with the idea of maintaining the United Kingdom. The other possible reaction, however, would be to suggest that the evidence of this chapter suggests it does not make sense for policymakers to ignore an identity, Englishness, that, it seems, is both widespread and now more popular than before. There is nothing inevitable about the association of Englishness with a more exclusive, ethnic conception of identity. Instead of being ignored if not discouraged by policymakers, it too could be promoted as a multicultural identity. At the same time it could be represented alongside Scottish and Welsh as one of a family of 'British' identities. Only then are we likely to be able to say that England really is both English and British.

Notes

1. It should also be noted that this 1997 figure, based unlike the data for other years on the British Election Study, is not replicated by that year's British Social Attitudes survey, which found 68 per cent saying they are British, 50 per cent English and 26 per cent both. We have opted, however, to use the election study data for 1997 because it is based on a much larger sample size that includes a deliberate over-representation of ethnic minorities, an attribute that is of advantage to us when later in this chapter we examine the national identity of those belonging to an ethnic minority.
2. Our interpretation here is not undermined by the results of the 1997 British Social Attitudes survey, which found 36 per cent saying they are English, 53 per cent British.

3. We tested whether the relationship between national identity and constitutional preference was significantly stronger in 2007 than in 2006 by undertaking a log-linear analysis of the pooled data for 2006 and 2007. In the absence of an interaction term for constitutional preference by national identity by year (i.e. a term that measures the difference between 2006 and 2007 in the strength of the relationship between constitutional preference and national identity) the residual chi-square was 8.86 which, with two degrees of freedom, is significant at p = .012. We can thus conclude that the relationship between constitutional preference and national identity is significantly different in the two years.
4. This was assessed by undertaking a log-linear analysis of the pooled data for attitude to the West Lothian question and national identity in 2000 and 2007. In the absence of an interaction term for attitude to the West Lothian question by national identity by year, the residual chi-square was 4.91, which, with four degrees of freedom, has a p value of .296. If answers to the West Lothian question are dichotomised into just two responses, strongly agree versus all other responses, the residual chi-square is 3.45, which, with one degree of freedom, has a p value of .063. We can thus conclude that the relationship between attitude to the West Lothian question and national identity did not significantly differ between the two years.
5. The pattern of responses to the question about Scottish MPs voting on English laws does not appear to be notably more strongly related to Moreno national identity either. For example, in 2007, 37 per cent of those who say they are English, not British strongly agree that Scottish MPs should not vote on English laws, only a little higher than among all those who say they are English in response to the forced choice question.

Bibliography

Anderson, B. (1983) *Imagined communities: Reflections on the origins and spread of nationalism.* London: Verso.

Bauman, Z. (2000) *Liquid modernity.* Cambridge: Polity.

Brubaker, R. (1992) *Citizenship and nationhood in France and Germany.* Cambridge, Mass.: Harvard University Press.

Bryant, C. (1997) Citizenship, national identity and the accommodation of difference: Reflections on the German, French, Dutch cases. *Journal of Ethnic and Migration Studies* (formerly *New Community*), **23**, 157–72.

Cantle, T. (chairman) (2001) *Community cohesion: A report of the Independent Review Team.* London: HMSO.

Cohen, R. (1995) Fuzzy frontiers of identity: the British case. *Social Identities*, **1**, 35–62.

Dalyell, T. (1977) *Devolution: The end of Britain?* London: Jonathan Cape.

Evans, G. (2000) The working class and New Labour: A parting of the ways? In R. Jowell, J. Curtice, A. Park, K. Thomson, L. Jarvis, C. Bromley and N. Stratford (eds) *British social attitudes: The 17th report.* London: Sage.

Gamble, A. (2003) *Between Britain and America.* Basingstoke: Palgrave Macmillan.

Goldsmith, Lord (2008) *Citizenship: Our common bond.* London: Ministry of Justice. Available at http://www.justice.gov.uk/reviews/citizenship.htm.

Hazell, R. (ed.) (2006) *The English question.* Manchester: Manchester University Press.

Heath, A., Martin, J. and Elgenius, G. (2007) Who do we think we are?: The decline of traditional social identities In A. Park, J. Curtice, K. Thomson, M. Phillips and M. Johnson (eds), *British social attitudes: The 23rd report: Perspectives on a changing society.* London: Sage.

Heath, A. and Roberts, J. (2008) *British identity: Its sources and possible implications for civic attitudes and behaviour.* (Report prepared for Goldsmith [2008]) Available at http://www.justice.gov.uk/reviews/research.htm.

Heathcoat-Amory, E. (2007) The new apartheid. *Daily Mail,* 16 June.

Heffer, S. (2007) The Union of England and Scotland is over. *Daily Telegraph,* 14 November.

HM Treasury (2008) *Public expenditure statistical analysis 2008.* (HC 489) London: The Stationery Office.

Joppke, C. (2004) The retreat of multiculturalism in the liberal state: Theory and policy. *British Journal of Sociology,* **55**, 237–57.

Kumar, K. (2003) *The making of English national identity.* Cambridge: Cambridge University Press.

McLean, I. (2005) *The fiscal crisis of the United Kingdom.* Basingstoke: Palgrave Macmillan.

McLean, I., Lodge, G. and Schmuecker, G. (2008). *Fair Shares?: Barnett and the politics of public expenditure.* London: Institute for Public Policy Research.

Meer, N. and Modood, T. (forthcoming) The multicultural state we're in: Muslims, 'multiculture' and the 'civic re-balancing' of British multiculturalism. *Political Studies.*

Moreno, L. (2006) Scotland, Europeanization and the 'Moreno Question'. *Scottish Affairs,* **54**, 1–21.

Parekh, B. (2000) Defining British national identity. *Political Quarterly,* **53**, 4–14.

Park, A., Curtice, J., Thomson, K., Phillips, M., Johnson, M. and Clery, E. (eds) (2008) *British social attitudes: The 24th report.* London: Sage.

Park, A. and Surridge, P. (2003) Charting change in British values. In A. Park, J. Curtice, K. Thomson, L. Jarvis and C. Bromley. (eds) *British social attitudes: The 20th report: Continuity and change over two decades.* London: Sage.

Russell, M. and Lodge, G. (2006) Government by Westminster. In R. Hazell (ed.) *The English question.* Manchester: Manchester University Press.

Scottish Government (2008). *Government revenue and expenditure Scotland 2006–2007.* Edinburgh: Scottish Government.

Stirling, S. (2007) Now let us turn to the English question … *Independent,* 1 May.

Tilley J., Exley, S. and Heath, A. (2004) Dimensions of British identity. In A. Park, J. Curtice, K. Thomson, C. Bromley and M. Phillips (eds), *British social attitudes: The 21st report.* London: Sage.

Tilley, J. and Heath, A. (2007) The decline of British national pride. *British Journal of Sociology,* **58**, 661–78.

4
Being Scottish

Frank Bechhofer and David McCrone

Here's tae us; wha's like us?
Gey few ...

It seems abundantly self-evident that people in Scotland have a strong
sense of being Scottish. After all, there is a powerful, and all too apparent
set of cultural icons: ruined castles, tartan, kilts, haggis and shortbread,
geared but not exclusively to the tourist industry. So omnipresent is this
Scottish cultural iconography that some have argued that it is detrimental
to a 'proper' sense of Scottish identity. Murray Grigor's famous festival
exhibition Scotch Myths (1983) managed to be both celebratory and con-
demnatory of the 'classic' icons. Sport also marks Scotland out as distinctive; having national[1] teams playing football, rugby, even, perhaps not
very successfully, cricket provides a vehicle for getting behind the national
team, especially if the opponents are the 'auld enemy', England. Cultural
iconography of this sort is intertwined into Scotland's politics, and in these
days of a (devolved) Scottish Parliament with a Nationalist government in
power, presenting Scotland as a nation is somewhat easier to do than, say,
50 years ago. To be sure, Scotland has long been distinctive in institutional
terms. It survived the Union with England in 1707 with most of its key
civil institutions intact: the legal system, education, religion, its banking
system with its distinctive banknotes, and its burgh politics which for a
long time were much more important in people's lives than the parliamentary variety, which until 1999 took place in faraway Westminster.

To bundle up cultural and political icons in this way is superficially
convincing but presumes that there is a seamless web of Scottish national
identity, and in particular that culture runs into politics. However, as
Ross Bond shows in his chapter, there is no simple connection between
people's sense of 'national' identity and how they do politics, whether

party or constitutional. Indeed, a prior question is whether Scots have a strong and coherent sense of their identity. Who, for example, is to say that they are even aware, never mind inordinately proud, of what may simply be a 'fact of life'? In the Introduction, we referred to Willie McIlvanney's wry observation comparing having a national identity to having an old insurance policy. One might conclude that if the Scots are 'pretty vague' about what it means to be Scottish, then national identity becomes an intriguing, even a problematic, concept.

Having a sense of who you are in national identity terms involves knowing who you are not. As Thomas Eriksen put it: 'We are not only because we have something in common, but perhaps chiefly because we are not them' (2004: 57). And 'them' to the Scots is the English. Scots define themselves *vis-à-vis* the English. That term *vis-à-vis* is the key. 'Against' implies being opposed to, and that is too strong. It means face-to-face with, as if looking in a mirror we see who we are in terms of our antithesis. Defining themselves as 'not English' has led some to pronounce that being Scottish is simply being anti-English, that somehow Scots have no 'content' to their identity except insofar as they dislike their southern neighbours. This misses the point. All sorts of social identities – gender, class, age, ethnicity and so on – involve 'othering', having a sense of self in terms of the other. This is not to imply that there is always symmetrical reciprocity involved. For example, a sense of being a woman or working class or black or young does not mean that those who are male, middle class, white or old have a similar and reciprocated sense of themselves.

Does Scottish mean 'not English'?

Without belabouring the point further, let us say that 'being Scottish' does not imply that 'being English' has to be its analogue. One cannot simply assume that 'English natives', people born and living in England have a common sense of being 'English' let alone that they define themselves as such *vis-à-vis* the Scots? To anticipate somewhat: our colleagues at Lancaster who carried out extensive interviews in England as part of this research programme concluded: 'Respondents in England were generally less inclined than those in Scotland to talk at length about national issues in general, and their sense of national identity in particular' (Condor and Abell, 2006:65). They make the point about the relative 'others':

> [W]hereas in Scotland the meaning of national identity was normally established in contrast to an external (English) other, in England individuals sought to establish the meaning of their personal claims

to national identity through a contrast with the 'typical' English case, or through a radical distinction between past and present. According to this system of accounting, English national identity effectively functions as its own 'other', being constructed *in relation to* (their emphasis) the other UK nations, but defined and evaluated *against* itself.

(Ibid.: 66)

In this chapter, although we are mainly concerned with 'being Scottish', this can only be done adequately with frequent reference to 'the other' and thus comparison with England. However, there are also important comparisons to be made between our prime focus, 'Scottish natives' (people born and living in Scotland), and where appropriate, Scottish migrants (those born in Scotland and living in England), and English migrants (born in England, living in Scotland).

We are interested in how people talk about and 'do' national identity, rather than what we might call 'top-down' identity, or 'state identity', that is, how the state defines its 'nationals' as citizens. This is an important distinction. In many countries, national identity and citizenship are coterminous. North of the border, people are more likely to tell you that they are 'Scottish' in national terms, and 'British' in terms of citizenship, because British is what it says on the passport they hold. Whether the English, who theoretically can also separate national identity from citizenship, would actually do so is a moot point, given the (con)fusion of England/Britain; in practice some would so do and others would not.

We focus on 'personal' national identity, on how people themselves articulate and define who they are and for which purposes. The social anthropologist Anthony Cohen has observed that the concept of 'nation' is something standing outside ourselves, but is

something which simply does not require to be well defined, first, because people presume that they know what they are talking about when they refer to it; and second, because the lack of definition allows them scope for interpretive manoeuvre in formulating or inventing or imagining the nation in terms of their selves for the purposes of personal identity.

(2000: 166)

His point is well taken. As we observed in our introductory chapter, we have long been influenced by an approach to self-definition and self-presentation derived from Erving Goffman (1959). Using both intensive interviews with the same people on two or three occasions a couple of years apart, as well as cross-sectional surveys, we have investigated three related questions: how actors define themselves; how they attribute national identity to others; and how, in turn, they think others attribute identity to them. We are trying to get away from the notion that national identity is an 'essence', something given, most often by the state or higher authority. We prefer to see national identity as a 'prism', through which processes, encounters and events are refracted: a frame of reference which people construct and apply for themselves.

Is national identity important?

How, then, do people articulate who they are (and are not) in national identity terms. The first, critical, question is whether national identity is or is not important. Does it matter compared with, say, being a parent, a partner, your class, religion, age, gender and so on? People like us who study national identity could be accused of thinking that because we think it important, it matters to 'ordinary people'. Back in 2001, we included in a survey a set of questions derived in part from qualitative interviews previous to the study. Respondents were shown a card with a long list of almost thirty social identities, as well as 'national' identities such as Scottish, British. They were then asked: 'Some people say that whether they feel British or Scottish is not as important as other things about them. Other people say their national identity is the key to who they are. If you had to pick just one thing from this list to describe yourself – something that is very important to you when you think of yourself – what would that be?' Respondents were also asked for the second and third most important things. Being a parent and being Scottish stood out as the most important. In Table 4.1, we give the percentages showing their first choice of identity, together with the percentage of the sample choosing the item as either first, second or third choices. The list gives the eight most cited identities. Were Scots any different from the English or Welsh who were also asked this question in comparable surveys in 2001?

The data (Table 4.2) show quite clearly that Scots are much *more* likely than either the English or the Welsh to give their national identity as one of the most important and they are far *less* likely to say that they are British.

One might argue that presenting these data in this way masks the fact that not everyone in the sample is, for example, a parent or a partner,

Table 4.1   Identity choices in Scotland (2001)

% choosing identity	First choice	All choices
Mother/Father	24	49
Scottish	17	45
Working person	9	29
Wife/Husband	5	27
Woman/Man	9	25
Working class	9	24
Retired	3	11
British	4	11
N	1605	1605

Source: Scottish Social Attitudes 2001.

Table 4.2   Identity choices in Scotland, England and Wales (2001)

% choosing identity	Scotland	England	Wales
Mother/Father	49	48	50
Wife/Husband	27	27	27
Woman/Man	25	30	22
Scottish/English/Welsh	45	20	33
British	11	27	23
Working class	24	19	23
Working person	29	32	26
N	1605	2786	1085

Sources: British and Scottish Social Attitudes 2001; and Welsh Election Study 2001.

and that specific subgroups may assemble identities differently. When we look at the extent to which subgroups say they are Scottish or British or defined by the subgroup identity, we find the following (Table 4.3).

Being Scottish matters to *all* subgroups with some variations. For example, while women are more likely than men to choose their gender identity, virtually the same proportion of men and women choose being Scottish. Similarly, the self-identifying middle class are considerably less likely than working class identifiers to choose their class identity but only slightly less likely to say they are Scottish.[2]

Not unreasonably, some critics pointed out that the preamble to this question foregrounded 'national' identity, which might have predisposed respondents to choose it. So in 2003 we omitted the preamble.[3] We found very similar results to those above in both Scotland and England and Wales. And then, to tighten the question even further, in

Table 4.3 Percentage within each social category choosing relevant identity (Scotland, 2001)

	% choosing Scottish	% choosing British	% choosing subgroup identity	Subgroup	N
Men	40	15	22	male	645
Women	41	8	35	female	960
18–24	57	8	53	young	136
65+	37	12	40	old	400
Married	40	11	44	wife or husband	805
Middle class identifier	40	15	15	middle class	392
Working class identifier	47	8	32	working class	1152
Protestant	46	13	12	Protestant	598
Catholic	44	6	33	Catholic	225
All	45	11	-		1605

Note: Percentages are those within each social category mentioning relevant identity as their first, second or third choice.
Source: Scottish Social Attitudes 2001.

Table 4.4 Identity choices for Scots and English* (2006)

% choosing identity	Scots	English
Mother/Father	55	49
Wife/Husband/Partner	43	41
Woman/Man	32	37
Working person	37	34
Working class	33	27
N	1286	2366

* categories 'Scots' and 'English' refer to respondents born and living in the respective countries. There was no comparable survey in Wales in 2006.
Sources: Scottish and British Social Attitudes 2006.

2006 we omitted 'national' identities – Scottish/English/British – from the original list and found the above frequencies (Table 4.4).

Respondents were then asked whether, if these had been available to them, they would have chosen Scottish or English or British *instead of* one of those identities originally chosen. Almost half (46 per cent) of Scots and one-third of English people would have done so. Further, among these people, nine out of ten Scots opted for 'Scottish' and only one in ten 'British', whereas 57 per cent of the English people chose 'English' and 49 per cent British. While these data are not strictly comparable with those from 2001 and 2003,[4] it is clear that this more rigorous test of national identity broadly repeats the earlier results. If we recalculate the figures as a percentage of the total sample (both those who would and those who would not have chosen national identity had they been offered it), 42 per cent of Scots choose 'being Scottish' (and only 5 per cent being British), compared with 18 per cent of the English who choose 'being English' (and 16 per cent 'being British'). Indeed, whichever way the question is asked – with or without preamble, with or without national identity in the list – we find that Scots place their national (but not their state) identity high on the list, the English considerably lower, although significantly both nationalities rate other social identities very similarly. In other words, we can be fairly sure that Scots rate being Scottish highly, and certainly more than the English do. Indubitably, being Scottish matters.

Does it matter to everyone equally, however? We saw from the 2001 data that young people and the working class were more likely to choose 'Scottish' than older people and the middle class. In terms of the 2006 data, there is a clear age gradient in both Scotland and England, from young to old and gender now also makes a difference as, by and large, men are more likely to choose 'Scottish' within each age group than women. Thus, while 48 per cent of young men in England choose national identity as an important way of identifying themselves, only 28 per cent of men over 65 choose to do so. Scots, unsurprisingly, are even more likely to choose national identity, with 68 per cent of young men and 40 per cent of older men doing so. In terms of those who do this, while English people split marginally in favour of 'being English' compared with 'being British (65 per cent to 57 per cent for the young, and 58 per cent to 42 per cent for the older people), in Scotland, both young and old opt for being 'Scottish' in massive numbers (96 per cent and 71 per cent respectively).

Whatever happened to being British?

Clearly, then, national identity matters, especially in Scotland, but even in England. We have also seen that the two populations balance up national identity (being Scottish/English) and 'state' identity (being British) in different ways. We have to be careful here, because in England there has been a history of confusing England and Britain, and at times treating them as synonyms. One way of refining the data – although we still cannot be absolutely sure that people in England properly understand the difference between English and Britain in their responses – is to use what has become known as the Moreno question,[5] a five point scale ranging from 'Scottish, not British; more Scottish than British; equally Scottish and British; more British than Scottish; to British, not Scottish'. We know, from in-depth interviews when we asked respondents to do so and then explain their decision, that it involves a calculation. This person captures the process nicely:

> No. 1 (Scottish, not British) is out, 'cos I do think of myself as British. No. 3 (equally Scottish and British) is out. I was looking at that one but I said I was Scottish first, and I stand by that. I live here; if I'd lived in England all my life I would probably have said 'more English than British'. But if I chose 'equally Scottish and British' it would mean I would accept a British football team which I wouldn't. I want a Scottish one.

Faced with the 5 categories on the scale, people narrow down their choices before choosing their final one. We also know from longitudinal studies – which go back and re-interview people periodically – that there is quite a lot of switching between national identity categories in Scotland, but rarely beyond the adjacent one. Thus, someone may say they are 'Scottish, not British' on one occasion, and 'more Scottish than British' at the next, and for perfectly good reasons, depending on the stimuli and context. For instance, the exclusively Scottish response may seem more appropriate to some people on sporting occasions when Scotland are playing or at typically Scottish occasions such as a Hogmanay party or Burns night. For others, a Scottish parliamentary election may evoke the more 'extreme' reaction. On other, less Scottish, occasions the same people may choose 'more Scottish than British'. Very rarely, however, do they jump two categories.

The data for 2006 (Table 4.5) show that in Scotland responses are massively skewed towards the 'Scottish' end of the spectrum, whereas in England there is more of a cluster around the mid-point. Nevertheless, a sizeable proportion, more than a third, of the English do prioritise their English identity. Yet this pales into insignificance when compared with the comparable proportion, just under three-quarters, in Scotland. Is this changing over time? As regards England, we can only go back

Table 4.5   National identity choices (Moreno scale) for Scots and English (2006)

% by column	Scots	English
Scottish/English, not British	38	21
More Scottish/English than British	35	16
Equally Scottish/English and British	21	46
More British than Scottish/English	2	7
British, not Scottish/English	1	6
N	1286	2366

Sources: British and Scottish Social Attitudes 2006.

to 1997 when the question was first asked in surveys, but we do find that whereas the mid-point has remained the modal one (45 per cent in 1997, compared with 46 per cent in 2006), the balance of 'English' to 'British' has shifted from parity (24 per cent 'only or mainly English', and 23 per cent 'only or mainly British', in 1997) to the 37 per cent and 13 per cent we see in the 2006 figures. In other words, people in England seem to be somewhat more willing to say they are 'English' these days at the expense of being 'British', and this may, in due course, have implications for the Scots and their strong sense of being Scottish.

An ever-increasing proportion of Scots choosing to prioritise their Scottishness is highly improbable because of what is often referred to as a 'ceiling effect'; the figure is already about as high as it is likely to get. However, the meaning of the statement and the content of this Scottishness could change. At present those prioritising their Scottishness tend to see this more culturally than politically. But this is a nice example of why it is so difficult to predict future, long-term developments. For instance, an increasing sense of Englishness south of the border might lead to an English Parliament or (perhaps more likely) reduced voting powers at Westminster for Scottish MPs. One might expect that, maybe only temporarily, this would enhance the political dimensions of Scottishness especially as such changes at Westminster would almost inevitably increase demands for increased powers for Holyrood as a quid pro quo. An increased political sense of being Scottish, if sustained, might well weaken the Union. While this is perhaps the more likely scenario, it is possible to paint a different picture where a stronger national identity on both sides of the border gave rise to a sense of greater similarity rather than difference, increasing the feeling that national identity is cultural, possibly even reducing pressure for constitutional change.

Our Scottish data take us back to 1992, when 59 per cent of Scottish residents described themselves as 'only or mainly Scottish', 33 per cent 'equally Scottish and British' and 6 per cent 'only or mainly British'. By 2006, then, there had been a considerable rise at the 'Scottish' end, little change at the 'British' end, and consequently a significant decline in the numbers describing themselves as equally Scottish and British. Perhaps the reader finds this relatively small proportional increase in those prioritising Scottishness surprising, given the turbulent constitutional politics of the last decade in particular, and the creation of the Scottish Parliament. It does not, on the face of it, seem that having a parliament in Edinburgh has led to a strengthening of people's sense of Scottishness, perhaps in part because so many had a strong sense of it anyway. However, as Ross Bond points out in his chapter, people's sense of 'national' identity is a poor predictor of their constitutional politics, and we should not be too surprised.

What does it mean to be Scottish?

When someone says, in answer to a question such as the one we have just discussed, that they have a strong sense of being Scottish, it does not necessarily mean that they have given it serious and lengthy thought. Nor does it tell us anything about what they mean by it, or indeed that there is not a variety of meanings under the single label. Here is an account from an extended interview with someone born and living in Scotland:

> I think birth is the key criteria because you have to have a logic, don't you? There has to be some form of logic that says 'this is it, this is what makes you whatever'. Ancestry I don't think matters. If they had to have everyone back here that had an ancestor that lived in Scotland, Scotland would sink. No, you're American if your parents are Scottish and you were born in America, you're American, of Scottish extraction.

If truth be told, most Scots usually take their Scottishness for granted, for reasons articulated by McIlvanney in his 'insurance policy' analogy. Why bother interrogating yourself if it's a taken-for-granted and 'banal' identity,[6] a point nicely made by one of the people we interviewed referring initially to the letter inviting them to talk to a researcher:

> But why should I need an envelope through my door to address whether I'm Scottish or not? But then again, it's like breathing, you

do it. You don't think it. It's what you do every day and then some-
body says to you 'why are you breathing?' then you've got to stop
and think about it. So for me to feel Scottish and then [for] some-
body just to come along and say 'why are you Scottish?' I maybe felt
like, it's a superficial thought that I've had before. But even the fact
that I've been given a week to think about it, I still think that I'm
Scottish because I was born here.

Over a decade ago at the start of the process of constitutional change,
we asked people in the 1997 Scottish election study about their criteria for Scottishness: straightforwardly, how important or unimportant
birth, ancestry (defined as having Scottish parents or grandparents)
and residence were to being Scottish. We chose these criteria because
our qualitative interviews strongly suggested that these were the main
markers in operation north of the border. Table 4.6 is a summary of how
people responded in the survey:
    We can draw various conclusions from these figures:

- that a clear majority of people living in Scotland accept all three
  criteria;
- that of the three, birth stands out as the strongest (82 per cent say it
  is very or fairly important, compared with 73 per cent for ancestry,
  and 65 per cent for residence);
- that almost two-thirds accept the most liberal criterion – residence – as
  a definition of a Scot.

That being born in Scotland is the key marker of one aspect of
national identity was to a large extent confirmed at the time of the
1999 election survey (for the first devolved Scottish parliament)
when we asked people to choose criteria for Scottish citizenship (in
terms of who should be entitled to a Scottish passport) in the event

Table 4.6   Criteria for being Scottish (1997)

% by column	Birth	Ancestry	Residence
Very important	48	36	30
Fairly important	34	37	35
Not very important	14	22	23
Not at all important	3	4	10
N	882	882	882

Source: Scottish Election Study 1997.

of Scotland becoming independent. Almost all (97 per cent) said anyone born and currently living in Scotland; 8 out of 10 anyone born
in Scotland but not currently living here; just over half accepted the
'residence' qualification without being born in Scotland; one-third,
that if you had a Scottish-born parent but weren't born nor currently
lived in the country; and half of that number – 16 per cent – on the
basis of a Scottish grandparent alone (McCrone, 2001: 173). What
this suggests is that people in Scotland adopt a more or less open
definition of being a Scottish *citizen*, possibly because it is politically
uncontentious, and all Scotland's political parties have supported an
open-door policy in the light of encouraging inward migration and
settlement.

Being Scottish is also a matter of culture and heritage. And judgements are usually made in comparison with others. Here, for example,
are comments from two 'Scottish nationals', that is, people born and
living in Scotland:

> I'm proud to be Scottish. I always have been and I always will be. It's
> a lot to do with our heritage and where we come from, a nice place to
> stay. I think Scottish people have got a certain personality to them ...
> you tend to find the Scottish people will take the back seat and they'll
> weigh up the situation. They don't jump in with two feet. They're not
> as mouthy as the people down south, you usually find they're quite
> knowledgeable but they're not prepared to push it as much as what
> the English are.

> It's daft but I guess I like the Scottish culture and, if there is such a
> thing as a Scottish culture, but I do think, in general, Scotland's a pretty
> welcoming culture compared to a lot of people, probably because a
> lot of Scots have travelled, throughout history. Generally I think Scots
> have got quite an open mind about what's happening in the world.

Culture is something of a catch-all term; so in the 2006 survey we gave
people a list of Scottish 'cultural' items, and asked them to choose the
most important (and then the second most important). Their responses
are given in Table 4.7.

The most important Scottish cultural icons are the Scottish landscape
(mentioned in all by 46 per cent), music and the arts (38 per cent), followed by a 'sense of equality' (35 per cent), language (30 per cent) and
the Scottish flag (27 per cent), and some way behind, Scottish sporting
achievements (14 per cent).

Table 4.7 Scottish cultural icons (2006)

% by column	Most important	2nd most important
Sense of equality	23	12
Scottish landscape	22	24
Scottish music and the arts	18	20
Scottish flag (Saltire)	14	13
Sporting achievements	6	8
Language (Gaelic or Scots)	12	18
N	1594	1594

Source: Scottish Social Attitudes 2006.

As Billig pointed out, the national flag is one of the most potent icons of national identity, and so it proves to Scots. Over seven in ten are very or a bit proud of the Saltire, the national flag (71 per cent in 2001; 76 per cent in 2003). What is perhaps more surprising, and a refutation of the idea that being Scottish is being anti-British, is that people's reaction to the state flag – the Union Jack – is indifference, not hostility. Thus, over half (60 per cent in 2001 and 55 per cent in 2003) say they don't feel much pride or hostility either way. Even among those who say they are Scottish not British we find little *hostility* to the Union Flag – 7 per cent (2001) and 12 per cent (2003). Just as with national identity, Scots opt for the Scottish over the British icon, but without seeing the choice as either/or.

So what can we say about the content of Scottish identity? Is it cultural, political or both? In 2006 respondents were asked: 'Some people say that being Scottish is mainly about landscape, music, sporting teams, language and literature and so on. Others say that being Scottish is mainly about, for example, the way Scotland is governed, the Scottish Parliament and how Scotland runs its affairs. Whereabouts would you put yourself on a scale between these two positions?' The median score for all those living in Scotland (where 1 is 'cultural' and 7 is 'political') was three (with a mean of 3.19); and nine out of ten saying cultural matters were very or quite important for being Scottish, compared with five out of ten saying political matters were very or quite important. Scottish natives, those born *and* resident in Scotland, were broadly on the same position on the scale (median of 3; mean of 3.17), with a similar view of the importance of 'culture' and marginally more in number thinking 'politics' very or quite important (66 per cent), suggesting that 'natives' are slightly more concerned than 'residents' as a whole to take the view that how Scotland is governed matters.

Can you become Scottish?

So far in this chapter we have emphasised that Scots have a strong sense of their national identity, and that most of the time it's a taken-for-granted thing, usually based on where you are born, something, of course, over which none of us has control. This takes us to an important issue: Can you become Scottish, especially if you weren't born in Scotland? We have seen that residence, living in Scotland, is an important criterion for being thought of as Scottish, but is it enough? In this section, we will do two things: explore, using qualitative data, how English migrants to Scotland tackle this question, and in turn how Scottish 'natives' react to such claims if they are made. Secondly, we will use survey data to look at how willing (or not) Scots are to accept the notional claims of people not born in Scotland, white or non-white, with or without Scottish ancestry. At the end of this section, we should have a clearer understanding of how Scottishness is acquired and/or ascribed.

Migrants are, in sociological terms, particularly interesting. According to the 2001 census, there are around 800,000 Scots-born people currently living in England, and 400,000 English-born people living north of the border. Being born, and usually brought up, in another country which may 'do' identity differently, they tend to have a more explicit awareness of national identity. Our data here are based on intensive interviews with people living in a large Scottish city as well as those living in small-town, rural communities. In a previously published paper (Kiely et al., 2005), we observed that many English migrants talked about their national identity in English as well as in British terms. Some used an 'English' frame when talking about family, history, language and sport; and 'British' when referring to the media, politics or matters of geography. Some, indeed, used 'English' and 'British' interchangeably. Above all, many encountered a different way of talking about national identity than they had been used to. Here are three examples:

> There's more of a sense of Scottishness [in Scotland]. In England it doesn't mean anything to be English. I don't think I thought that much about being English.

> I've never really thought about it before but I do think that the English don't have a strong sense of Englishness.

> I think it's a peculiarly English trait. I find it quite frustrating that we, the English, I, as an Englishman or the English, as a generic group of people, probably don't have an identity that you're proud of. We don't kind of have a heritage that we're proud of.

Given this weak sense of being English, did migrants want to or think they could become Scottish? Most did not make belonging claims to being Scottish, despite the fact that many regarded Scotland as home and had no plans to leave. They spoke of what prevented them from being Scottish, and then went on to articulate what made them English. We then asked: 'Can you become Scottish?'

For most, their English nationality was essentially a fact of birthplace; for many, simply an accident of birth, and not something to which they attached importance or pride. Ancestry seldom figured in their ideas of national identity and was never prioritised over birth. Here are two typical examples, one using the telling phrase 'accident of birth':

> I'm just aware that I was born in England so I'm English only through my birth.

> Nationality is really an accident of birth. I don't see it as something to be ashamed of but I don't see it as something to be terribly proud of.

Migrants, when talking about England, made fewer connections than Scottish nationals between birth and early upbringing on the one hand, and a sense of attachment and commitment to place, on the other. Because for such migrants, nationality and identity derive strictly from birth, most English migrants found it impossible to think of themselves as Scottish, however much they wished to do so; it was literally unthinkable, and many saw it as tantamount to making a false claim.

Some went further, seeing Scottish national identity as deriving from blood as well as birth, as in this exchange between interviewer (I) and respondent (R):

I: Can I ask why you don't think that you can claim to be Scottish?

R: Because I'm being honest. I like being here, I like being associated with the people but I don't like to go out into the street and say 'Yeah, I'm a better Scot than you'. Because people could quite rightly turn round and say, 'You're an Englishman'.

I: So it's because of your place of birth that you can never think of yourself as being Scottish?

R: Not really, because I think it goes back to where you were born. It doesn't have to be I suppose but I think if you are here, born in Scotland and your name is

Mc-something it's 10:1 you'll have a tartan attached to your name and you can find lists of them. So people can go 'Oh aye, he's a McDiarmid or he's a Cameron' and you can practically then identify it with a part of Scotland also, that the name histori-cally came from.

I: There's no sense that because you're living in Scotland, you're then Scottish?

R: Not really, I live the Scottish way, let's put it that way but that doesn't make me a Scotsman.

I: Even if you might choose to want to make that claim?

R:(pause)   There's a possibility that could be so but to me if you were to cast it down in writing there's an element to it not being true. If I'm writing a thing down it should be factually correct.

Some migrants, however, particularly those who had lived in Scotland for some time, articulated a strong sense of commitment to Scotland, and were, in fact, claiming to be Scottish by *living* the identity as illus-trated by these two people.

I don't think of myself as English at all. Really, I feel, as much as any-thing, Scottish, if you want to … because I've been here so long now, 35 years. My wife's been here longer than she lived in England. Our home is here now. We're not moving from here. I'll die here and, as I say, 3 of my children are living here and I identify with it. The chari-ties I contribute to, the charitable things I try to do, are for Scotland. Scotland's given me a lot and I owe something.

I'd probably say I was Scottish because I've lived here mostly … I have a stronger sense of being Scottish but then that's a culture thing. It's more the things you do, the people you see, the places you're used to going to, to the kind of lifestyle we lead. I think the Scottish way of life is slightly different to the English way of life. It's much faster down south unless you're in a really rural area, I would say. I find we have a lot more personal space in Scotland.

Migrants commonly stressed living in Scotland out of *choice*, for instance saying 'It's not just an accident of birth that I live here, I chose to live here', in contradistinction to many 'native-born' Scots who choose to live else-where, showing neither commitment nor direct contribution to Scotland.

Belonging claims to Scottishness are often heavily qualified and tentative. Phrases such as 'I *feel* I am Scottish' or 'I *think* I am Scottish' are
used, but very rarely the definitive 'I *am* Scottish'. Migrants also tended
to temper their Scottish claims by saying that they weren't 'true' Scots
or 'real' Scots.

> I'm very proud that we live in Scotland even though I'm perhaps
> not entirely Scottish but I'd like to think of me as Scottish, because
> I do live here.

The qualified nature of their claims sometimes reflects a perception that
Scots by birth or blood judge the claims to be weak. This person went
on to say:

> I don't think we can say we're truly Scottish because we were born
> in England, we've still got that nationality, you know, originally,
> because you were simply born in England, you can't take that, you
> can't scrub it out and say you're Scottish. Once you've been born in
> England, *they* will still think of you as English.

So what do 'they' think? Is this last respondent right or are Scottish
nationals willing to accept such claims? Can migrants become Scottish,
we asked 'native Scots'? The most common response was to deny that
it was possible. It is a dramatic confirmation of the salience and importance of Scottish identity to Scots that some could not even compre-
hend that anyone would want to claim a nationality other than one
based on their birthplace. Here are two examples:

> I think if somebody was born in England, they'd always class ther-
> selves as English. Well personally, I was born in Scotland. There
> is no way I'd ever class myself as being English or British. I'm
> Scottish.

> R: I have a friend that was born in Ireland, raised in Bath, has
>   moved all over the place and he sounds very English when you
>   speak to him but he has spent longer in Scotland than he has
>   anywhere else and he thinks of himself as Scottish.
> I: Would you think of him as being Scottish?
> R: I don't think of him being Scottish, no. That's because he doesn't
>   sound Scottish. It's because he speaks with a very posh English
>   accent.

Scottish nationals think of national identity as a matter of birth, and to a lesser extent, belonging. They also assume that others 'do identity' in similar ways to themselves. Claims by migrants based on belonging would then probably be rejected by most nationals, given the emphasis on birth. Consider this national's comment:

> They can't become Scottish, they can be integrated into a Scottish community. I think that's fine but as far as becoming Scottish. To go back to what I said before, not that generation but then the next generation. So if their kids are born in Scotland, if they choose to become, I think that's fine.

This national clearly challenges the right of a first generation (non-birth) belonging claim to Scottishness, yet sees the next generation as having full rights to claim Scottishness by birth. There is, however, a belonging element involved, given the active choice to commit to Scotland. This was the majority view of our nationals when assessing the nationality of migrants' children born in Scotland. A number of nationals said that migrants to Scotland might see *themselves* as Scottish but they would not share this perception.

> Become Scots? I would say no, myself, but there are certain people I've met, from other countries, that they just seem to fall in love with Scotland and they've been here for quite a few years and they like to sort of think thersel as Scots and I wouldnae knock that. I would accept it but I think deep down, I would accept it to their face but I think deep down I would say to masel 'well he wants to be Scots, he loves it up here' and I wouldnae knock but he'll never be Scots.

Making a belonging claim, then, would not necessarily be challenged or rejected *overtly* by Scottish nationals. Such claims, anyway, tend to be of a qualified nature reducing the likelihood of overt rejection. A few nationals, however, *were* willing to a degree to accept belonging claims, sometimes with reservations. For example, it would apply only in very specific personal circumstances such as coming to live in Scotland at a very young age, or attempting to erase a negative experience of living elsewhere as suggested by these two respondents:

> From an early age, yes. I don't think if they're in their 20s and 30s and they move up here, and they're up here for another 20 or 30 years then they are still English more than Scottish. I think your first

years, up to 10 years old or so, really is where you learn about where you live and the culture you live.

If you didn't have a strong association with wherever you did come from to start with, I suppose it would be, over a lot of time. Yeah, I suppose so but then you'd have to have presumably not a lot of pride in wherever you did come from, to be willing to become Scottish, I think.

Accepting the claim of migrants to be Scottish also depended on context:

I: Do you think it would be possible for someone to become Scottish?

R: Absolutely. John [pseudonym], the English guy, he's English but his father was Asian and he becomes more and more Scottish every day. He's just basically one of the boys and the only time basically it's remembered that he's English is when we play them at football and that's it, suddenly John's English again. But his accent has even changed, he's as Scottish as anyone else, because now he's lived here for this long that this is his patch as well.

I: Would he, in any way, describe himself as being Scottish?

R: He probably could do if the boys didn't remind him, at times, as I say, usually sporting times, that he was English. He probably could do. Put it this way, to his mates in Bradford, he's like Scottish John. They'll wind him up about his accent or just the way that he talks and does things because he does things Scottish, stupid things. Aye, to his Bradford mates he's became Scottish John but to us he has became Scottish John but really he's still English John, I know it sounds daft but [pause] [laughs].

So can English migrants become Scottish? It seems that many do not try, because they share the Scots' view that national identity is a matter of where you are born, a view reinforced by Scottish nationals' responses to such claims. Some migrants, on the other hand, do make tentative claims based on choice and commitment to Scotland, what we might call 'living the identity', and were gratified to find in some cases that their claim as 'adopted' Scots was accepted. This was especially so for those whose children had been born north of the border, and who could claim to be Scottish through (birth) association.

Claiming Scottishness

The interviews which generated such comments were a rich source of ideas for us in our survey work on national identity. It became clear that many, nationals and migrants alike, were making calculations based on multiple criteria. What if, for example, you were born elsewhere, but your parents were Scottish? What if the person had a Scottish accent? Did it make a difference if the person making the claim was white or non-white? Accordingly, we set up a suite of questions asking respondents whether they were more or less likely to accept claims if the putative claimant had various known characteristics.

In the 2006 survey, people were asked:[7]

'I'd like you to think of a white person who you know was born in England, but now lives permanently in Scotland. This person says they are Scottish. Would you consider this person to be Scottish?' They were given a card showing four possible responses plus 'Don't Know'(DK). These were: 'Definitely would'; 'Probably would'; 'Probably would not'; 'Definitely would not'.

Respondents, except those who said 'Definitely would', were then asked (and offered the same choices): 'What if they had a Scottish accent? Would you consider them to be Scottish?'

Finally, excepting those who said 'Definitely would' to the previous question, they were asked: 'And what if this person with a Scottish accent also had Scottish parents? Would you consider them to be Scottish?' The results appear in Table 4.8.

There is some, but not a large, difference as regards rejecting a non-white as opposed to a white person. Thus, while 55 per cent would reject the white claim, 59 per cent would reject the non-white one, and as we progressively introduce accent and parentage, we find the differentials are 40 per cent to 48 per cent, and 18 per cent to 29 per cent respectively. We might conclude that lowering the barriers steadily increases the acceptance rate of someone born in England and slightly raises the white/non-white differential. The biggest shift is when parentage is introduced, a rise of 23 per cent for white claimants, to four out of five people (81 per cent), and rather less than 18 per cent for non-white to two thirds (68 per cent).

Is Scotland different from England in these regards? Suffice it to say that the similarities far outweigh the differences in the way that respondents accept and reject hypothetical claims, whether from white or non-white persons. While there is a slightly greater tendency for Scots to reject non-white claims, in both countries those who say they are

Table 4.8 Acceptance and rejection of claims by a white person born in England, but living permanently in Scotland

% by column	White	White with Scottish accent	White, Scottish accent, and Scottish parents	Non-white	Non-white with Scottish accent	Non-white, Scottish accent, and Scottish parents
Definitely would	14	19	37	12	15	26
Probably would	30	39	44	26	35	42
Probably would not	30	24	12	31	26	18
Definitely would not	25	16	6	28	22	11
DK/NA	1	1	1	3	2	2
N	1302	1302	1302	1302	1302	1302

Source: Scottish Social Attitudes 2006.

Scottish and English respectively – and not British – what we might call the 'exclusive nationals' – are equally likely to reject claims from non-white people if they are not born in the appropriate country. Possibly this is racism, but they are also likely to reject claims from white people who are not born there. What does stand out is that thinking of yourself in exclusively national terms, as 'Scottish, not British' or as 'English, not British', makes you less willing to accept claims, possibly because you think of national identity as an exclusive club, and are more likely to scrutinise applicants more carefully. The ambivalence about accepting a non-white person as Scottish is nicely put by an English migrant, so we get a doubly reflexive comment from a 'migrant' on a non-white person being (or not) accepted by the host Scots:

I: Do you think that being white is a very prominent marker of being Scottish?

R: Yeah, I think it is and I think it shouldn't be. I'm not happy that it's that way. But again it's not something that you notice until you are faced with someone who isn't white. Meeting someone who is ethnically Chinese with a Scottish accent was like a revelation, because he didn't look like he sounded. And I found it quite hard, he called himself Scottish and he wore kilts and he did Scottish things and he looked Chinese. And it took a bit to adjust to it. Whereas if he'd said I'm British I would have said 'yeah, fine'. But he said 'I'm Scottish' and I thought 'Oh no you're not'.

I: Almost that, I don't know, the colour of skin would be seen as contradictory to that.

R: Yeah, but the accent was what really threw me and the kilt, that was too much ... If I see a white person who says that they are Scottish I don't think about it all I just accept it. If I see someone with a different colour who says that they are Scottish I do think about it.

We have, then, both survey and in-depth interview material which shows that people make quite careful and gradated judgements about who is or is not to be counted as Scottish, and, in passing, that the evidence shows the English are not that different, even though they 'do' national and state identity differently, having an apparently weaker, but growing, sense of 'being English'.

That leaves us with an obvious question: what do Scots-born migrants do when they go to live in England? Would they, like some

English migrants, wish to be taken for English? How do you 'do' Scottish south of the border? Crucially, migration to England, even long residence there and strong feelings of being at home, does not lead to migrant Scots claiming to be English. Take for example this account:

> But English, it's all to do with the thing, it's to do what's in your guts you know. And I will never be English. Um, I will be more comfortable in England and I will understand a bit more about what makes the English tick. But I think the English themselves are rather a diverse group of people. Um, but um no I'll not become English and I'll never say that I'm English I don't think.

Almost without exception, they still claimed to be Scottish, saw that in positive terms, and did not consider themselves in any way 'English'. Some commented that they were less vociferously 'Scottish' in England, and had a greater awareness that 'the English' were rather more diverse as a national group than they had expected. They denied that they had become anglicised, but some admitted to having modified their accents for English ears, something they noticed when they went back to Scotland to visit people. Here is a comment by one Scottish migrant to England when asked if he thought he was becoming anglicised:[8]

> I don't know. Other people would probably better answer that question than I. It's never been said to me when I've gone home, I've heard it said of other people, 'Oh, you're losing your accent, you sound English'. No one has ever said that to me. I know I do sound differently, you know, when I'm with friends, I talk faster, probably use more colloquialisms from the local area than I ever would do where I live or where I work, simply because no one would understand me. But from that point, it's not a concession, it's how you live, you have to deal with it. If you were that stupid or that ignorant, that you spoke that faster than that sort of broad, then you wouldn't get by, no one would understand. That's changed, but, again, it's not a conscious thing, I don't sort of suddenly get back and think, 'Oh, it's time to talk like this rather than that, it just, it just happens'.

Neither do Scottish migrants indicate that they felt under pressure to become English. Most thought that, as Scots, they had been well received. Scotland is frequently described as 'home' and in emotional terms, even after people have long settled in England. Take this encounter:

I: Can you become English?

R: I suppose if you want to you can perceive yourself. If you've got the feeling inside that you are, I guess you can but I don't think that I'll ever think I'm English or become English no matter how long I stay here. But that might just be me, I don't know.

I: I was wondering if other people see them as Scottish?

R: I just can't see a Scottish person ever saying that they were English, it's just too much. But also you know that England, the reputation of England and what is English it's got a lot of negative things, too many, because obviously English people are not, they are not even that different really we're not different. But there is a negativity, which Scottish don't have, and I think Scots are seen quite positively. So I can see why people would want to say that they were Scottish.

I: What feels different?

R: I don't know, I notice it mostly when I go back to Scotland and just feel something, just something different, something inside, I can't really explain it, you know. And um, even though I'm starting to call it home here I'll never be, ever describe myself as coming from England. You know if anybody ever asked, 'where are you from?' 'I'm from Aberdeen but I live in Manchester', you know.

Being Scottish is normally taken as a given, an essence, as in this comment from someone who has lived 30 years in England:

I: What about your feelings about being Scottish? Have they changed in recent times?

R: What, about me being Scottish?

I: Yeah, or your general feelings of Scottishness. Have they changed?

R: No, it's just there. Yeah. It's always there in the background. It's always part of the kernel of – the kernel of me.

Migrants to England had, then, lost none of their Scottishness but a minority had also adopted a heightened sense of being British.

I: Do you feel more Scottish now you've moved here?

R: I feel more British now I've moved here.

I: That's interesting.

R: 'Cos, I know, when I was a teenager, you know, filling in forms I would always put that I was Scottish, and then you put British. And, I'm Scottish first and British second. And then, always been that, in England it's British first and English second. And I never thought about that way. Erm. I'm probably more proud of being Scottish, here than when I was at home, it's just one of those things.

The 'umbrella' aspect of being British had an appeal to those Scottish migrants who assumed that 'British' would not be taken, as it some-times is in England, as a synonym for 'English' but many are reluctant to say they are British, recognising as this person does, that its meaning, in England at least, is not clear cut:

R: I guess, erm, you know, if ever I'm asked to state my national-ity, it's Scottish and always will be.

I: What about British? Have you any sense of being British?

R: Don't think so, to be perfectly honest, cos, I can't really explain why or why not. I don't see it as being one or the other, it's just Scottish not English, you know, but, we have, we have the usual story about when something's good, it's always English, and when something's not good, it's er, if you got your soccer hooligans, they're all of a sudden British and not English.

When Scottish migrants talk about 'the English' and Englishness, they tell of their initial bewilderment that they did not encounter strong feelings on English national identity matching those they knew in Scotland. Several made the point that they were more likely to celebrate certain iconic aspects of Scottishness in England – Burns' suppers, St Andrews Day, wearing national dress – than 'back home'. They com-mented that these expressions of Scottishness seem to be positively valued by English people, and are subject, like sport, to banter and jok-ing relationships. By and large, however, the consensus is that England is regarded as an identity context in which issues of national identity are much less salient than north of the border, and of greater English concern are migration, asylum, ethnic minorities and the politics of 'race'. Some observed that, post-devolution, there are tensions. 'How come that English MPs cannot vote for Scottish matters, but Scottish MPs can vote on English matters? I do see there is a problem with that now', said one Scottish migrant, in a neat exposition of the West Lothian question.

Conclusion

So what does it mean to be Scottish today? First of all, our evidence suggests that there is no practised litany of Scottishness as such, although Scots are more likely than the English to talk the talk if the evidence of our colleagues' work in England is anything to go by (Condor and Abell, 2006). Nevertheless, national identity in Scotland is an unquestioned fact of birth and upbringing in the main, and most people carry it around with them in a taken-for-granted way. They articulate certain common features of being Scottish. They possess and mobilise shared identity markers such as: birth and upbringing, ancestry and parentage, residence, accent, a sense of commitment and belonging, as well as a set of cultural symbols – sport, humour, recognition and appreciation of Scotland's culture, its heritage, landscape and languages. They seem to be familiar with and share a general sense of comfort with aspects of everyday living; what one English migrant to Scotland called 'living the Scottish way', how civil institutions operate in Scotland. There is a perception of Scotland's image outwith the country, notably when people travel abroad. Travelling with an 'Ecosse' sticker on your car is deemed to be a positive thing, in part to ensure not being taken for 'English'. For example, in our 2006 survey, more than half (52 per cent) of Scottish natives said that they would reply 'Scotland' when asked where they came from when travelling abroad (compared with only 18 per cent of English natives replying 'England'). Similarly, many English migrants in Scotland chose to say, when asked, that they 'came from Scotland' when on holiday abroad, a nicely ambiguous distinction compared with saying they were 'Scottish'.

We do not get a sense of competing ways of being Scottish, with the possible exception of an older form of Unionism which separates out 'cultural' from 'political' matters; wearing the kilt and voting Conservative would be good examples of the 'cultural' and the 'political', perhaps. As we have remarked earlier there is no clear-cut association between how you vote and your constitutional preference on the one hand, and how you construe being Scottish on the other. Thus, while most people who identify with the Scottish National Party (SNP) and who prefer independence (by no means the same thing) say they are 'Scottish, not British', most 'Scots' in these terms do not identify with the SNP, nor want independence. Likewise, most Conservatives are happy to prioritise being Scottish, and prefer devolution to having no Scottish parliament. In other words, few people see 'political' identity as necessary and sufficient for being a Scot. Likewise, the historic 'Protestant' meaning of Scottishness no longer operates, with Catholics and people with no religious affiliations being just as likely to say they are Scottish as those with an affiliation to Protestant churches.

If being Scottish is largely implicit and uncontentious, what can we say about the cultural and social boundaries of Scottishness? While it is the case, as we saw earlier, that non-white people are somewhat more likely to have their 'Scottish' claims rejected than white people, valuable research by, for example, Asifa Hussain and Bill Miller (2006) suggests that people of Pakistani origin in Scotland, by far the largest non-white group, are far more likely than their counterparts in England to adopt hybrid identities – Scottish Pakistani, or Scottish Muslim, for example. They observe that 'English immigrants [to Scotland] crowd the "British" end of the scale and Pakistanis the "Scottish" end (even if not quite so much as "majority Scots" do)' (2006: 148). The evidence south of the border is quite the reverse, that is, among ethnic minorities 'being British' is seen as much more open than 'being English'.

Scotland's largest 'minority' – although they would not describe themselves in this way – are people born in England. English migrants in our studies confirm the strength and depth of Scottishness, from Scottish icons, celebrations and events, a distinctive media, and so on. They are very aware that, par excellence, it is 'Englishness' that is the Scottish other. This, and the strength of identity markers such as birth and upbringing, make it unlikely that English migrants feel they could ever claim full Scottishness, something confirmed by the Hussain and Miller research cited above. Thus, for most English migrants, Scottishness is a fairly closed identity, even though many see it as positive and something to which they aspire; to be taken for Scots, either abroad or when visiting friends and relatives, is spoken of positively. They also attribute to Scottish identity, far more, ironically, than Scottish natives do themselves, an ancestral link, a perception that Scottish 'roots' is a powerful identity marker.

Migration seems to play a different role north of the border. Scotland's population politics, the perceived shortage of labour as well as a low birth rate has encouraged Scottish governments since devolution, unionist and nationalist, to encourage 'New Scots' to settle. All the major political parties buy into the policy, and those who, in England, oppose similar policies such as the British National Party (BNP) and the United

Kingdom Independence Party (UKIP) consistently lose their deposits in all elections in Scotland.

Relatedly, the Scottish diaspora, people of Scottish origin living outwith the country, plays an important part in constructing Scottish national identity, much, but not quite on the scale of the very large and powerful Irish diaspora, especially in the United States. Encouraging inward investment through annual events like 'Tartan Week' in New York, or the 2009 programme of 'Homecoming' organised by the Scottish Government reflects both the economic importance of the diaspora as well as the large numbers of Scots with relatives living abroad, in Canada and the United States, Australia and New Zealand. This, perhaps, helps to reinforce the impression that 'ancestry' is an important identity marker in Scotland, even though in practice most Scots place it well below birth and upbringing.

Finally, and lying behind the programme on which this research and this book are based is constitutional change. What impact, if any, has it had on Scottish national identity? The short answer to this important question is that, while a growing sense of being Scottish helped to fuel the demand for greater self-government in the 1980s and 1990s, during the last decade there has been no significant rise in the number of people saying they are Scottish. This may seem a surprising finding, but it reflects the previously mentioned 'ceiling effect', that so many Scots already prioritise being Scottish over being British, though not at its expense, that few are left to change their views. If the broad proportion saying they are Scottish has not changed a great deal, has the content of Scottishness changed? Has, for example, it become more 'political'? This, of course, is a question which only time will answer, and, in the classic phrase, it is too soon to tell. Nevertheless, there are indications that people have not become more Scottish as a result of devolution. For example, in the 2006 survey, we asked people whether having a Scottish parliament had made them feel more Scottish. Focusing on Scottish natives, people born and living in Scotland, fewer than one-third (28 per cent) of those who gave priority to being Scottish (that is, said they were Scottish, not British, or more Scottish than British) said it had, but fully 40 per cent that it hadn't, with 30 per cent saying neither. We might note in passing that English natives who prioritised being English were more likely to think devolution (whether the Scottish Parliament or the National Assembly for Wales) had made them feel more English (34 per cent compared with 30 per cent who did not think it had).

Neither does the strong sense of being Scottish imply that Scots are hostile to being British. These days fewer may opt to describe themselves as British, but it still represents around two-thirds of people's self-description, albeit in the minor key. In our paper in *Political Quarterly* (Bechhofer and McCrone, 2007) we noted that well over half (56 per cent) of Scots said that they were proud of Britain's past, not ashamed of the Empire (57 per cent), and take a positive view of 'British' as a unifying symbol (59 per cent). Even those who thought themselves Scottish, not British were not uniformly negative, with around half taking a positive view of these aspects of Britishness. Here is a comment from one of our respondents in the in-depth interview study who makes the point for us:

> I'm not at all ashamed of being British, not at all. I suppose every country had a go at getting what it could for itself, at one time and making other people suffer. I'm not really ashamed but I'm very conscious of the fact that everything Britain did is not something we should be proud of.

One might perhaps naively ask: if the Scots and English have quite similar social and political values, why do they not share a common sense of Britishness? One error here is to see such values as 'British' per se, rather than Scottish, or indeed English, in the respective countries. In truth, one can go further. Most Western liberal capitalist countries would sign up to similar values – the rule of law, freedom for the individual, mutual trust and tolerance – without implying that they have the same national identity or indeed wish to be part of the same state. What is clear in the British context is that while Scots do not feel hostile to the idea of Britain and Britishness, they do not define themselves primarily in this way. Attempts by politicians to impose a common sense of being British assume erroneously that it is a moral-cultural identity rather than a political-institutional one. Asking the Scots, or the English for that matter, to sign up to 'British' values in lieu of Scottish (or English) ones is to commit a category error which might, under appropriate circumstances, have serious consequences.

Will having a Scottish Parliament eventually make a difference to national identities? We might construe the Parliament as another brick in the wall of national identity, without assuming that its existence will propel Scotland out of the Union. Indeed, unlike public opinion a decade ago, most Scots according to our surveys think that if independence comes about, it will not be the direct result of having a devolved parliament. It could be, of course, that devolution will drip-feed its way into Scottish consciousness through greater institutional and policy

differences compared with England, notably in health and education and social care. There is also evidence that Scots see the Scottish
Parliament as *the* way of doing politics, witness complaints from Scottish
MPs at Westminster that they have been rendered invisible in the media
by devolution. It might seem odd to say that Scotland, a country which
has been around for a millennium, has an ongoing process of nation
building, or perhaps more accurately, of nation transformation.

National identity and nationalism have a deeply personal quality.
We 'do' national identity in a myriad of intimate and personal ways,
as well as in a macro-social way. In other words, 'nation' is a symbol
mediated through self, and understandings of self and self-presentation,
and is not an external 'object' as such (Cohen, 2000). Thomas Eriksen
has observed that '"nation" is the metaphorical space in which people
locate their personal histories, and thereby their identities' and hence
personal identity is synonymous with national identity (in Cohen,
2000: 152). In saying this, we are not saying that people simply make it
up as they go along, but that there is sufficient sharing of metaphorical
space for a common currency to be developed and recognised: appeals
to shared symbols, ideas, memories, for example. As a symbol, the
nation has the capacity to mean different things to different people, but
with sufficiently shared meanings to do the work. In other words, 'who
one is' is also about who 'we' are; it is not simply a matter of *me-ness* but
we-ness that matters; people making a claim to some shared collectivity
generated through, and in the course of, social and (small p) political
interaction. 'Gey few' – maybe, in crude numerical terms, but in terms
of helping us understand more generally how people 'do' national identity, accepting some claims and rejecting others, gey many.

Notes

1. Where the context makes the term ambiguous we use 'national' to mean any
   of English, Scottish or British, and national (without quotation marks) when
   we mean English or Scottish.
2. For a discussion and further analysis of the 2001 data, see Rosie and Bond,
   2003.
3. In the 2003 surveys, respondents were asked: 'People differ in how they think
   of or describe themselves. If you had to pick just one thing from this list to
   describe yourself – something that is important to you when you think of
   yourself – what would it be?'
4. The question was asked of those born in Scotland and England rather than
   all respondents in Scotland and England as in 2001 and 2003. In practice,
   more detailed analysis suggests it makes little difference which sample is
   used.

5. Strictly this should be called the Juan Linz question, as the political scientist was using the five-point scale in Spain in the 1970s, whereas Luis Moreno used it in a Scottish context in the late 1980s (see Moreno, 2006).
6. The notion of 'banal nationalism' was coined by Michael Billig (1995), to refer to the fact that, like the national flag on buildings, most people took it (and their national identity) for granted and without a second glance. Nevertheless, comments Billig, such implicit national icons reinforce the taken-for-granted.
7. These questions were developed from an earlier sequence of questions in 2003. Although the 2006 questions were somewhat different and, we believe, improved, the results were very similar.
8. Quotes from interviews with Scots in England come from the work of our colleagues Susan Condor and Jackie Abell at Lancaster University who were part of the Leverhulme research programme. Responsibility for the way we use the excerpts is of course entirely ours. We have also edited the quotes very slightly by removing symbols indicating a slight pause by the respondent.

Bibliography

Bechhofer, F. and McCrone, D. (2007) Being British: A crisis of identity? *Political Quarterly*, **78**, 251–60.

Bechhofer, F. and McCrone, D. (2008) Talking the talk: National identity in England and Scotland. In A. Park, J. Curtice, K. Thomson, M. Phillips, M. Johnson and E. Cleary (eds) British social attitudes: The 24th report, 81–104.

Billig, M. (1995) *Banal nationalism*. London: Sage.

Cohen, A. (1994) *Self consciousness: An alternative anthropology of identity*. London: Routledge.

Cohen, A. (2000) *Signifying identities: Anthropological perspectives on boundaries and contested values*. London: Routledge.

Condor, S. and Abell, J. (2006) Vernacular constructions of 'National Identity' in post-devolution Scotland and England. In J. Wilson and K. Stapleton (eds) *Devolution and identity*. Aldershot: Ashgate, 11–32.

Eriksen, T. (2004) Place, kinship and the case for non-ethnic nations. *Nations and Nationalism*, **10**, 49–62.

Goffman, E. (1959) *The presentation of self in everyday life*. New York: Doubleday Anchor.

Grigor, M. (1983) Scotch myths: An exploration of Scotchness [an exhibition devised by Murray and Barbara Grigor, with Peter Rush], Edinburgh International Festival.

Hussain, A. and Miller, W. (2006) *Multicultural nationalism*. Oxford: Oxford University Press.

Kiely, R., Bechhofer, F. and McCrone, D. (2005) Birth, blood and belonging: Identity claims in post-devolution Scotland. *Sociological Review*, **53**, 150–71.

McCrone, D. (2001) *Understanding Scotland*. London: Routledge.

Moreno, L. (2006) Scotland, Catalonia, Europeanization and the 'Moreno Question'. *Scottish Affairs*, **54**, 1–21.

Rosie, M. and Bond, R. (2003) Identity matters. In C. Bromley, J. Curtice, K. Hinds and A. Park (eds) *Devolution – Scottish answers to Scottish questions*. Edinburgh: Edinburgh University Press, 116–36.

5
Political Attitudes and National Identities in Scotland and England

Ross Bond

> Nationalism is primarily a political principle, which holds that the political and the national unit should be congruent. Nationalism as a sentiment, or as a movement, can best be defined in terms of this principle
>
> (Gellner, 1983: 1)

These are the opening sentences of Ernest Gellner's *Nations and Nationalism*, one of the most famous books on the subject, by one of its leading scholars. Gellner's words highlight the fact that any study of nationalism and national identities must consider their political significance, and it is the purpose of this chapter so to do. But in this chapter, and indeed this book, we are concerned with nationalist sentiment of a different kind, that which can more usefully be termed national identity. This relates to a more subjective sense of belonging or attachment to a particular nation, one which the individual assumes is shared with other co-nationals. The chapter will assess the degree to which such sentiments are indeed related to political attitudes.

The chapter will highlight and develop three particular features of 'political' attitudes. Firstly, political attitudes may be represented by people's beliefs about the most appropriate *constitutional* arrangements for the government of the nation within which they are resident: in stark terms, national independence, some form of devolved government at a national level, or centralised government at a state level. This has, self-evidently, been the essence of debates about UK devolution and its possible futures, and, as stated in the introduction, national identities have been an important element of these debates. One might assume that constitutional change in the UK was inspired to a considerable degree by national identities in the 'non-English' territories of the UK and that, in turn, the establishment and further development of the devolved political institutions might change conceptions of national identity in the UK, including in England. Are people's national identities closely aligned with those political attitudes which have constitutional significance? That is the first question which this chapter seeks to answer.

The second kind of political attitudes concerns the degree to which people living in one of the national territories of the UK post-devolution feel solidarity with, or dissociation from, those living in the other national territories. States – even devolved states – need a certain amount of 'glue' to hold them together. The extent to which national identities are shared between the people of Scotland and England is examined elsewhere in this volume, and certainly shared identities are one important element of solidarity, but so too are certain political opinions. To an extent, these cannot be divorced from the constitutional attitudes outlined above. For example, the attitudes of people in England towards Scottish independence may provide an indication of weakening identification and/or increasing antagonism between these different parts of the UK. However, so too might opinions about the economic and fiscal benefits which each of these 'partners' in the Union derives from the continuation of this partnership. Such attitudes may not have a specifically constitutional character, but may nevertheless have important constitutional consequences if evident grievance weakens the glue which holds the state together. Also important in this sense, although less obviously political in character, is the degree to which people identify on a personal level with those who live in a different nation within the UK. So the second central question to be addressed is the extent to which there is evidence of solidarity or dissociation.

In turn, the third dimension also relates to some extent to the issue of identification and may also have constitutional import. These are what we might call 'ideological-legislative' political attitudes. They are less concerned with constitutional issues and more with normative beliefs about social justice and morality and the ways in which governments might exercise power in accordance with these norms. Rather than examine a series of distinct social issues or policy preferences, it is more useful (and economical) to address ideological-legislative preferences in a broader sense. This will be done through utilising two well-established scales, one of which places individuals on a left–right political spectrum, and the second on a libertarian–authoritarian dimension. If the political character and normative beliefs of people from different national units within the same state show profound differences, then once more this might raise questions about the future stability of that state. Thus the third and final question to be answered concerns whether there are any evident ideological divides between different parts of the UK.

The broader question to be addressed, then, concerns what national identities and political attitudes, and the relationships between them, can tell us about the likelihood of further constitutional change in the post-devolution UK. While recognising that Wales and Northern Ireland are an important part of this post-devolution context, in common with the rest of the book the focus will be on England and Scotland. The evidence, which will be drawn upon and evaluated, is taken from questions in large-scale social and political surveys. This represents a contrast and complement to much of the other evidence considered in this book. As Bechhofer and McCrone (2007: 253) point out, surveys are a necessary tool when attempting to assess patterns of national identity across broad populations, but it is also important that we are alive to the limitations of this approach, and these will be discussed briefly below.

Many of the survey questions we draw upon were inspired by constitutional change itself and by associated research programmes, not least The Leverhulme Trust programme upon which the book is founded. However, the sheer diversity of questions which constitutional change has generated (and the resource limitations within which even the most generously funded programmes must work) means that some relevant questions have been asked more frequently, and more recently, than others. The chapter uses the most up-to-date data available with respect to each question. All data are taken from the Scottish and British Social Attitudes Surveys.

National identities and the constitution

This section investigates whether national identities in Scotland and England are related to three issues of constitutional significance: opinions about the best means of governing the respective countries (what might be called constitutional preferences); political party support; and trust in the institutions of government. As has been discussed elsewhere in the book, there are a number of different ways of measuring national identity in survey questions. The method used in this chapter is the 'multiple choice' question which allows people to select as many national identities as they believe apply to them. This question has been consistently asked on an annual basis in the British and Scottish Social Attitudes surveys during the entire period since devolution. Here we use it to identify three categories of respondents in both Scotland and England: those who identify as Scottish or English but *not* British; those who identify as Scottish or English *and* British; and those who identify as British but *not* Scottish or English.[1] So the question allows us to identify whether people adopt an exclusive 'sub-state' national identity (Scottish or English), an exclusive 'state' national identity (British), or whether they adopt both of these and thus have a dual national identity. Others have described this distinction as 'state'/'national' (Bechhofer et al., 1999; McCrone et al., 1998) or 'state'/'ethnonational' (Heath and Kellas, 1998; Kellas, 1998) or 'supranational'/'national' (McCrone, 1997). However, describing both 'sub-state' and 'state' identities as *national* identities is helpful because it makes the important distinction between two different territorial levels while still recognising that, for many people in the UK, Britishness will be conceived of as a national identity in a similar fashion to the 'substate' identities of English, Scottish and Welsh (Bryant, 2006; Gallagher, 1995; Langlands, 1999).

It should, however, also be recognised that for a number of different reasons (historical, geographical, political, cultural, demographic), the state/substate distinction is likely to be more keenly appreciated in Scotland (and indeed in Wales and Northern Ireland) than in England, where many people tend to conflate English and British identities (Kumar, 2003; Langlands, 1999; Rose, 1982). Moreover, the potential limitations of assessing national identities in the UK through survey questions do not end there. As Wyn Jones (2001: 46) points out, even subtler survey measures of national identity do not allow for change in identification based on different social or political contexts. Nor do they uncover the various *meanings* national categories might hold (Brand et al., 1993; Heath and Kellas, 1998; Henderson, 1999), although some survey-based and experimental studies have sought to address this question (see Bechhofer and McCrone, 2007; Haesly, 2005). Nevertheless, surveys have established consistent patterns of difference in national identities between different parts of the UK as well as correlation with other key social and political variables (see, e.g., McCrone et al., 1998; McCrone, 2001) and with alternative measures of national identity and sentiment (see, e.g., Heath et al., 1999; Heath and Smith, 2005). The consistencies are such that one can be confident that, notwithstanding their limitations, these means of measurement are methodologically robust: they are assessing something 'real' about national identities in the UK. Moreover, there is evidence of convergence in findings between studies utilising primarily quantitative and qualitative methods (Bechhofer and McCrone, 2007).

The ways in which respondents to the latest available surveys (2006) in England and Scotland divide between the three categories of national identity previously outlined are shown in Table 5.1. These data reflect differences in patterns of national identities in the two countries discussed elsewhere in the book. Broadly, English and British identities have a much more equal salience in England than do Scottish and British identities in Scotland, where Scottish identity is clearly much more prominent, although dual identities also account for one-third of respondents.[2]

Table 5.1 Dual and exclusive national identities in England and Scotland (2006)

% by column	England	Scotland
English/Scottish, not British	22	51
English/Scottish and British	45	33
British, not English/Scottish	23	10
Neither English/Scottish nor British*	10	6
N	3666	1594

Note: People in this category (*) are not examined separately in subsequent tables but are included where data are given for all respondents and also in reported measures of association.
Source: British and Scottish Social Attitudes 2006.

How then are these identities associated with key constitutional attitudes in both countries? In England, respondents are asked the question below about direct constitutional preferences. Table 5.2 shows how responses to this question vary by national identities.

'With all the changes going on in the way the different parts of Great Britain are run, which of the following do you think would be best for England:

• for England to be governed as it is now, with laws made by the UK Parliament;
• for each region of England to have its own elected assembly that makes decisions about the region's economy, planning and housing;
• or, for England as a whole to have its own new parliament with law-making powers?'

Table 5.2 National identities and constitutional preferences in England (2006)

% by column	English, not British	English and British	British, not English	All
Westminster status quo	50	57	58	55
Regional Assemblies	15	18	18	18
English Parliament	27	22	16	21
N	182	448	213	923

Note: All the associations between national identities and political attitudes shown in Tables 5.2–5.7 are statistically significant at a level of p < 0.01. The *strength* of any such associations is of course another matter, as will become clear.

In some tables the overall sample size is smaller than the survey as a whole because only a sub-sample of respondents was asked the question. Similarly, column percentages in some tables do not sum to 100 because those answering 'none of these', 'don't know' etc. have been excluded.

Source: British and Scottish Social Attitudes 2006.

Table 5.2 shows that, regardless of national identity, the Westminster status quo is clearly the most popular constitutional preference in England. Substantial minorities in each category do favour constitutional change but, especially in the dual identity and exclusively British groups, supporters of change are divided fairly evenly between the two options. This is somewhat less true of the exclusively English category, with support for an English parliament highest in this category (but still little more than one-quarter). There is evidence, then, that English identity is associated with stronger support for an English parliament while British identity is more closely associated with the status quo, but the variation is fairly weak. Nevertheless, these data do suggest a possible shift because, if anything, previous surveys tended to show an even weaker association between national identities and constitutional preferences in England.

In Scotland, the preferred constitutional options are of course different. Respondents are offered the options of Scottish independence, either within or outside the EU; the status quo of devolution, either with or without the current taxation powers; or a return to the pre-devolution position of no elected Scottish parliament and government from Westminster. Table 5.3 shows how responses vary by national identity. Responses favouring independence or devolution in either of the preferred forms have been amalgamated in the table.

Table 5.3   National identities and constitutional preferences in Scotland (2006)

% by column	Scottish, not British	Scottish and British	British, not Scottish	All
Scottish Independence	42	20	15	30
Devolution status quo	45	65	60	54
No Scottish Parliament	5	12	23	9
N	798	523	178	1588

Source: Scottish Social Attitudes 2006.

Table 5.3 shows an immediate contrast to the findings from England in that national identities and constitutional preferences are much more closely associated. This is reflected in the statistical measure of association for each table: 0.133 for England, 0.197 for Scotland.[3] Those in the exclusively Scottish category are much more likely to support Scottish independence than are those with a dual or exclusively British identity and, in turn, those in the latter group are unlikely to support independence but more likely to favour a return to centralised Westminster government. It is the exclusively Scottish group which stands out as being most distinctive in their opinions, particularly with regard to support for independence. Indeed if we focus specifically on exclusive Scots and compare them with all other respondents treated as one category, then the contrast in measures of association between the Scottish and English data becomes much more obvious, with Cramer's V rising to 0.293 for Scotland. However, this only tells half the story. In Scotland as in England the status quo is the most popular option in all three identity groups, albeit only marginally so in the exclusively Scottish category. It is particularly striking that half of those who profess no British identity believe that Scotland should continue to be governed within the United Kingdom, while three-quarters of those who profess no Scottish identity favour some form of Scottish government (in most cases devolution). So, in Scotland, what might be termed the 'alignment' of national identities and constitutional preferences is certainly stronger than it is in England, but as the correlation coefficients indicate, it is hardly strong, especially if we consider all categories of identity separately rather than comparing the exclusively Scottish with all others.

This is even more evident in the views concerning the political institution that people believe *should* have the most influence over the way their country is run. In Scotland in 2006, 67 per cent of those with an exclusively Scottish identity believed that the Scottish

Executive (prior to the 2007 name change to 'Scottish Government') should be most influential compared to only 8 per cent who thought the UK government at Westminster should have most influence over the way Scotland is run. The differential narrows when we consider those in the dual identity and exclusively British categories – from around 8:1 to 4:1 and 3:1 respectively – but it is clear that there is a broad consensus on this question in Scotland which encompasses those of all national identities.[4] This question was not asked in England in 2006, and one has to go back to 2003 for comparative data. A very similar finding emerges: even though people with an exclusively English identity are more likely to believe that a new English parliament should be the most influential institution, even among this group this option is only favoured by around one in six respondents, and indeed comes below local councils which are chosen by around one in five. In contrast to Scotland, the UK government at Westminster is the most popular choice regardless of national identity, and its prevalence only varies marginally between those with an exclusively English national identity (47 per cent) and those with an exclusively British identity (51 per cent).

A second way to assess the constitutional significance of national identities is to examine their association with support for particular political parties. Of course in England – in contrast to the other UK territories – there is no political competition between 'nationalist' parties which are the most obvious advocates of radical constitutional change and 'unionist' parties which seek to limit the extent of such change. The Conservatives have, to some degree, assumed the mantle of an 'English' party, both in terms of their core electoral support and their advocacy of 'all-England' solutions to the constitutional anomalies created by devolution. Under William Hague in the late 1990s the possibility that the Conservatives in government would establish an English Parliament was briefly on the agenda, but this lacked the support ever to become official party policy (Ward, 2004: 159). They currently favour more modest constitutional changes with respect to 'English-only' legislation which would not fundamentally alter the Westminster model in England. Labour and the Liberal Democrats have shown more appetite for further constitutional change along regional lines but it is doubtful whether their positions on the constitution would be reflected in disproportionate support among any particular national identity group. However, while overall one might not expect party support to vary greatly by national identity in England, examining any such associations provides a useful benchmark for a similar exercise in Scotland, where the Scottish National Party (SNP) in particular are much more obviously associated with radical constitutional change.

Table 5.4 shows how supporters of the principal political parties in England break down across the categories of exclusive and dual national identities. The measure of party support used combines questions which ask respondents whether they support any particular party and then, for those who do not, asks whether they feel closer to any party. Of course, many people decline to nominate a party in response to either question, and they are represented by the 'None' category. Those who supported a party other than Labour, Conservative or Liberal Democrat (e.g. the Greens) are not represented as a separate category in the table, but they are included in the final column which shows data for all respondents. As expected, although Conservative supporters have a somewhat more English than British profile (as indeed do those who support no political party) and the opposite is true of Labour and Liberal Democrat supporters, any differences are small: there is only a very weak association (0.093) between party support and national identities in England.

Table 5.5 shows the kind of associations between 'nationalist' and 'unionist' parties and identities which might be expected in Scotland. SNP supporters are the most likely to identify as exclusively Scottish, and Conservative supporters as exclusively British. Liberal Democrat supporters also have a relatively British profile. However, although the

Table 5.4 Party support and national identities in England (2006)

% by column	Labour	Conservative	Lib Dem	None	All
English, not British	20	25	16	27	22
English and British	48	48	47	38	45
British, not English	23	22	26	22	23
N	1192	1030	447	536	3650

Source: British Social Attitudes 2006.

Table 5.5 Party support and national identities in Scotland (2006)

% by column	Lab	Con	Lib Dem	SNP	None	All
Scottish, not British	51	32	33	65	58	51
Scottish and British	38	38	44	29	25	33
British, not Scottish	8	25	18	3	6	10
N	529	206	142	270	214	1588

Source: Scottish Social Attitudes 2006.

correlation coefficient for the table is 0.207 – notably stronger than for the English data in Table 5.4 – once more this does not support the conclusion that national identities and party support in Scotland are strongly associated. This is most evident with respect to Labour supporters, more than half of whom are exclusively Scottish (indeed, given the relative size of the two parties' support in the 2006 survey, Labour supporters contribute a larger proportion to the 'Scottish, not British' category than do SNP supporters). It is also true that although Conservative supporters are more likely to hold an exclusively British identity than those from other parties, a larger proportion have an exclusively *Scottish* identity than are exclusively British. Thus while both Conservative and Labour *parties* strongly emphasise their British credentials and would contemplate further constitutional change only within a broadly British framework, their perspectives on constitutional policy do not necessarily map on to the identities of their *supporters*. Moreover, it is also true that around one-third of SNP supporters professed some form of Britishness, and therefore the SNP's status as an explicitly *non*-British party is again not always reflected in their supporters' identities.

The final issue to be considered in this section is the relative trust which people have in institutions of government and how, if at all, this might vary by national identity. In Scotland, in 2006, people were asked how much they trusted the Scottish Executive and the UK government to work in Scotland's best interests. The different degrees of trust invested in both institutions, and across different categories of national identity, are shown in Table 5.6.

Table 5.6 Trust in the Scottish Executive and UK government to work in Scotland's interests (Scotland, 2006)

% by column

Trust Scottish Executive (UK government in brackets) ...	**Scottish, not British**	**Scottish and British**	**British, not Scottish**	**All**
Just about always/ Most of the time	46 (15)	55 (25)	62 (37)	51 (21)
Only some of the time/Almost never	51 (82)	43 (73)	38 (62)	46 (76)
N	798	523	178	1588

Source: Scottish Social Attitudes 2006.

The first thing to note in Table 5.6 is that people overall, and in each identity category, have much more trust in the Scottish Executive than they do in the UK government. Secondly, the degree of trust in each institution varies by national identity. With respect to the UK government, this association has a predictable character: the exclusively Scottish respondents are the least trusting, followed by those with a dual identity and then the exclusively British who are the most trusting. But even among the 'British' a clear majority of respondents (62 per cent) would trust the UK government only some of the time or almost never. In terms of trust in the Scottish Executive, the relationship with national identity is rather different from what might be expected. Those in the British, not Scottish category show the highest degree of trust in the distinctively Scottish institution, and indeed are far more trusting of this body than they are of the UK government (62 per cent to 37 per cent). Of course there are many other factors which may influence trust in political institutions and it is not my purpose here to explore these. However, one obvious conclusion might be that the reason that the exclusively Scottish are less trusting of the Scottish Executive than those in other categories of identity relates to the party political character of the Executive at the time of the survey in 2006: a Labour–Liberal Democrat coalition. But this does not provide an entirely satisfactory explanation, firstly because we have already observed that those with an exclusively Scottish identity are most strongly represented among *Labour* supporters, and secondly because a similar question in previous surveys which asked about trust in the Scottish *Parliament* as opposed to Executive produced broadly similar results. For example, in the 2003 Scottish Social Attitudes survey, the exclusively British showed a greater degree of trust in the Scottish Parliament than did the exclusively Scottish, albeit that the difference between them was less than in 2006. In 2003, levels of trust among the exclusively Scottish were rather higher than in 2006, with 59 per cent saying they would trust the Parliament at least most of the time compared to 67 per cent among the 'British' group. Despite some decline in trust among the exclusively Scottish in recent years, overall these data indicate that national identities in Scotland are not strongly associated with trust in the key political institutions of the post-devolution UK. This is reflected in the correlation coefficients of 0.158 (trust in Scottish Executive) and 0.265 (UK government).[5]

What of England? An obvious difference is that, aside from the London Assembly, there are no devolved institutions about which to gauge trust, so analysis is limited to trust in the UK government and how this relates to national identities. The most recently available data

Table 5.7 Trust in the UK government to work in England's interests (England, 2003)

% by column	English, not British	English and British	British, not English	All
Just about always/ Most of the time	42	54	55	55
Only some of the time/Almost never	54	42	41	44
N	212	364	316	975

Source: British Social Attitudes 2003.

(Table 5.7) are also rather more dated than in Scotland, coming from 2003. Overall, trust in the UK government in England is much higher than in Scotland (this is also true if we compare with 2003 Scottish data, which are very similar to 2006) and only a little lower than trust in the Scottish Executive in Scotland (although lower still if we compare with 2003 Scottish data, which nonetheless relates to *Parliament* rather than *Executive*). The degree of association between trust and national identity is also less than in Scotland (correlation coefficient = 0.147), although as in Scotland it is those with an exclusively 'sub-state' (English) identity who are the least trusting of the UK government. Even if we were to accept, then, that lack of trust might suggest an appetite for some kind of constitutional change (and, as was noted above, political trust is likely to relate to many other factors) there is only weak evidence that it may be those with the strongest English identities who support constitutional change the most.

Many of the findings discussed in this first section substantiate previous survey research. Work carried out in Scotland in the predevolution period (Brand et al., 1993, 1994; Brown et al., 1998; McCrone, 2001) showed a clear association between national identities and constitutionally significant political views with, for example, those with an exclusively Scottish (rather than British) identity more likely to support the SNP and to favour Scottish independence.[6] However, such relationships were not straightforward. For example, many supporters of the SNP and of independence were not 'exclusive Scots', and even those with the most unionist political attitudes (i.e. supporters of the Conservatives and opponents of devolution) were more likely to prioritise a Scottish rather than British identity. Such findings revealed a non-alignment between identities and political attitudes in Scotland (Bond, 2000).

Similar post-devolution research continued to highlight this non-alignment (see, e.g., Paterson et al., 2001; Bond and Rosie, 2002). With respect to England, Heath and Kellas's (1998) analysis showed that those who adopted exclusive identities displayed a stronger appetite for constitutional change than those with dual identities, but research on national identities and constitutional attitudes in England in the post-devolution period has indicated that associations between them are rather weak (see, e.g., Curtice and Heath, 2000; Curtice, 2006).

Solidarity or dissociation?

The degree to which national identities and national differences might be politically significant relates not only to self-conceptions of identity and constitutionally significant political attitudes *within* given UK territories but also to how people view the political status of other parts of the UK. If there is an evident desire for the dissolution of the union, or substantial grievances about the relative benefits of continued union in a post-devolution context, then the continuance of the UK state might be called into question. This section considers the views of people in Scotland and England about the best means of governing the other country. Do people in Scotland believe that England should now be governed by its own parliament? Do people in England feel that it would be better if Scotland were fully independent? Are people in both countries broadly supportive of the current constitutional arrangements? Or are people in Scotland and/or England in fact largely indifferent to the constitutional fate of their neighbours? After considering these questions, the views of people in both countries concerning the economic and fiscal benefits (or disbenefits) which they believe their own nation derives from the Union are examined. Finally, a rather more direct measure of solidarity which explores whether a shared sense of social class is more or less important than a shared nationality in each country is considered. Much of the data we examine in this section is taken from surveys carried out in 2003, around the end of the first Scottish parliament. While this certainly allows one to consider the potential impact of devolution upon feelings of solidarity between people in Scotland and England, it is also possible that further change in opinion may have taken place over the course of the second Scottish parliamentary period up until 2007, and beyond.

Table 5.8 shows the constitutional preferences of people in Scotland for the government of England in 2003. The pattern of response to the same question among respondents in England in the same year is

Table 5.8   Constitutional preferences for government
of England (Scotland and England, 2003)

% by column	Scotland	England
Westminster status quo	53	55
Regional Assemblies	17	24
English Parliament	18	16
Don't know	10	4
N	1508	975

Note: The version of the question asked in Scotland in 2003
was somewhat different from the 2006 version outlined
above. In this version, the regional assemblies would 'run
services like health'. Around one-third of the sample in
England in 2003 was also asked this version, and to ensure
direct comparison only these respondents are represented in
Table 5.6 (although in fact response to the version related to
'economy, planning and housing' was very similar).
Sources: Scottish and British Social Attitudes 2003.

also shown in the table. This shows that in both countries, desire for
constitutional change of any sort was outweighed by support for the
status quo. The only notable differences are a somewhat higher level
of support for regional assemblies in England and a higher proportion
of 'don't knows' in Scotland, but overall the pattern of response is very
similar.[7] Examining these data according to respondents' national identities does not reveal any striking differences. In Scotland, the status quo
is the most popular option for each of the three categories of national
identity, although comparatively speaking those with an exclusive
Scottish identity are rather more likely to believe that England should
have its own parliament while for the exclusively British the opposite
is the case. In England there is a pattern that is very familiar from
Table 5.2: the status quo is supported by a majority in each identity
category and those with an exclusively English identity are somewhat
more likely to support an English parliament than those in the other
identity categories.

If the views of people in Scotland with respect to England's constitutional status were broadly similar to those of people in England – at
least in 2003 – is the same true of corresponding opinions regarding
Scotland's constitutional status? Table 5.9 indicates that this is indeed
the case, with devolution supported by a majority in each country.

The most notable difference is that support for independence is somewhat higher in Scotland, but this merely establishes that support for the

Table 5.9 Constitutional preferences for government of Scotland (England and Scotland, 2003)

% by column	England	Scotland
Scottish Independence	17	26
Devolution status quo	59	56
No Scottish Parliament	13	13
Don't know	12	6
N	1917	1508

Sources: British and Scottish Social Attitudes 2003.

union is, if anything, even stronger in England and so there is not much evidence of dissociation in the post-devolution period. Similar to the Scottish respondents in Table 5.8, the proportion of 'don't knows' is also higher for people in England who are asked to state their constitutional preference for Scotland. Do national identities make a difference? With respect to Scotland, the answer is similar to our conclusions regarding Table 5.3 above: yes, but only to a degree. Only 10 per cent of those in the exclusively British category support Scottish independence, while 23 per cent do not support any form of Scottish parliament. Equally, 39 per cent of the exclusively Scottish support independence and only 4 per cent believe there should be no Scottish Parliament. But the status quo of devolution is the most popular option in each category including the exclusively Scottish, where it is favoured by 50 per cent of respondents. As one might expect, differences related to national identities in England are even smaller. The exclusively English are somewhat more likely to believe that Scotland should be independent (22 per cent) but there is majority support for devolution in each category of identity. Overall, then, at least with respect to 2003 data, it is not the case that people in England think that it would be better if Scotland went its own way, and nor is it true that they believe that constitutional change has already gone too far and that there should be a return to centralised Westminster government. It is also interesting to note that in 2003 people in England were also asked how they would feel if Scotland and Wales were to become independent: would they be pleased, sorry or neither? Only a small minority (less than 10 per cent) said they would be pleased while nearly half said they would be sorry, once more certainly not offering positive evidence of a lack of solidarity. However, a large minority (42 per cent) said they would be neither pleased nor sorry, perhaps suggesting a large measure of

Table 5.10   Whose economy benefits more from having Scotland in the UK? (Scotland and England, 2003)

% by column	Scotland	England
England benefits more	30	7
Scotland benefits more	24	39
Equal	40	40
Don't know	6	12
N	1508	1917

Sources: Scottish and British Social Attitudes 2003.

indifference in England with respect to the constitutional future of other parts of Britain.

If political disaffection cannot be found in people's direct opinions on the constitution, perhaps they might be more obvious in their beliefs about economic and fiscal justice? Once more in 2003, respondents were asked which economy, England's or Scotland's, benefited more from having Scotland as part of the UK, or if the benefits were about equal. The patterns of response in Scotland and England are compared in Table 5.10.

An identical proportion (four out of ten) in both countries believes that the benefits are equally shared and this is also the most common response on both sides of the border. However, in England a similarly large minority believe that Scotland benefits more from its place in the UK, far outnumbering the small minority who believe England benefits disproportionately. In Scotland nearly one-quarter think that their own country benefits more from the union, not far short of the 30 per cent who feel this about England. Overall then, there is some evidence here of grievance and this is more marked among respondents in England. Here national identities (not shown in the table) make an evident difference, once again more marked in Scotland. Forty-two per cent of those with an exclusively Scottish identity believe that England benefits more as against 10 per cent of those with an exclusively British identity. Correspondingly, 41 per cent of the exclusively British believe that Scotland benefits more compared to only 16 per cent of the exclusively Scottish. It should be noted, however, that in each identity category a large minority believe that the benefits are equal. In England, it is those with an exclusively English identity who are the most likely to believe that Scotland benefits most from the union: 45 per cent compared to 35 per cent of the exclusively British, but once more the differences are

Table 5.11 Does Scotland receive a fair share of UK government spending, or more or less than this fair share? (Scotland and England, 2003)

% by column	Scotland	England
More than fair share	11	22
Fair share	35	45
Less than fair share	47	8
Don't know	8	25
N	1508	1917

Sources: Scottish and British Social Attitudes 2003.

much smaller than in Scotland. Overall, then, perceptions of economic injustice are clearly related both to national location and national identity, particularly in Scotland.

How about the analogous issue of differences in attitudes to government spending under the union? In 2003 respondents were asked whether, compared to other parts of the UK, Scotland received a fair share of government spending or whether it received more or less than this fair share. Again the different patterns of response in England and Scotland are shown in Table 5.11. Once more, response varies by country, although this time the sense of grievance at fiscal injustice is much stronger in Scotland. Less than a quarter of people in England felt that Scotland received more than its fair share of public spending but nearly half of people in Scotland believed that the country received less than its fair share. However, large minorities in both countries do think that Scotland gets pretty much its fair share and no fewer than one in four people in England did not feel equipped to give a definite response to the question, which once more may reflect indifference or ignorance. In England, those with an exclusively English identity are somewhat more likely to believe that Scotland gets more than its fair share of government spending, but differences are not great and the most popular response in each identity category is that Scotland receives its fair share. In Scotland, however, differences across identities are much more evident. While 63 per cent of exclusive Scots believe that Scotland gets less than its public spending entitlement, only 28 per cent of the exclusively British think likewise. In this group, and indeed in the dual identity category, the most common response is that Scotland receives its fair share.

There is, then, some evidence of grievance on both sides of the border but, especially from the English perspective, this is not represented by profound dissatisfaction with the economic and fiscal arrangements in the post-devolution UK. In Scotland too there is a fairly widespread recognition that Scotland is not fundamentally disadvantaged by maintaining its place in the UK. However, the questions thus far relate solidarity or dissociation to political arrangements at a 'macro' level, and it is interesting to draw on data showing how people on both sides of the border might relate to each other at a personal level. On this occasion, the same question was asked in 2006 in both Scotland and England. The question asks respondents to say whether they feel they have more in common with people of the same (Scottish or English) nationality as them who come from a different social class, or with people from the same social class but different nationality.[8] Moreover, as well as comparing patterns of response between the two nations, because this question has some historical pedigree in Scotland, we can also assess whether solidarity based on shared social class seems to be declining with respect to national differences or not. The data for 2006 are shown in Table 5.12.

The table shows that levels of class solidarity are very similar in both nations, with around a quarter of respondents saying they would have more in common with people from the same social class but the opposite nationality. National solidarity is stronger in each country, but particularly so in Scotland, where nearly half of respondents feel they would have more in common with people of the same nationality but a different social class. This is true of about one-third of respondents in England. A quarter in England and a fifth in Scotland do not give a decisive answer either way. One might expect that individuals' national identities would make a difference to the response they give to this question, and this is certainly true in Scotland. Among those with an

Table 5.12 More in common with same class, different nationality or same nationality, different class? (Scotland and England, 2006)

% by column	Scotland	England
Same class, different nationality	25	26
Same nationality, different class	47	34
No preference	19	25
Depends on the individual	5	6
Don't know/not answered	5	10
N	1494	2775

Sources: Scottish and British Social Attitudes 2006.

exclusively Scottish identity, the differential between the two main categories of response is wider, with only 20 per cent saying they would have more in common with English people of the same class compared to 53 per cent who would have more in common with Scottish people of the opposite class. For those with an exclusively British identity, on the other hand, the differential is reversed, with a higher proportion (38 per cent) saying they would have more in common with English people of the same class than Scottish people of the opposite class (27 per cent). The figures for those with a dual identity are broadly similar to those for respondents as a whole. Differences by national identity in England are much less obvious. There is little variation in the proportions saying they would have more in common with Scottish people of the same class, but those with an exclusive English identity or a dual identity are significantly more likely to say they would have more in common with English people of the opposite class compared to those with an exclusively British identity, who are rather more likely not to choose either way. Overall though, once more we find that national identities in Scotland make more of a difference in terms of key social and political attitudes than is true in England.

This leaves the question of whether the period of devolution has coincided with an increase in national solidarity at the expense of class solidarity in Scotland. In fact there is very little evidence for this. An identical question asked in 1997 produced very similar results, with 23 per cent of respondents saying they would have more in common with English people of the same class compared to 46 per cent with Scottish people of the opposite class.

Ideological-legislative attitudes

Finally, are there any evident ideological divides between the people of Scotland and England which might imply that further constitutional separation is desirable or necessary? Are any such divisions based on people's subjective sense of national identity? Two well-established political scales, each derived from a series of survey questions, can be used to address this question. The first measures the degree to which respondents are left wing or right wing in their political outlook. It is based on the following five statements:

Government should redistribute income from the better-off to those who are less well off.
Big business benefits owners at the expense of workers.

Ordinary working people do not get their fair share of the nation's wealth.

There is one law for the rich and one for the poor.

Management will always try to get the better of employees if it gets the chance.

For each statement, respondents are asked to indicate their level of agreement (agree strongly; agree; neither agree nor disagree; disagree; disagree strongly) with each response given a value from 1 (agree strongly) to 5 (disagree strongly). These responses are then summed and divided by 5 to give an average point on the scale. The left–right scale can therefore run from a minimum of 1 (for someone who agrees strongly with all statements) to a maximum of 5 (for someone who disagrees strongly with them all). Table 5.13 shows the mean value on the left–right scale for all respondents in Scotland and England in 2006, and also how this value varies for each of the three categories of national identity.[9]

The table shows that, overall, there is very little difference in the degree to which people living in Scotland and England might be considered left wing or right wing on this measure. There is a prominent perspective in Scotland which emphasises the nation's 'social democratic' credentials. Data such as those in Table 5.13 do not necessarily contradict such beliefs – there remain good reasons to think that Scotland is a social democratic country (see McCrone and Keating, 2007) – but they do indicate that there is no strong evidence that people in Scotland are much more social democratic in their perspectives than are their southern neighbours in England. In fact there is more variation between categories of national identity within each nation than there is between the nations. Once more, however, such variation is very

Table 5.13   Mean values on left–right scale (Scotland and England, 2006)

	Scotland	England
All respondents	2.61	2.64
Scottish/English, not British	2.50	2.56
Scottish/English and British	2.70	2.70
British, not Scottish/English	2.75	2.65
N	1408	3152

Sources: Scottish and British Social Attitudes 2006.

limited in England and indeed there is no clear pattern of association, with the *dual* identity group, rather than those in either of the exclusive categories, showing the most right-wing profile.[10] In Scotland the key group would appear to be those who have an exclusively Scottish identity, who are noticeably more left-wing than their counterparts with a dual or exclusively British identity. Indeed the difference in mean values between these two latter groups is not statistically significant, and even the degree of difference between the exclusive Scots and the others hardly amounts to a fundamental division on the basis of national identity. Both aspects of these findings largely reflect previous survey research concerning such political values. Where differences between Scotland and England do emerge, either with respect to specific attitudes or the type of multi-question scale utilised above, these frequently disappear when attitudes in England are disaggregated on a regional basis (Brown et al., 1998; Hearn, 2000; Rosie and Bond, 2007). Social democracy is related more to the leftward slant of the party political structure in Scotland (Paterson, 2002; Rosie and Bond, ibid.) than it is to the attitudes of the people. It is also argued that social democratic values are related to national identity in Scotland (Hearn, 2000: 3) and the analysis bears this out to some degree at least, and in doing so once more mirrors earlier analysis (Rosie and Bond, ibid.).

The second summary scale with which to assess ideological divides between and within Scotland and England measures the extent to which people hold a predominantly libertarian or authoritarian position on social issues. It is based on the following six statements:

Young people today don't have enough respect for traditional British values.
People who break the law should be given stiffer sentences.
For some crimes, the death penalty is the most appropriate sentence.
Schools should teach children to obey authority.
The law should always be obeyed, even if a particular law is wrong.
Censorship of films and magazines is necessary to uphold moral standards.

The same response options and method for calculating the final scale value for each respondent are used as with the left–right scale outlined above. In this scale, value 1 represents the most libertarian position and 5 the most authoritarian. Table 5.14 shows the mean value on the libertarian–authoritarian scale for all respondents in Scotland and England in 2006, and also how this value varies for each of the three categories

Table 5.14   Mean values on libertarian–authoritarian scale
(Scotland and England, 2006)

	Scotland	England
All respondents	3.69	3.73
Scottish/English, not British	3.76	3.84
Scottish/English and British	3.65	3.71
British, not Scottish/English	3.62	3.71
N	1420	3195

Sources: Scottish and British Social Attitudes 2006.

of national identity. The table shows that people in both countries are more socially conservative (as measured by the libertarian–authoritarian scale) than they are politically conservative (as measured by the left–right scale): the values in all categories are markedly higher than in Table 5.13. But the difference between the two nations is once more very small.[11] This finding is virtually identical to previous analyses based on 2003 and 2004 data (Rosie and Bond, 2007). Those with an exclusive Scottish or English identity in the respective nations are somewhat more authoritarian than are their counterparts with dual or exclusively British identities, but again the differences are relatively small.[12] Overall then, there is little evidence to suggest that people in Scotland and England diverge fundamentally in terms of ideological–legislative political attitudes, nor that national identities in either nation are strongly associated with such attitudes.

Conclusions

This chapter began by setting out three specific questions and one broader question. These questions have been addressed using data from Scotland and England in the post-devolution period. The first question asked whether people's national identities were closely aligned with constitutionally significant political attitudes. In England, there was little evidence of any such alignment. It is true that there is some consistent evidence that those who identify as English rather than British are more likely to favour constitutional change, most specifically the establishment of an English parliament, but in fact their constitutional views are not much different from their counterparts who have a dual English/British or exclusively British identity.

Support for the continuation of Westminster government, more or less in its current form, is strong across all three groups. The findings in relation to Scotland are similar in that the status quo (of a devolved Scottish parliament) is also strongly supported among the exclusively Scottish or British and those with a dual identity. Associations between identities and attitudes (including party support and trust in governments at state and substate level) are much more evident than in England, and for the most part they have a predictable character. People who feel Scottish rather than British are more likely to support independence and/or the SNP and have low levels of trust in UK government. But evidence of non-alignment is also extensive, not least with respect to the large proportions of people with an exclusively British identity who show high levels of support for Scottish institutions and those respondents who do not profess any British identity but who nevertheless do not favour constitutional changes or parties which would divide Scotland from Britain politically.

The second question concerned the extent to which there was evidence of solidarity or dissociation between people living in Scotland and England. This was examined with respect to constitutional, economic, fiscal and interpersonal attitudes. The significance of national identities was also considered in each case. To the extent that dissociation might be represented by a desire among people in England for Scotland to be independent, or for people in Scotland to believe that England should have its own parliament, there is little evidence of this. A majority of respondents in both countries favour retaining the current constitutional status of their neighbour. There is some evidence of widespread perceptions that the economic benefits of the Union are not shared equally between Scotland and England, but it is also true that only a minority in each nation believes that the other nation's economy benefits more. A similar pattern is observable with respect to the degree to which public spending is distributed equally, although in this instance, and in contrast to views about economic benefit, it is people in Scotland who have the greater sense of injustice. There is some evidence that solidarity with one's substate counterparts represents a challenge to the continued coherence of the state to the degree that substate nationality appears to be a more powerful focus of association than does social class. But again this applies only to a minority of people in both Scotland and England, and large minorities are unwilling to profess that substate nationality 'trumps' statewide social class as a general rule or vice versa. It is also true that, in Scotland at least, there is no evidence that solidarity based on one's nation is increasing at the expense of class-based association. People's national identities do make a difference to the patterns of response to all these questions and, although often these differences are not large and do not represent fundamental cleavages in opinion, it is consistently true that those with exclusive substate identities in both Scotland and England are the most likely to be discontented with the current constitutional settlement and the least likely to feel solidarity with those in the neighbouring nation.

The third question asked whether there were any evident ideological divides between people in Scotland and England. This was addressed by using two scales designed to place people on a left–right and a libertarian–authoritarian dimension. There was no evidence of any substantial ideological differences between the two nations. Indeed there was greater variation between those with different national identities *within* each nation. Once more, although those with an exclusive substate identity are distinct to some degree, they are not fundamentally different from their counterparts with dual or exclusive state identities.

The broader question concerned what national identities and political attitudes in the post-devolution UK might tell us about the likelihood of further constitutional change. Overall, there are some consistent associations between identities and attitudes, although these are not uniformly evident. Particularly in Scotland, but also to some degree in England, it is those with exclusive substate identities whose attitudes are most consistent with a desire for change. However, and perhaps most importantly, such differences in attitudes are not so fundamental as to suggest that even profound shifts in conceptions of national identity in Scotland and England would necessarily lead to very strong demands for constitutional change. The pattern of response to some of the questions in England also suggests that there is a substantial degree of indifference with respect to Scotland's status and whether this might occasion the need for constitutional change in England. Of course if national identities changed so radically that only small minorities continued to hold a state-level identity, then this might in itself have profound constitutional implications, but that is both a doubtful proposition and an issue which this chapter does not address directly. Finally, it is also true that not only national identities but political attitudes too may shift. Although much of the data discussed in this chapter is consistent with previous research from recent years, this does not preclude future change. After all, relatively speaking, post-devolution United Kingdom is still quite a young country.

Notes

1. Note that the analysis concerns only those who identify as Scottish in Scotland or English in England, not those who identify as English in Scotland or Scottish in England.
2. In fact this is an unusually low figure for dual identities in Scotland compared with other recent surveys. In the three Scottish Social Attitudes surveys from 2003–5, the figure ranged from 39–47 per cent.
3. The correlation coefficient used is Cramer's V, which is commonly applied to cross-tabulations of this kind. The coefficient may run between 0 (no association whatsoever between the two variables in the cross-tabulation) and 1 (a perfect association). It should be noted, however, that for categorical data of this kind, it is rare to achieve strong correlation coefficients. For example, for this to be achieved, Table 5.3 would require the vast majority of respondents in the 'Scottish, not British' category to support independence, and for similar majorities in the 'Scottish and British' and 'British, not Scottish' groups to support devolution and no parliament respectively. It should also be noted that a somewhat stronger correlation coefficient (0.316) may be achieved with respect to the Scottish data if one applies a measure which is appropriate to ordinal data ('gamma'). This may be done for the Scottish data because both variables have an evident rank order, from more to less Scottish and from high to low Scottish political autonomy. The constitutional options in England cannot be so ordered.
4. In each case, most of the remaining respondents said that local councils should have most influence. Indeed in each identity category more people gave this response than chose the Westminster government.
5. An ordinal measure of association has again been used since the response options for trust follow a rank order from more to less trusting. The coefficients are based on the full tables in which each option – just about always, most of the time, only some of the time, and almost never – is represented separately.
6. Some of the previous studies discussed here use a five-category scale to measure national identity, in which respondents choose one option ranging from 'Scottish, not British' to 'British, not Scottish'. This contrasts somewhat with the simpler three-category measure used in this chapter, which is constructed from responses to the multiple choice national identity question outlined above. However, patterns of association between identities and political attitudes are broadly similar regardless of which measure is used.
7. This question was asked of some respondents in Scotland in 2006, but they were participating in the *British* Social Attitudes Survey, and because less than 100 people in Scotland were asked this particular question one must be cautious about the validity of the data. Nevertheless, even allowing for a large margin of error in such a small sample, they do suggest a substantial increase in support for an English Parliament – 39 per cent, compared to 44 per cent in favour of the Westminster status quo and 12 per cent Regional Assemblies. It should however be noted that the data from England also show an increase (albeit more modest) in this support between 2003 and 2006 (compare Tables 5.9 and 5.2).

8. The measure of class used for this question is subjective rather than objective. That is, the question is phrased in accordance with which social class respondents chose to identify with in a previous question, rather than their occupational status. Thus, for example, someone in England who had previously identified as working class would be asked whether they felt they had more in common with middle-class English people or working-class Scottish people. Those who did not identify with any social class are excluded.

9. People who did not respond to one or more of the questions are excluded. This also applies to Table 5.14.

10. In fact the difference in mean values on the scale between the two exclusive identity categories is not statistically significant.

11. To put the difference of 0.04 between the countries into perspective, we might take the example of educational qualifications where, in both Scotland and England, the mean score of those with a degree is about 0.7 lower than those with no qualifications.

12. Similarly to the analysis for the left–right scale, the difference in means between the 'Scottish and British' and 'British, not Scottish' categories is not statistically significant. The same is true in England, where the difference in means between the dual and exclusively British identity categories is not statistically significant either.

Bibliography

Bechhofer, F., McCrone, D. Kiely, R. and Stewart, R. (1999) Constructing national identity: Arts and landed elites in Scotland. *Sociology*, **33** (3), 515–34.

Bechhofer, F. and McCrone, D. (2007) Being British: A crisis of identity? *Political Quarterly*, **78** (2), 251–60.

Bond, R. (2000) Squaring the circles: Demonstrating and explaining the political 'non-alignment' of Scottish national identities. *Scottish Affairs*, **32**, 15–35.

Bond, R. and Rosie, M. (2002) National identities in post-devolution Scotland. *Scottish Affairs*, **40**, 34–53.

Brand, J., Mitchell, J. and Surridge, P. (1993) Identity and the vote: Class and nationality in Scotland. In D. Denver, P. Norris, D. Broughton and C. Rallings (eds) *British elections and parties yearbook 1993*. London: Harvester Wheatsheaf, 143–57.

Brand, J., Mitchell, J. and Surridge. P. (1994) Social constituency and ideological profile: Scottish Nationalism in the 1990s. *Political Studies*, **42**, 616–29.

Brown, A., McCrone, D. and Paterson, L. (1998) *Politics and Society in Scotland*. 2nd edn. Basingstoke: Macmillan.

Bryant, C. G. A. (2006) *The nations of Britain*. Oxford: Oxford University Press.

Curtice, J. (2006) A stronger or weaker Union?: Public reactions to asymmetric devolution in the United Kingdom. *Publius*, **36** (1), 95–113.

Curtice, J. and Heath, A. (2000) Is the English lion about to roar?: National identity after devolution. In R. Jowell, J. Curtice, A. Park, K. Thomson, L. Jarvis, C. Bromley and N. Stratford (eds) *British Social Attitudes: The 17th report*. London: Sage, 155–74.

Gallagher, M. (1995) How many nations are there in Ireland? *Ethnic and Racial Studies*, **18** (4), 715–39.

Gellner, E. (1983) *Nations and Nationalism*. Oxford: Blackwell.

Haesly, R. (2005) Identifying Scotland and Wales: Types of Scottish and Welsh national identities. *Nations and Nationalism*, **11** (2), 243–63.

Hearn, J. (2000) *Claiming Scotland: National identity and liberal culture*. Edinburgh: Polygon.

Heath, A. and Kellas, J. (1998) Nationalisms and constitutional questions. *Scottish Affairs*, Special Issue: Understanding Constitutional Change, 110–28.

Heath, A., Taylor, B. Brook. L. and Park. A. (1999) British national sentiment. *British Journal of Political Science*, **29** (1), 155–75.

Heath, A. and Smith, S. (2005) Varieties of nationalism in Scotland and England. In W. L. Miller (ed.) *Anglo-Scottish relations from 1900 to devolution and beyond*. Oxford: Oxford University Press, 133–52.

Henderson, A. (1999) Political constructions of national identity in Scotland and Quebec. *Scottish Affairs*, **29**, 121–38.

Kellas, J. (1998) *The politics of nationalism and ethnicity*. 2nd edn. Basingstoke: Macmillan.

Kumar, K. (2003) *The making of English national identity*. Cambridge: Cambridge University Press.

Langlands, R. (1999) Britishness or Englishness?: The historical problem of national identity in Britain. *Nations and Nationalism*, **5** (1), 53–69.

McCrone, D. (1997) Unmasking Britannia: The rise and fall of British national identity. *Nations and Nationalism*, **3** (4), 579–96.

McCrone, D. (2001) *Understanding Scotland:The sociology of a nation*. 2nd edn. London: Routledge.

McCrone, D., Stewart, R. Kiely, R. and Bechhofer, F. (1998) Who are we?: Problematising national identity. *Sociological Review*, **46** (4), 629–52.

McCrone, D. and Keating, M. (2007) Social democracy and Scotland. In Keating, M. (ed.) *Scottish social democracy:Progressive ideas for public policy*. Brussels: P.I.E. Peter Lang.

Paterson, L., Brown, A., Curtice, J., Hinds, K., McCrone, D., Park, A., Sproston, K. and Surridge, P. (2001) *New Scotland, new politics?* Edinburgh: Polygon.

Paterson, L. (2002) Governing from the centre: Ideology and public policy. In J. Curtice, D. McCrone, A. Park and L. Paterson (eds) *New Scotland, new society?* Edinburgh: Polygon.

Rose, R. (1982) *Understanding the United Kingdom: The territorial dimension in government*. Harlow: Longman.

Rosie, M. and Bond, R. (2007) Social democratic Scotland? In M. Keating (ed.) *Scottish social democracy: Progressive ideas for public policy*. Brussels: P. I. E. Peter Lang.

Ward, I. (2004) *The English constitution: Myths and realities*. Oxford: Hart.

Wyn Jones, R. (2001) On process, events and unintended consequences: National identity and the politics of Welsh devolution. *Scottish Affairs*, **37**, 34–57.

6
Drifting Apart?
Media in Scotland and England after Devolution

Michael Rosie and Pille Petersoo

Given its multinational nature, the United Kingdom offers a useful test case by which to explore media assumptions about 'the nation'. As part of the *Nations and Regions* project, we[1] investigated the relationship between national identities and mass media. When people talk about events happening 'here' or about what constitutes news relevant to 'us', just *where* and *who* might they mean? Much research on mass media within the UK takes as its starting point the existence of a singular (and relatively) homogenous 'British media'. In the context of devolution, that starting point is very problematic.

A number of authors have claimed that mass media (and news media in particular) are crucial to the legitimacy of both states and nations. Such accounts assume that news media reproduce a *national* culture, reporting about 'home' events to a 'domestic' audience. Moreover, media outlets themselves routinely and explicitly nationalise news: networked television news bulletins in the UK, for example, routinely divide their content between 'national and international news'. In the case of news media output, their content, production, distribution, as well as the characteristics of their audience, provide useful evidence for examining perceptions of nations and national identity. Benedict Anderson (1983) argued that newspapers (and other media) facilitate how national communities are *imagined*. In reading their newspaper, each reader becomes aware that many others are reading the same news, thus creating (*imagining*) a common community. However, Anderson's assumption that the boundary to that community is a 'national' one depends on several implicit conditions, notably that the newspaper is (and is known by the reader to be) nationally (rather than locally, or internationally) distributed. Michael Billig's *Banal Nationalism* (1995) argued that nations are 'reproduced' on a daily basis through routine and often unnoticed assumptions about who and where 'we' are. We are reminded of our nationality in mundane (rather than explicit) ways, ranging from unnoticed flags on public buildings, to the habits and shortcuts of everyday speech. Crucially, within the selection and presentation of 'the news' by mass media such habits *point* at the nation, subconsciously underpinning our sense of national identity.

Multinational contexts pose inherent problems here since such accounts all too casually slip between concepts of 'nation' and 'state'. In such contexts – like the United Kingdom – the national community 'imagined', or 'the nation' we are reminded of is open to question. To a newspaper reader in, say, Wrexham, is the community imagined in reading a newspaper: local (Wrexham), regional (North Wales) or national? And if the community is a national one, does it comprise Wales or Britain? Indeed, such a reader might conceive of themselves as belonging to some or *all* of these communities simultaneously. The nation, here, may well be *both* Wales *and* Britain.

Our first challenge was defining those media we would investigate – after all, mass media comprise institutions and forms as diverse as popular film, celebrity gossip magazines and talk radio. Given that different forms of media would require the collection of different sorts of evidence (text, audio, video) we chose to focus our initial energies on examining the production and content of daily morning newspapers. There were a number of reasons for doing so, not least the less complex challenges involved in analysing textual (rather than visual) data, and the extensive availability of circulation and readership figures. Once we had conducted and analysed a series of 'day surveys' of the morning press in both England and Scotland, we carried out a series of interviews with editors and journalists. We also conducted more modest content studies of news bulletins from BBC Radio 4 and BBC Radio Scotland as well as observing the newsrooms of these stations, watching bulletins and stories develop and talking to newsroom staff and management. In this chapter we wish to briefly reprise the background to issues of national identity and mass media, report the overall results of our study and fashion some concluding questions.

We have developed much of our detailed analysis elsewhere (Rosie et al., 2004, 2006; MacInnes et al., 2007; Petersoo, 2007). Here we wish to draw a rather broader picture incorporating our main findings, and also evidence not discussed elsewhere. We focus first on the *presentation* of news, how it is 'framed' and how this may, or may not, 'flag' a readership/audience belonging to a particular nation; we then examine the *content* of news and its national 'habits'; finally we look at the *production* of news agenda and contents, drawing on both interviews with producers and our own observations from BBC newsrooms. We conclude by examining whether our findings *matter*. First, we offer a brief discussion of the 'geography' of relevant news media.

The geography of the UK news media

The 'British news media' often pass for a homogenous and clearly defined set of institutions. Television's long-running current affairs programme *What the Papers Say* treated 'the papers' as an unproblematic term – although the titles/editions in question invariably belonged to 'Fleet Street'.[2] In fact, the UK's media form a complex web of public and private concerns whose readership/audience (in media-speak, their 'reach') is sometimes UK-wide, but more often spills beyond or spreads only partially within it.

In terms of ownership and control, media outlets are often part of wider, and increasingly global, corporations. Let us take an 'archetypically' British newspaper as an example. *The Times* is a subsidiary of News International in turn owned by the US-based News Corporation. As well as several UK titles, News Corp owns film studios, television stations, magazines and newspapers throughout Europe, Asia, Australasia and North America. Far from being a straightforwardly British institution, *The Times* is one cog within a *global* media network. We face serious problems in finding a definition for a 'British' newspaper (or for 'British media' more generally) which captures the shifting international complexities of ownership and control.

Neither does the 'reach' of media institutions neatly coincide with either national or state boundaries. British television and radio broadcast outwith the UK through 'accidents' of geography (e.g. Irish viewers of Channel 4 or Dutch listeners to BBC Radio 2) and through intentional transmission (such as BBC World television or the World Service). While 'overseas' audiences might be quite marginal in the broader scheme of UK broadcast media, we cannot say the same for newspapers. Every Fleet Street daily publishes editions for sale abroad. While many such editions are directed at holidaymakers and expatriates, this is not entirely the case. The *Financial Times*, for example, sells most of its copies – about 70 per cent – to investors and business people outwith the UK. Many 'British' papers also target one specific foreign market: Ireland. The *Mirror*, for example, sells twice as many copies per day in the Irish Republic than it does in Scotland. The *Sunday Mirror*, the *People* and the *Sunday Times* also enjoy higher sales in Ireland than in

Scotland. How is it that some newspapers do better outside the United Kingdom than in some parts within it, and what does that tell us about their assumed 'Britishness'?

Ireland illustrates a key limitation to any assumption that 'national' and 'media' boundaries coincide. UK-based newspapers such as the *Mirror* do well in Ireland because to some extent they *become* 'Irish'. This is explicitly flagged by the adoption of the prefix 'Irish' (becoming the *Irish Mirror*), investment in editorial and reporting staff in Dublin and the production of 'Irish news'. Crucially, this suggests that readers are not simply conceived of as 'readers *in* Ireland' but *as* Irish. We will return to this territorial versus national distinction later. Probably the most successful national rebranding has been achieved by the *Sun*. The *Sun* might seem an unlikely candidate to be the best-selling tabloid in both Scotland and Ireland given its jingoistic Little England associations – yet each day it sells 100,000 dailies in the Republic and 400,000 in Scotland. It does so because it has successfully discarded its 'Little England' persona and succeeded in becoming (more acceptably) *Irish* and *Scottish*. Newspapers and other media deliberately (if not always self-consciously) manipulate presentation, agendas and content to address different national audiences in different 'nationalising' ways.

Presentation of news and 'national' framing

Crucial here is an understanding of those linguistic habits and short-cuts, the smallest of words – 'here', 'us', 'we' – which point towards the nation. We also need to pay attention to the *absence* of words: often it is sufficient to refer to 'the people' or 'the country' on the assumption that the audience will understand the unstated context. As Billig (1995: 107) puts it: 'Which country? Which people? Which nation? No specification is necessary; the nation is this nation, "our" nation'.

That such a position is, in the context of a multinational state, rather problematic can be illustrated through the following pieces of routine media text/speech. To each the reader should bring the questions 'Which country? Which people? Which nation?'

☐ The **Sky News** website carried the following headline:

Queen's Costs Rise Above Inflation: The Queen is the latest victim of rising prices according to official accounts as her spending has risen by an inflation-busting 5.26 per cent.[3]

☐ **Channel 4 News** trailed a filmed report ('Brown in school sport pledge') with the following introduction:

> The amount of time children spend doing sport in school will increase to five hours a week under new government plans to get children more active. Currently pupils are required to do only two hours of sport a week. The prime minister this morning announced a new national school sport week.[4]

☐ The **Daily Mirror** reported a delay in delivering secondary school exam results ('Marking delay hits million kids'). The text in full was as follows:

> More than a million pupils will start their holidays without knowing school test results as private firm ETS struggles to mark scripts. The National Assessment Agency said results of Key Stage 2 tests taken by 10 and 11 year-olds will be out a week late on July 15. It is not clear when 14 year-olds will get results from Key Stage 3 tests in English, Maths and Science. Schools Secretary Ed Balls promised a probe into the fiasco and said the delay was 'clearly unacceptable'.[5]

☐ The **Press & Journal** newspaper routinely carries a claim, under its masthead, to be 'The Voice of the North'.

These examples have been chosen because they are perfectly ordinary, and unremarkable. Each contains pointers toward a national context that would pass, for the most part, unnoticed. All assume some common understanding (indeed imagining) of *who* and *where* 'we' are, as well as a shared perspective on the world around 'us'. The first example assumes that 'we' know just who *the* Queen is – that is, that we are not talking here about, say, Queen Beatrix of the Netherlands. Readers in any doubt (can we imagine such doubts?) are helped by references within the report to Buckingham Palace.

The second and third stories are excellent examples of reports with no direct indication of context. Few hearing the Channel 4 report or reading the *Mirror* article however, would have assumed that they related to children everywhere, to children in a specific town or village or to children in France. Such reports relate to *our* children, *here*, sitting exams in *our* schools. This is indicated with reference to 'government plans', 'the Schools Secretary' and 'the prime minister'. Readers can be expected to understand, *without being told*, that this is the government of the United Kingdom (the '*British* government'), the *British* education secretary, the *UK* Prime Minister. Here, following Billig (1995) 'readers could be expected to recognise their national selves'.

However, there is a problem. While the answer to our questions (Which country? Which people? Which nation?) seems reasonably clear in the first example, it is not so clear in the second, third and fourth. If the answer for the first example leads on from the context of '*the* Queen' being understood as Elizabeth, head of the state of the United Kingdom then we have a clear answer: country = UK; people = British; nation = UK. It might seem, at first glance, that the same holds true for the second and third stories – after all 'the Prime Minister' is head of the *British* 'government'. However, education policy is a *devolved* matter. Neither the prime minister nor the 'Schools Secretary' has responsibility or authority for children's education in Scotland, Wales or Northern Ireland. Therefore 'the children' in these articles are, on reflection, *not* clearly 'British' but are children at schools in England. Since these articles are about English schools and children in England both appear to be pointing at the '*wrong*' context (the UK) and to the 'wrong' people (the British)! The reports refer to a 'national sports week' and to the 'National Assessment Authority' (NAA), but it is unclear whether 'national' should be interpreted as the UK or England. The NAA, it should be noted, has responsibility only in England – though there is no reason why the *Mirror*'s 'ordinary reader' would be aware of that. It is thus difficult to assume that readers 'could be expected to recognise their national selves' since there are *two* nationalities at play here (English and British). Further, given that the Channel 4 school sports item was broadcast throughout the United Kingdom, how might viewers in Scotland, Wales or Northern Ireland have perceived their national selves (if at all) in the context of the story?

This is further exemplified by our final example. The *Press & Journal* may well be 'The Voice of the North' – but 'north of *what?*' Published in Aberdeen, the paper primarily circulates around North East Scotland and in certain parts of the Scottish Highlands. This area is, simultaneously, the geographic north of Britain *and* the geographic north of Scotland. Anyone with a passing acquaintance with the *Press & Journal*, however, will know that the missing qualifier here is 'of Scotland'.

What these examples demonstrate is that in answering our questions – Which country? etc. – there is room for doubt. The nation is not obvious and singular, but – at least potentially – debatable and plural. The United Kingdom is made up of a multiplicity of nations and nationalities, both mutually exclusive *and* overlapping (English; Scottish; Welsh; British).

Where individuals may have more than one national self (British *and* Scottish for example) or more than one national homeland (England *and* the United Kingdom) then the 'pointing' habits we find in UK media are more complex and fuzzy than is allowed for by some accounts.

So far we have described both 'micro' and 'implicit' aspects of news presentation and noted how the national context need not be as singular, nor as 'obvious' as some theorists have assumed. However, much news presentation is *explicitly* framed in ostentatiously 'national' ways. We have already noted that some London-based newspapers have rebranded specific editions as Irish or Scottish. Newspapers routinely make claims to national status through their titles, insignia and straplines. This is less obvious and explicit in Fleet Street titles distributed in England than is found in other parts of the UK. The only masthead on Fleet Street with an 'obvious' national referent is the *Express* crusader (with England's St George Cross emblazoned on his chest), frequently accompanied with a byline mentioning Britain (e.g. 'Crusading for a Fairer Britain'). There are also some allusions to location in the labelling of regional editions within England, for example, 'the North West edition' of the *Daily Mail*. This is unlikely to be understood as the North West *of Britain*.

Explicit national referents, by contrast, are common in the symbolism and sloganeering of newspapers sold in Scotland and, to a lesser extent, Wales and Northern Ireland. With the exception of *The Times*, the *Guardian* and the *Independent*, all Fleet Street titles distributed in Scotland make reference to Scottishness through masthead, logo or strapline. The *Daily Star* appends '*of Scotland*' to its title, while the other tabloids acquire the adjective 'Scottish'. The *Scottish Sun* sports a thistle while the *Scottish Daily Express* replaces its 'crusader' logo with a rampant Scottish lion brandishing Scotland's Saltire flag. The *Telegraph* simply adds the caption 'Scottish Edition'. In Wales the *Mirror* (briefly) adopted the prefix *Welsh* and, featured a Red Dragon flag with the strapline 'For all that matters in Wales'; while the *Western Mail* proclaims itself 'The national newspaper of Wales'. In Northern Ireland, the *Mirror* is 'Northern Ireland's paper'; the *News Letter*, 'At the heart of Northern Ireland'; and the *Belfast Telegraph*, 'Northern Ireland's favourite newspaper'.

This suggests at least three territorial levels at which we need to consider 'national framing' and presentation. The first is that of the entire United Kingdom, populated by 'network' news media (such the BBC's *Six O'Clock News*, *Channel 4 News*, *Sky News*) or those newspapers existing in one single edition (i.e. the *Guardian*, the *Independent*, the

Independent on Sunday). 'Home news' in these media *usually* implies UK/
British news, and banal invocations of 'the country' will generally mean
the UK. Here, though, there may well be considerable slippage between
'Britain' and 'England'. The second level comprises clearly defined areas
within the UK in which newspapers (or specific editions of newspapers)
or broadcast media are distributed/transmitted. This includes territories
understood as 'regions'. For example, Yorkshire enjoys both Yorkshire
Television and the *Yorkshire Post*; the 'North West' receives BBC North
West television, including the daily *North West Tonight* news and the
weekly *Politics Show*. Other territories might be regarded as nations:
England, Scotland, Wales, Northern Ireland. Three of these have autonomous media 'pointing' to an imagined Scottish, Welsh or Northern
Irish 'community'. England, however, seems to have no self-consciously
national media. England, in fact, rather better falls into a third level,
comprising whatever parts of the UK are *not* covered by substate media.
For example, the *Mirror* produces specific editions for Scotland, for Wales
and for Northern Ireland. Its remaining territory, defined in terms of
'what is left' is in effect (though it may not be consciously thought of as)
England. Other titles that remain after substate national editions are
excluded might be England and Wales (e.g. the *Daily Mail*) or, indeed,
England, Wales and Northern Ireland (e.g. the *Telegraph*).

Altogether, then, the 'British' news landscape is far more complex
than existing theorising about media and nation allows for. Notions
of 'British' pointing are perceptive and plausible in *some* UK media
contexts, but less so in others. In some contexts media language may
point simultaneously in different 'national' directions. Elsewhere
(Rosie et al., 2006; Petersoo, 2007) we have described how the
national context of newspaper articles can 'wander', even within a
single paragraph or sentence, between different conceptions of who
'we' might be. If presentation of media content is routinely remind-
ing us of our 'national' selves, it is certainly not doing so in a straightforward manner.

News content

In this section we show the extent to which different (and sometimes
overlapping) national frames exist in newspapers in Scotland and
England. We do so through a content analysis of newspapers across
twelve 'day surveys' between October 2000 and January 2003 and comprising over 2500 articles. These were drawn from the nine Fleet Street
titles bought in both England and Scotland, and from the five main

Scottish daily titles.[6] Here we offer the broadest contours of our results regarding explicit spatial or national markers (locations, institutional titles, national nouns and adjectives) reported in more detail in Rosie et al. (2004). We found considerable differences between Scotland and England (and *within* the press in Scotland) in two respects: the patterns of national nouns and adjectives explicitly mentioned in articles, and the locations mentioned in them.

Table 6.1 shows the number of explicit national markers in both countries, with the newspapers bought in Scotland differentiated between the 'indigenous' Scottish and 'Fleet Street' titles. For each category of national marker, we have noted the proportion of articles containing at least one relevant adjective or noun:

References to 'Britain' and 'British' occurred quite frequently, but there are several caveats, not least that they are a little less frequent in Scotland. In England we found broadsheets more likely to use British terms, perhaps because they maintain a more formal tone than tabloids. In Scotland we found differences in the frequency of 'British' terms between indigenous Scottish newspapers and Fleet Street titles. The key difference here, however, was that newspapers bought in England mentioned *only* Britain/Britishness with any great frequency, while other national nouns and adjectives were largely absent. Papers bought in

Table 6.1   Summary of national 'flags' in newspapers in England and Scotland

| | England: | Scotland: | |
% of articles containing:	All titles	Indigenous	Fleet Street
Any 'British' term (Britain, UK, British, Brits, Britons)	36	26	32
Any 'English' term (England, English)	12	12	11
Any 'Scottish' term (Scotland, Scots, Scottish)	6	47	17
Any 'Welsh' term (Wales, Welsh)	4	3	3
Any 'Northern Irish' term (Northern Ireland, Ulster; N. Irish)	2	2	2
N	1026	518	985

Source: From data collected by The Leverhulme programme's Media & National Identity team.

Scotland, on the other hand, used 'Scottish' terms at least as frequently as 'British' ones. Indigenous Scottish titles were much more likely to flag up Scotland. Here, we found considerable variation. 'Scottish' terms were frequent in those Fleet Street tabloids investing most resources in 'Scotticisation' (the *Sun, Mail, Express* and *Mirror*) and infrequent in the Fleet Street broadsheets.

In neither country, it might be noted, were 'Welsh' or 'Northern Irish' terms found with any frequency. Finally, the relative absence of 'England/English' should be noted. Of the few articles mentioning 'English', around one-third actually referred to the English *language* and most of the remainder were concerned with England's national sporting teams. Similarly one-third of those articles which contained the noun England were concerned with sport. We found very little evidence that newspapers bought in England routinely used 'English' to denote either an explicit or a banal national 'we'.

We also found significant national differences in *locations* mentioned (see Table 6.2). Over half the articles from England mentioned a city, town or county in England, compared to just over a third of articles from Scotland. Again we found considerable variation in Scotland, with a Scottish location cited in a majority of indigenous newspaper articles. In short, newspapers bought in England tended to report events occurring *in* England while papers bought in Scotland – with some variation – most frequently reported events *in* Scotland. Hardly any of the sampled

Table 6.2   Summary of locations mentioned in newspapers in England and Scotland

% of articles containing:	England: All titles	Scotland: Indigenous	Scotland: Fleet Street
London	22	12	19
Other location in England	41	21	30
Any location in England	*51*	*28*	*40*
Edinburgh	1	13	5
Other location in Scotland	3	30	29
Any location in Scotland	*5*	*54*	*20*
Any location in Wales	*3*	*1*	*2*
Any location in N. Ireland	*	*1*	*1*
N	1026	518	985

Note: *less than 1%.
Source: From data collected by The Leverhulme programme's Media & National Identity team.

stories from either country referred to locations in Northern Ireland or Wales.

Echoing our earlier findings, the extent to which some Fleet Street titles have 'become Scottish' is manifested in the frequency of their citing locations in Scotland. In the case of the *Scottish Sun*, for example, two-fifths of articles mentioned at least one Scottish location. This contrasts sharply with the *Guardian* and the *Independent* (neither of which produce Scottish editions) which were no more likely to mention a Scottish location than the England-bought press.

We found similar patterns in our (more modest) study of BBC Radio news bulletins. Here again we found that Radio Scotland emphasised 'Scottish stories' (broadly speaking stories located in Scotland, involving a person or institution defined – implicitly or explicitly – as 'Scottish', or of some other relevance to Scotland and the Scots) or highlighted Scottish 'angles' on broader UK or international stories. While there was no overt 'nationalisation' of Radio 4 news bulletins, we did find routine 'pointing' towards the United Kingdom. There were, however, frequent stories on Radio 4's bulletins in which the 'national focus' was unclear (Britain? England?). In this sense we were confident that our arguments about newspapers could be carried over into other forms of mass media.

While these findings might seem understandable – indeed 'obvious' – there are two distinct interpretations that could be made. The first is that media producers have a clear conception of *where* readers/ listeners are, and strive to meet preferences for relatively *localised* news. The *Scottish Sun*, for example, aware that its readers are *in* Scotland, offers them news from Scotland as a *geographical* (rather than national) selling point. There are two problems with such a view – first, is it simple coincidence that the boundaries of this understanding are national? Further, if 'local people want local news' why does there seem to be no prospect of successful *regional* English editions of Fleet Street titles (the *Yorkshire Sun*)?

The second interpretation is that, continuing with our example, the *Scottish Sun* thinks of its readers in national terms, believing these readers want *Scottish* stories in which Scottish locations and actors are central. Such a view is supported by the fact that the *Scottish Sun*'s distinctiveness extends into its editorial line. The *Scottish Sun*'s 1992 relaunch saw it flirting with (if never truly embracing) Scottish independence and the Scottish National Party (SNP). A car sticker enjoined Scottish readers to 'rise now and be a nation again' (the refrain of *Flower of Scotland*, a popular Scottish patriotic song). There was no change in policy on the part of the *Sun's* parent edition which maintained a directly opposing political line. The reaction of Scotland's (then) most popular title, the *Daily Record* was revealing. Insisting that '*Real* Scots Read the *Record*', it routinely disparaged the *Sun* – and the Scotticising *Daily Mail* – as 'London dailies'. Similarly in the late 1970s the *Record* dismissed the claim of the *Scottish Daily Express* to be 'The Voice of Scotland' as 'impertinence' accusing the 'English Express group' of 'political humbug' in its claims to Scottishness.[7] The point is that these tabloids do not see themselves as offering local news (which just *happens* to be Scottish) in a broader British context. Instead they engage in a fierce commercial rivalry over Scottishness with disputed claims of 'authenticity' at its core.

Such overt media 'nationalising' simply does not occur in England. Indeed, it is not at all clear that the *Sun*, in its England-wide guise, routinely thinks of its readers as 'English' (since that is a term the *Sun* – and its rivals – seldom commits to print). Nor is there any dispute over national 'authenticity'. There is, therefore, an asymmetry between Scotland and England reflected in, and reproduced by, newspapers and, to a less explicit extent, other media. Any assumption that 'the nation' is, indeed must be, Britain *may* be a dominant, rarely criticised common sense in England, or (as we shall see) in UK-wide media such as 'network' television news. Elsewhere the nation does *not* necessarily mean Britain. In some contexts 'the' nation may be 'Scotland *and/or* Britain'; in others 'Britain (but perhaps England)'. Where there is a question mark over the nation, in what sense might it be *routinely* 'imagined'?

News production

In an influential study of Britishness, Linda Colley (1992: 43) noted the tendency of seventeenth- and early eighteenth-century newspaper editors to

> borrow ... heavily from the London press, filling ... columns with accounts of ... parliamentary debates, the vicissitudes of the stock market, the latest court gossip, the chances of war with foreign states, or the prospects of peace. Scottish newspapers were no different from the English in this respect. They, too, reprinted swathes of south-of-the-border news culled from the metropolitan press, grimly substituting the words 'Great Britain' in place of the more parochial references to 'England'.

Colley suggests that the availability and topicality of 'metropolitan' news for resource-starved newspapers helped tie 'the provinces' into the new British state, inculcating a common identity – citizenship – along the way. Yet this probably understates the longstanding and often powerful local, regional and national interests of newspapers. The *Yorkshire Post*, for example, declares itself 'Yorkshire's National Newspaper'. This is not a claim towards Yorkshire's nationhood but of providing 'national' news through a clearly defined 'local' or 'regional' prism. Scotland's press has long pursued a rigorously 'Scottish' agenda viewing Scottishness and Scotland as an integral part of the British 'project'. The opening paragraph of the very first issue of the *Scotsman*, published in 1817, made this agenda clear:

> Before proceeding to the ordinary business of our paper, we beg to observe, that we have not chosen the name of Scotsman to preserve an invidious distinction, but with the view of rescuing it from the odium of servility. With that stain removed, a Scotsman may well claim brotherhood with an Englishman, and there ought now to be no rivalry between them, but in the cause of regulated freedom. In that cause it is our ambition to labour.[8]

There has never been a single news agenda within the UK's press, nor in more modern forms of mass media. While it might be tempting to presume that media within a given state (such as the UK) pursue a broadly similar 'national' (e.g. 'British') news agenda and work within a similar 'news culture', the evidence suggests otherwise. To explore this further we interviewed senior editors and journalists from a range of Fleet Street and Scottish-based newspapers, as well as observing the putting together of morning bulletins in BBC radio newsrooms in London and Glasgow. In all these contexts we found a striking rejection of deliberately 'national' or 'nationalist' agendas in the production of news. It became clear, however, that many journalists held a 'national' understanding of their readers/listeners. For London-based journalists this often amounted to a 'banal' understanding of their audience as 'British' (though sometimes British seemed to mean 'English'). For journalists in Scotland (and Scottish journalists now in London) the situation was more complex, and showed recognition of different levels of national understanding (Scottish, British) and the difficulties in managing these. All the journalists, regardless of media institution or location stressed a professional ethos that prized 'journalistic instincts' above 'national knowledge'. In practice, however, these two concepts overlap. As one journalist told us:

> [Y]ou write for your readership. At the end of the day, that's all that matters. You know? ... the *Scottish Daily Mail* was set up to try and eat into the Scottish market at a time when a lot of the papers were moving up here and tartanising their editions, and because, I think, most people would accept that the *Daily Mail* in England wouldn't be to the taste of your average Scottish ... reader.
>
> (*Donaldson*, Glasgow)[9]

'Knowing the audience' had direct consequences on content. Discussing the south-of-England focus of some Fleet Street titles, for example, one senior editor noted that this reflected knowledge about where readers actually were (implying reinforcement between readers' locations, their interest in 'relevant' stories and the provision of spatially relevant content):

> Some papers like ... if you look at the circulation profiles, like *The Times* and *The Independent* are really vestigial in the north of England. They don't exist there very strongly at all. *The Independent* more or less stops at Watford.
>
> (*Ormiston*, London)

Another senior editorial figure was blunt about the prospects of raising the circulation of his Sunday broadsheet in different parts of the UK, and how a metropolitan focus was in the immediate self-interests of some titles:

> [I]t's easier, much easier to put on 20,000 inside the M25 [the Greater London orbital motorway] than it is to put on 20,000 outside the M25. There's definitely that. I think it's true actually. You put a CD out in the paper, and your circulation will jump 50,000 and nearly all [that increase will] be inside the M25.
>
> (*Smith*, London)

For these experienced journalists a degree of commercially led 'parochialism' (though they would not have used this term) was a crucial, though not necessarily conscious, strategy. While this might be explicit and obvious in the Scottish media, it also occurred within Fleet Street, even though producers themselves might hesitate to recognise or admit it: 'The *Observer* tends to think of itself as writing about Britain. Even when it's *not* writing about Britain, it will still *say* it is writing about Britain' (*Smith*, London).

The situation in Scotland is quite different with many journalists describing a deliberate process of 'tartanisation' or 'putting a kilt on' stories. One journalist, trained in England but now working for a Scottish title, told us:

> So we're always looking for a good Scottish angle. That's not to say that we won't carry a story if there's no Scottish angle to it because a good story is a good story, whatever the nationalities involved. But we try and pick up Scotland if you like. At first when I moved up here I couldn't get my head round this problem, because I – because English newspapers don't big up England.
>
> (*Inglis*, Glasgow)

There was evidence of some discomfort at this process, not least because 'nationalism' might imply, to some at least, narrow-mindedness. The journalist above sought to defend his readers from such a charge:

> I can see why [newspapers are] doing that because it's a marketing ploy, but I don't really think – I would like to think that most readers think beyond nationalities these days and they – they buy a newspaper, not because they want to be reminded how great Scotland is but because they're interested in what's going on in the world. We're a Scottish newspaper, not a British newspaper. I mean that's a geographical fact. We don't – you know, we only sell a few copies on the other side of the border. So yeah. It's always the word 'Scots', never the word 'British'.
>
> (*Inglis*)

Likewise our observation of and conversations within the BBC newsrooms found a reluctance to describe any of the processes of story selection or presentation in explicitly 'national' terms. Nevertheless it was clear that some key (and prized) journalistic skills – notably 'knowing the audience' and 'moving the story on' – comprised 'banal nationalistic' assumptions about where listeners were, the stories that would interest them, and – just as importantly – the stories that would not interest them. In Glasgow (although we deliberately avoided directly raising issues of 'nation' or 'Scotland') we were immediately met with accounts about 'Scottish' news. It was a commonplace that what made Radio Scotland 'distinctive' was the 'unique selling point' of its Scottish coverage. BBC Scotland's position as the only television and radio broadcaster to Scotland *per se* was emphasised. While Radio Scotland's bulletins have a responsibility to cover 'the news', and often lead with global and/or UK stories, it was deemed important to have a Scottish story prominent in the running order.

Accounts of what makes a story Scottish varied from the 'common sense' of events happening in Scotland, to people from Scotland, or which affect Scotland, to the more obscure and 'intuitive'. The team, for example, mentioned 'dietary studies into salmon consumption' and 'US relations with Libya' as *Scottish* issues given the importance of fish farming to the Scottish economy and the legacy of the Lockerbie bombing. A number of journalists volunteered that they routinely *put a kilt on* stories; sometimes the team hedged their bets by working on stories with no apparent Scottish angle *in case one emerged*. News items resistant to this strategy were often judged less newsworthy. As one journalist commented, 'some stories are just a bit "England" for us'.

It was generally felt that devolution had brought a specifically Scottish news agenda more sharply into focus, but in talking to editors and journalists we discerned an unexpected consequence of this. Some (in both London and Scotland) held the view that now that Scotland had its own Parliament, and a semi-autonomous media to report upon it, there was *less* rather than more obligation on media to relay news from Scotland to audiences in England. From the perspective of London-based editors and journalists, routine stories from Scotland were deemed of little interest to a 'general' audience, and the assumption was made that those who *would* find such stories interesting (i.e. people in Scotland) were well served by Scottish media:

> [O]ne of the particularly pronounced effects of devolution on ... the Press as a whole and possibly even broadcasting ... is that there is now, there's actually kind of less interest in what's going on in Scotland than there was before ... [The Scottish edition] have a page for the Scottish Parliament rather than a page for the Westminster Parliament and they will sometimes change the front page and they will certainly change some of the stories and that happens more than it did beforehand. But one of the consequences of that is the Scottish stories tend to be restricted to the Scottish editions more than they were in the past.
>
> (*Fox*, London)

If Scots are really passionately interested in what's going on in Scotland, they're buying *The Herald* or *The Scotsman* or something anyway and they're certainly watching all the Scottish News ... my own view is that Scotland is, if anything, rather less well covered now [by Fleet Street/networked bulletins] than it was before devolution.

(*Ormiston*)

Scottish-based journalists unanimously agreed that a 'Scottish' story was only likely to receive coverage in Fleet Street editions, or on network news bulletins, if it was *extraordinarily* newsworthy, or unusual and exotic. An example of this was Madonna being welcomed at Inverness airport with a bagpiped medley of her hits. While the *Sun's* front page headlined 'Piper don't screetch', the *Scottish Sun* was more attuned to Scottish sensibilities, asking: 'Who's that skirl?'[10] This was not a story about Scotland but about a world celebrity: its Scottish aspect was reported in the English-based press merely to 'add colour'. A consequence of devolution, therefore, seems to be that audiences in England are less likely to have regular access to news about Scotland and, to a lesser extent given the (natural) dominance of English-based events in networked news bulletins, Scottish audiences will receive less news about ('non-British') events in England: 'Scottish stories ... have fallen off the London, not just London, British agenda to a considerable extent and I think that's a terrible pity' (*Ormiston*, interview).

Concerns over how far the 'British' media are adequately reporting news from across the United Kingdom have particular resonance for the BBC since they are legally bound to represent 'the UK, its nations, regions and communities'. In 2008 (as we wrote the final draft of this chapter) the BBC Trust published an independent assessment of *BBC Network News and Current-Affairs Coverage of the Four UK Nations*.[11] Professor Anthony King, in summarising the various strands of the research, emphasised several notable findings, including the following:

Network news stories concerned with devolution, or with policies closely associated with devolution, 'were found to be vague and confusing' and often 'simply assumed that a story applied to the whole UK when it did not. Very often, it was left unclear to which parts of the UK a story applied and to which it did not';

News presenters and interviewers frequently used terms such as 'we' or 'this country' when referring to England (and not the whole UK);

In reporting stories relating only to England presenters would frequently highlight that at the beginning of the report 'but then never ... mention that fact again, even in the course of a lengthy programme'.

Most viewers or listeners 'could be forgiven for not realising that the story in fact related only to England'. In sharp contrast, stories relating solely to other parts of the UK 'were almost invariably flagged up as such, often several times';

London or Westminster were routinely used 'as the implicit or explicit point of reference' in reporting and discussing 'UK' news.

(BBC Trust, 2008)

All of these findings echo our own and, further, demonstrate that many of our findings – based as they were on a survey of the press and of more limited investigation of radio news – are mirrored in network television news and current affairs.

Media effects?

One thorny question which did not form part of our research, but which is, nevertheless, a crucial one, is that of 'effects'. We can show that there are national differences in the kind of habits of explicit language, of reporting and of 'pointing' – but do these serve to nationalise the readership/audience? In other words, *does this matter*? There are a number of ways that we could begin to answer this question. Our own research suggests that it matters, at least in the context of Scotland, in a very concrete way. Those Fleet Street titles which have gone furthest in 'putting a kilt on' their Scottish editions have also proved most successful in increasing their circulation. The *Scottish Sun* is now Scotland's biggest-selling title. Producing a genuinely 'Scottish' edition had concrete rewards for News International. In short, 'Scotland' sells newspapers – at least in Scotland.

Likewise, a survey conducted for the BBC Trust research found that respondents in Scotland were most likely to feel that network broadcast news stories were 'irrelevant to the area where they live' and to be annoyed by this. Further, people in Scotland were most likely to 'rely on local newspapers for their local news'. The research also found that viewers/listeners in some regions of England, in Wales and, in particular, Northern Ireland were poorly served by network news coverage. It is not so much that such coverage has an Anglocentric bias, but a *metro*-centric one – that is, London disproportionately dominates news reports and the 'network' news agenda. This has at least three consequences:

- Many people will feel ill-served (indeed annoyed) at the level of 'national' service they receive from 'network' news sources;

- Some will thus turn to (or continue to rely upon) other sources of news – this helps to explain why the Scottish newspaper market remains vibrant and distinctively *Scottish*;
- The conjunction of poor network coverage of non-metropolitan news and the existence (at least in some parts of the UK) of alternative sources of news may serve to strengthen a *fragmentation* of news in the UK. As the BBC Trust survey demonstrated, many people seem ill-informed about key policy issues (health, education etc.) in other parts of the UK, in large part because no one is informing them!

Research carried out elsewhere in this programme touched upon aspects of media effects with particular reference to Scotland (see Kiely et al., 2006). That study found that Scottish 'nationals' (respondents born and resident in Scotland) tended to possess

> a taken-for-granted, non-contentious aspect to the media. What they read, watch and listen to is mainly the result of habit, often focusing on local matters. Yet their preference for the Scottish press suggests that a sense of Scottishness is important. Identity and media consumption become contentious when something in the media challenges their sense of identity.

Such challenges, it will be appreciated, come from the kind of metro-centric habits criticised by the BBC Trust. Most Scots who read newspapers either read 'indigenous' titles (which account for around half of all daily sales) or the most Scotticised editions of Fleet Street titles. That is, they read newspapers in which a Scottish 'frame of reference' is present (although it will not be the sole frame of reference they encounter). Revealingly, the same research illustrated how 'migrants' (those born in England but now resident in Scotland) renegotiate their identity, in some part relating to 'the stance taken by the Scottish media on Scottish, British and English national identity'. In terms of media this negotiation ranges from those who accommodate themselves to a more Scottish positioning; through those who try to claim an inclusive Britishness (but 'struggle to find media compatible with being British in Scotland'); to 'Those in Scotland who describe themselves as English [and who] often complain about a Scottish national frame of reference in the Scottish media' (Kiely et al., 2006: 488).

What is striking about the material from the study of 'nationals' and 'migrants' is how taken for granted national 'frames of references' within media are, and how disorienting a shift in that frame can be.

As newcomers to Scotland may struggle with, be puzzled by and in some cases resent the unfamiliar Scottish 'pointing' within Scotland's media, so too people in Scotland, Wales and Northern Ireland (and to a less marked degree some regions of England) will chafe at, and feel misrepresented by the Anglocentric and/or metro-centric habits of the 'British' media. All of this brings us back to the ideas that media in some way tie us together in an imagined community through banal 'reminders' of who and where we are. Our research, other research within the Leverhulme Nations & Regions programme and the research by the BBC Trust suggest great variation in just which community – or indeed communities – are invoked and imagined through media in different parts of the UK.

Conclusion

Our findings suggest that in the aftermath of devolution, newspaper reporting in England and Scotland is characterised by a high degree of concentration on the respective countries in which the newspapers are sold. The clear emergence of a 'Scottish political agenda' has not seen that agenda reported on networked broadcast media or in 'Fleet Street' editions – rather, it seems, Scottish news is reported by the Scottish media. In this sense news agendas within the United Kingdom are fragmented. Residents of Scotland may well have more reportage about the Scottish parliament but, as a consequence, have relatively little information about Welsh, Northern Irish and even (non-British) English current affairs. Residents of England, in turn, have little daily access to news about Scotland, Wales or Northern Ireland. Perhaps paradoxically, devolution has reinforced this trend rather than reversing or weakening it.

How aware are media producers about various national audiences? How sensitive are they to subtle differences in audience preferences (and in particular to differences that might be understood as 'national')? And, perhaps most importantly, what are the possible consequences of the paradox that devolution appears to have entrenched and expanded *different* information spaces in different parts of the United Kingdom?

We do not believe that these are simply 'academic' questions without relevance to broader social, political and commercial processes. Indeed, these questions have immediate political relevance to the relationship between Scotland and the rest of the UK. In 2007, as we began thinking about this chapter, the Scottish Government (led by the SNP) reopened the debate on a 'Scottish Six', an hour-long evening news bulletin on

BBC One which would opt out of the current networked BBC news. The *Daily Mail* derided the proposal as 'The Tartan Opt-Out', while the *Daily Star of Scotland* argued 'Telly plan is turn off'.[12] The proposal, however, found a number of influential supporters, including a former BBC director general.

The details of the proposal, and the pros and cons outlined by proponents and opponents are unimportant here. Rather, the key issue lies in the underlying consensus that there *is* a 'Scottish perspective' on news, and that existing network bulletins are failing (fully) to address that. The BBC Trust research confirms that the existing arrangements for network news and current affairs are not adequately reporting on, or to, the UK's 'nations and regions'. Consequently, news agendas in Scotland and 'London' (and to an extent Belfast and Cardiff) have been drifting apart. Without a radical rethink on how 'network' or 'home' news is constructed and delivered this is likely to continue.

We return then to the earlier arguments about media's role in (re)imagining national communities. If *different* communities are being imagined, and if imagining is *increasingly different* in separate parts of the United Kingdom, then we might plausibly expect concrete political and social consequences. Without a unified public media space, and without a clear communicative field, can the UK retain (or regain) its primary political legitimacy throughout the four nations? If not, might we see this drifting apart of media spaces joined by increasing pressure on the British state itself?

Notes

1. As well as the authors, the research team comprised Susan Condor (University of Lancaster), James Kennedy (University of Edinburgh), and John MacInnes (University of Edinburgh).
2. London's Fleet Street was long a centre of the British newspaper industry and, despite the relocation of newspaper offices to elsewhere in London, 'Fleet Street' remains a useful shorthand term for 'the British national press'.
3. The Sky News, 27 June 2008.
4. Channel 4 News, 13 July 2007.
5. The *Daily Mirror*, 5 July 2008.
6. 'Fleet Street': *Daily Express, Daily Mail, Daily Mirror, Daily Star, Daily Telegraph, Guardian, Independent, Sun, Times*. Scotland: *Courier & Advertiser, Daily Record, Herald, Press & Journal, Scotsman*.
7. The *Daily Record*, 08 February 1979.
8. The *Scotsman*, 25 January 1817.
9. All interviews carry pseudonyms.

10. The *Sun*; The *Scottish Sun*, 19 December 2000.
11. Available online at: http://www.bbc.co.uk/bbctrust/research/impartiality/nations.html.
12. The *Daily Mail*, 11 August 2007; the *Daily Star of Scotland*, 09 August 2007.

Bibliography

Anderson, B. (1983) *Imagined communities: Reflections on the origin and spread of nationalism*. London: Verso.

BBC Trust (2008) BBC Network news and current affairs coverage of the four UK nations.

Billig, M. (1995) *Banal nationalism*. London: Sage.

Colley, L. (1992) *Britons: Forging the nation*, 1707–1837. London: Pimlico.

Kiely, R., McCrone, D. and Bechhofer, F. (2006) Reading between the lines: National identity and attitudes to the media in Scotland. *Nations and Nationalism*, **12** (3), 473–92.

MacInnes, J., Rosie, M., Petersoo, P., Condor, S. and Kennedy, J. (2007) Where is the British national press? *British Journal of Sociology*, **58** (2), 185–206.

Petersoo, P. (2007) What does 'we' mean?: National deixes in the media. *Journal of Language and Politics*, **6** (3), 419–36.

Rosie, M., MacInnes, J., Petersoo, P., Condor, S. and Kennedy, J. (2004) Nation speaking unto nation?: Newspapers and national identity in the devolved UK. *Sociological Review*, **52** (4), 437–58.

Rosie, M., Petersoo, P., MacInnes, J., Condor, S. and Kennedy, J. (2006) Mediating which nation?: Citizenship and national identities in the British press. *Social Semiotics*, **16** (2), 327–44.

7
Small Fortunes: Nationalism, Capitalism and Changing Identities
Jonathan Hearn

Introduction

National identity is a moving target. Although we are used to using familiar, well-established stereotypes in our daily 'identity talk' – the Scots are reticent, the English are confident – not only are these unreliable generalisations at any given time, but they are history-bound notions. Far from revealing a stable inner essence that persists over time, what we say about our identities actually reflects particular aspects of the times we are living in, which frame and animate what we have to say about identity.

It is easier to remind ourselves of this point when we look back over longer stretches of time. Intense and severe religiousness was once a Scottish characteristic, but now Scotland shares in European trends towards secularism (Rosie, 2004). Enthusiastic support for the empire, queen and the union (Finlay, 2002; Morton, 1999) were once part of what made Scots who they were, but no more. However, the shifting nature of identities goes out of focus when we move towards the present. In recent decades much of the impetus behind and justification for devolution in Scotland has come from the idea that Scots identify particularly strongly with principles of egalitarianism, democracy and socialism (Hearn, 2000; McCrone, 2001; Paterson, 1998), but this too is an historical pattern, an abstraction, that is susceptible to change, and may perhaps be changing significantly, while we are not looking.

Two macrohistorical processes have a particularly powerful shaping effect on social identities. One is capitalism, with its restless drive towards the pursuit and concentration of profit, and generation of new forms of markets. The other is nationalism, that is, the growth of nations and states as fundamental ways of claiming, contesting and negotiating political control and linking this to territories. Intertwined and evolving, these processes set the conditions under which identities, including national identities, get conceptualised and mobilised. In the case of Scotland, much of the recent discourse about Scottish identity has been shaped by the development of mid-twentieth-century welfare state and associated social democratic politics in Europe, and the subsequent struggles over the relative roles of the state and the market in social provisioning since about 1980. Emblematic of this was the strong association made between Scottish home rule politics and anti-Thatcherism, Thatcherism being cast as the antithesis to a whole set of deeply embedded Scottish values. But Scots in their twenties today have little or no personal memory of Margaret Thatcher's political career, and have grown up in the wake of deindustrialisation, and amid the normative reassertion of the legitimate power of private capital. Scotland does not stand where it did, so neither can conventional notions of Scottish identity. This has implications for politics and political rhetoric under the new and still evolving constitutional settlement in Britain, and how parties and other political actors lay claim to Scottishness in their appeals for support. I will return to this point in the conclusion.

To make these generalisations more concrete, I explore the influence of capitalism and nationalism on national identity below, through an ethnographic case study of the first year of merger of the Bank of Scotland (BoS) and the Halifax, to form HBOS. Amid the usual tensions and strains of corporate merger, staff from both banks used notions of national identity (among other things) to make sense of the encounter and their personal situations. I believe aspects of these data help us understand the ways national identities interact with and get moulded by macrosociological changes. Obviously longitudinal data are invaluable for tracing historical transformations of such things as national identity. But key moments of institutional change in which issues of identity are highlighted and rendered problematic also provide insights into this process, as people are forced to relate their identities to the tension between the *status quo ante* and the new order of things.

Thinking about identity

So how can we conceptualise identity in a way that encourages us to be sensitive to its historical nature? We should always think about identities, national and otherwise, as having three interacting and interdependent dimensions (see Hearn, 2007). First, there are identities in the sense of common linguistic categories that we use to organise our social world.

Just as there are tables, chairs, cows and pigs 'out there', we talk as though the world is also straightforwardly populated by Scots, English, men, women, deviants, 'toffs' and so on. Sometimes we appropriate these categories, and sometimes they are thrust upon us by circumstances and social forces. This points to the second dimension. We also have unique personal identities attached to our bodies and individual biographies. We build up and maintain a sense of self partly by relating our personhood to wider social categories, however easily or uncomfortably. Much of what we call 'ideology', matters of moral and political suasion, has to do with how people associate their personal identities with the wider social identities on offer. Finally, the interaction of personal and social identities is heavily mediated by the myriad of social organisations and institutions – families, workplaces, associations in civil society, the state – through which people pursue and negotiate their lives. It is these mediating organisations that determine the practical power people have (or do not have) over their lives, in the process influencing how they understand themselves and situate themselves in relation to collective identities (Webb, 2006).

It is this third dimension that particularly helps us get a handle on how identities respond to social change, for it is this dimension that most directly manifests the ongoing developments of capitalism and nationalism. Social organisations provide the most fundamental practical means through which people achieve control over their lives. As organisations adapt to changing conditions in order to survive, and possibly thrive, people must adjust their personal identities to the organisations they find themselves a part of, and the salience of wider social identities will wax and wane, and their construal will evolve, accordingly. Identities involve distinct psychological and sociological dimensions, and both these dimensions are influenced and shaped by the fates of social organisations.

Talking about social change

Before I launch into the case study, let me pose the underlying issue. Göran Therborn has suggested that defining modernity simply in terms of its characteristic institutional features, such as industrialisation, science and the bureaucratic nation state, misses an important 'cultural' dimension. He prefers to define modernity

> [A]s an *epoch turned to the future*, conceived as likely to be different from and possibly better than the present and the past'; thus

'modernity ends when words like progress, advance, development, emancipation, liberation, growth, accumulation, enlightenment, embetterment, avant-garde, lose their attraction and function as guides to social action.

(1995: 4, emphasis in original)

For Therborn modernity is not just period of history marked by the rise of new political-economic forms, but an attitude towards time itself that systematically privileges the new over the old. The material presented below illustrates Therborn's general point in a specific way. On the surface it is simply an account of the routine institutional change that characterises the modern economy. But more deeply it is about how modernity's repetitive, omnipresent, disembodied call to change infuses a particular social environment. In this process, value-laden notions of progressiveness and backwardness shape people's under-standings and assessments of the organisations they work for, their national cultures and ultimately their selves. 'Scottishness' was rendered problematic, and associated with being parochial and unable to adapt and keep up with the times, and because the ascription of Scottishness applies to persons, the organisation (BoS) and a collective national identity all at once, this evaluative atmosphere was strangely pervasive.

Ethnographic data does not normally lend itself to the proof or refuta-tion of tidy hypotheses. Instead, it is suited to the rather dense descrip-tion of specific social settings, conveying a holistic sense of how various social pressures and motives interact in that setting. In what follows, after a brief introduction to the case, I work through a number of inter-penetrating themes and situations: staff reflections on the contrasting organisational cultures of the two banks; experiences of staff-training courses concerned with organisational change; the idea of a contrast between Scottish parochialism and English progressiveness; evaluative perceptions of the Scottish accent by Scots; and notions of Scottish char-acter traits and their adaptability to the modern business environment. With this composite I aim to portray a general, diffuse atmosphere of anxiety, specific to the early days of this corporate merger, in which the adaptability of Scots and Scottish culture too was put in question.

Big mergers and small fortunes

The merger resulted from increasing competitive pressures in the financial sector. After World War II, BoS specialised in lending to the Scottish industrial sector, especially shipbuilding and later North Sea oil development. But since about 1980, with the decline of heavy industries and growth of a service economy, like other clearing banks, BoS was obliged to expand further into small business lending and new retail products (e.g. residential mortgages, financial services, credit cards, etc.). Competition was intensified by banking deregulation, which led to the growth of a secondary banking sector, the transformation of many building societies (including Halifax) into banks, and new amalgamations into ever larger banks (see Leyshon and Thrift, 1997). During this period, there was increasing concern in the Scottish banking community about the potential for takeovers to erode a distinctive Scottish banking sector (Saville, 1996: 717–40). In September 1999, BoS surprised the City by making a £20.85 billion bid to take over NatWest, in effect striking first in an environment where further bank mergers seemed inevitable. Many in the financial press were quick to point out that under these new terms, BoS and other Scottish banks could not expect to have their future 'independence' protected. In late November the Royal Bank of Scotland, BoS's main competitor, made a successful counter bid of £25.1 billion. The City now anticipated a takeover of BoS, compelling BoS to keep pace with the Royal Bank. BoS and Halifax began merger negotiations in April 2001, and the new banking group, HBOS, began trading on the stock market on 10 September, 2001, the day before terrorists flew two airliners into the Twin Towers in New York City. Billed as a 'merger of equals', Halifax was nonetheless twice the size of BoS, with around 36,000 employees to BoS's 19,000, and a market value of around £18 billion compared to BoS's £10 billion. Several times I heard BoS staff wryly refer to the event as a 'merge-over'.

My fieldwork was originally planned and negotiated with the Bank of Scotland before the merger happened, and as a result the research was primarily based in and focused on the BoS part of HBOS. The emphasis is on the Scottish perspective. Nonetheless I did participant observation and interviews with staff from both sides of the new organisation, primarily in the division of HBOS concerned with staff training and development and human resources. One line of inquiry I pursued with staff concerned their perceptions of the 'organisational cultures' of the two banks, and of the new organisation. I begin by sampling responses to this question as posed in an open-ended email questionnaire I sent to mid-level managerial staff (all quotes come from informants who were BoS staff before the merger, except where otherwise noted). One respondent, a man in the Corporate division, who had worked for the bank for many years, gave this particularly long and reflective reply, which introduces the key themes I will be exploring here. In this passage 'the Bank' refers specifically to the Bank of Scotland:

> The organizational culture of the Bank I believe is partly a factor of the nature of the Scottish people. It contains characteristics typically associated with that such as a sense of history, conservatism, loyalty, prudence and self-deprecating humour! With that as a basis, the Bank is also very hierarchical and historically it was not the done thing to 'get ahead of yourself'. You would have a job for life if you didn't rock the boat. Consequently, within the Bank there were ways of not doing things, not challenging superiors, not saying what you mean (in case you were rewarded with a posting to Benbecula) [a small remote Hebridean island], and using implied and informal 'grapevine' communication. The organizational culture has been perpetuated by typically long-serving staff/senior executives and the knowledge base and contacts they have, formed part of one's progression within the organization. Whilst I think there has been an overall continuing culture, certain people have influenced this more directly because of their personalities – some good, some not so good. The organizational culture has also been accused in the past of being too self-contained, too independent, limiting its future and not giving enough consideration to the demands of the City.
>
> I believe these factors are changing. A lot of attention is now given to the analysts' needs, which in turn drives the means of meeting those. Growing market competition, consumer demands, technology and the recent merger have accelerated the process further. Isolated independence has been relinquished bringing an influx of new executive personalities; there are more opportunities for/influences from non-traditional/non-long-serving Bank of Scotland colleagues; communication methods are becoming less stuffy in their approach; revised staff incentives/remuneration packages are creating new cultures, and history is less important than where you are going. I think some staff are learning that they have to be more accountable and learn to perform rather than be shielded under a historically benevolent culture. Banking as a financial service commodity, increased use of technology and a greater willingness of young educated consumers to switch providers has also led to a cultural change.[1]

I start here because this passage nicely brings together themes that I repeatedly encountered during my fieldwork, often in very similar terms. It gives a good rough sketch of the conventional wisdom within the BoS about its overall situation at the time of my research. These reflections on organisational culture simultaneously invoke notions of national identity and character, and a larger sense of structural and ideological imperatives to adapt to the pressures of capitalist markets. Informants regularly characterised BoS as having a Scottish culture, frequently associating Scottishness with various characteristics, such as: traditionalism and conservatism (with a small c); a Presbyterian and Calvinist ethos; risk aversion, cautiousness and canniness; and paternalism and male domination. A long-term male employee in the Insurance division offers a fairly typical description of BoS culture:

> Careful, conservative, surefooted, proud, heritage, historical, Scottish, stability – are all words that come to mind when describing the culture of Bank of Scotland as was. I feel that it is changing for the better and the realisation is slowly sinking in that we are now in a truly global market which is being pressured from new and previously inconceivable sources – supermarkets, internet, building societies etc. Also the size of the organisation prior to the merger meant that senior individuals had too much influence on how the business operated and developed which set but stifled the culture and influenced decisions too significantly.

As this statement suggests, there was a widespread sense that this Scottishness was waning, or becoming more attenuated, postmerger. Other traits that were associated with the Bank's Scottishness are also more generally associated with traditional banking prior to the acceleration of business in recent decades, but seemed to resonate with Scottishness for some informants. These included: formality, status awareness, hierarchy; orientation to service (frequently contrasted to Halifax's 'orientation to sales'); and an ethos of professionalism. Thus as one woman from the Corporate division, fairly new to the Bank assessed the matter:

> The majority of departments and branches in Bank of Scotland are traditional and operate very distinct hierarchies. The Bank (along with the Royal Bank of Scotland) has the vast majority of the Scottish retail market and business market and there is a definite complacency generated by this. The culture has a strong customer service tradition with an emphasis on the relationship. However there are a number of newer departments in the bank which are bucking this trend; innovation, being competitive are very important in these areas,

e.g. integrated finance, structured finance and some of the corporate departments in England. BoS was typically shy of publicity but has recently been actively seeking out PR and advertising more strongly. Furthermore a sales culture is being introduced into branches and this is encouraging a more aggressive, dynamic culture.

The last point about 'sales culture' in the branches specifically reflects the impact of Halifax on BoS through the merger, in that the marketing of retail/personal banking was seen as a strength that Halifax brought to the merger. So Halifax practice in this area quickly radiated through-out the BoS branches postmerger. Correspondingly, unlike BoS, the organisational culture of the Halifax was not connected to notions of national culture, but rather to a 'youthful', 'informal/casual', 'assertive' and 'sales-oriented' approach to business. As one male BoS staff member in the Corporate division said:

> Halifax from an outside perspective re-invented itself in recent years, now an aggressive youthful organisation which has embraced culture of change.

Here the term 'culture of change' comes in from contemporary corporate discourse, disseminated through training courses and internal communications. As another BoS staff member, a man in the same division, but with more years in the Bank, put it:

> I have only had exposure to the fledgling corporate side of the Halifax. It is relatively wide thinking, open to suggestions, and proud of its own achievements in a very short time. It seems very London focused and much more focused on bonuses. Almost by definition most of the people in it have been there for a very short time and were bought in from the market at or above market rates. This makes them a very different animal from the typical BoS corporate employee who has been with BoS for many years. It also has a flatter structure that allows much younger staff into positions of seniority.

And a male Halifax staff member working in the central HR part of the bank offered this rather unflattering characterisation of the Halifax culture:

> Fast, cut throat, bottom line driven, sales centric, job for a while – burn out, informal, greedy. Yes, the culture has moved from where

I described BoS within 3 or 4 years, and is still changing, moving towards a polarised version of the current culture.

However, as this last quote from another male BoS staff member in Corporate implies, many noted that in its earlier guise as a traditional building society the organisational culture of Halifax was probably more similar to that of BoS:

> I would say that the Halifax was a conservative, traditional very Yorkshire organisation that was dragged into the 20th Century about 5 years before Bank of Scotland following demutualisation. Now it is an aggressive, sales orientated business.

The opinion was frequently expressed that the organisational culture of HBOS would come to resemble that of Halifax, albeit with divisional variations based on the premerger strengths of the two banks indifferent areas. A woman from BoS's Treasury division speculated:

> Overall I expect it to be akin to that of Halifax. Very sales orientated – if targets are not achieved then the threat of dismissal looms, however in reality this culture will probably prevail in Retail whereas Business and Corporate will more likely be predominately a BoS type environment. In summary it will largely depend on where you work.

Many informants also observed that organisational culture is significantly determined by matters of size and structure. A repeated refrain was that the much larger merged organisation, with stronger divisional separation, was unlikely to maintain any cohesive culture across the group. Instead staff widely seemed to expect that there would be different localised cultures within divisions, to some degree reflecting the differing influences of BoS and Halifax in those divisions, as suggested above. A man who had been working in the HR division of BoS for several years said:

> I would hope that it would maintain the paternal approach which both BoS and Halifax originally subscribed to. I expect that no overarching culture will develop. There is insufficient input from the top to create such. The culture will reflect the approach within each fiefdom.

These questionnaire responses exemplify a way of talking that I encountered more widely in my fieldwork, in interviews and daily casual conversations. I draw heavily on them here simply because they provide vivid instances of the wider conversations going on at the time, in people's own words. As these comments indicate, conceptual oppositions such as 'old/young', 'stasis/change', 'parochial/progressive' and so on, seemed to provide a basic frame for making sense of the contrasting organisational cultures of BoS and Halifax. It is worth noting a certain paradox within the notion of a 'Halifax culture' often employed by bank staff. On the one hand, this culture is characterised in terms of youthfulness, informality, dynamism, aggressiveness, as we have seen. But on the other, because it was larger and more 'modern', with a more fluid staff, Halifax is seen as having less of a culture *per se*, exemplifying the modern business organisation in which staff commitments to the organisation are strategic and ephemeral.

It is not surprising that Therborn's modernist ideology of change, in addition to framing and infusing local discourses about organisational cultures and national identities during the merger, was also very explicitly present, in a more distilled form, in several of the BoS staff-training courses I participated in. There was continual talk in regard to staff training not just about 'managing' and 'coping with change', but about developing a 'culture of change' within organisations such that staff are habituated to and even welcoming towards a flexible and fluctuating working environment. The instructors for these courses were clearly alert to the pressures that merger was placing on staff, incorporating this knowledge into their delivery of the courses. Instruments such as the Holmes Rahe Social Readjustment Scale were frequently employed to assess personality types and how one personally tends to cope with the stress of change. In a course I attended on 'Coping Strategies', participants shared stories about older BoS staff having troubles adjusting to new regimes, and older participants contrasted their perceptions of a BoS career for life with those of younger staff who expect to change jobs many times during their careers. During another course I had a discussion with an instructor who seemed to see his own situation as a self-employed consultant as exemplary, and believed that there was a need for a fundamental shift in attitudes towards employment among BoS staff. He felt that 'change' was the norm for him, and BoS staff needed to learn to be more comfortable with this. What was striking in this and all these encounters was the dominant view of change as an inevitable natural force that must be coped with and adjusted to, and of Scots and BoS as constitutionally resistant to change. Some found this proposition welcome and stimulating, others, probably the majority of those I met across BoS, regarded it with an air of resignation and acceptance.

One of the training courses in which I participated, called 'Creativity and Innovation', brought out the themes I have been discussing with peculiar vividness. A new course designed by a couple of young and energetic staff trainers soon to be deployed to other parts of HBOS, it sought to be experimental, both fun and serious at the same time. Alternating between whole-group and small-group activities, the course programme sought in various ways to encourage participants to 'think outside the box' and tap into hidden powers of creativity. The organising conceit was that one of the two trainers was by nature 'left-brained', the other 'right-brained', and thus they tended to approach problem solving in different ways, each with its own strengths and weaknesses. Over two days the mornings involved the presentation of ideas about mental habits that stifle creativity (e.g. defeatist inner voices) and 'limbering' exercises such as solving maths problems counter-intuitively, using visualisation to aid memorisation, and learning to juggle, and then the afternoons would turn to more 'applied' activities, such as brainstorming to design a new product for the bank using randomly generated stimuli or learning to pitch a new idea to a partner in the role of sceptical and unreceptive manager.

The participants, about 27 in number, were drawn widely from the various divisions of the bank. Most had simply elected to take the course out of personal curiosity, but some had been advised to take such a course by a line manager who felt that they might benefit from it in terms of personal career development. The mood of the group tended to be light-hearted – some were probably seeking diversion during a period of uncertainty about their future paths in the merged organisation. But I noted that by the end of each day, especially the second day, anxiety tended to displace the momentary enchantment of adult playfulness, and talk tended to turn to comparisons of uncertainty, a degree of discomfort with the mildly infantalising nature of the course instruction, and questioning of the ultimate utility of such training. The trainers valiantly struggled to negotiate several competing demands of their task: be fun, entertaining and inspiring; make the participants feel that their time was being put to good use; facilitate open and realistic communication about participants' concerns; present a positive message in regard to the bank. Their overriding message was that all those present could benefit themselves and the bank by letting go of inhibition and releasing their creative potential. This struck a dissonant note against common perceptions, expressed at various points in group discussions, that the very bank that was indirectly urging them to improve themselves had a reputation for being overly cautious and stifling creativity from on high. While the talk over the two days acknowledged that some problems of 'innovation and creativity' lay with the organisation and its leadership, rather than personnel, the exhortation to embrace change was ultimately being translated into a message of personal moral reform. In this way the modernist ideology of change, while encountering resistance, percolated down to beleaguered selves seeking some greater purchase on their circumstances.

I turn now from accounts of the organisational cultures of the two banks to how people used notions of Scottishness and Englishness to talk about national identity at both general and personal levels. I would emphasise that when I explicitly asked staff about whether they perceived differences between Scottish and English people, I frequently encountered resistance to the proposition, and counterarguments to the effect that national differences are cross-cut by other, perhaps more salient differences – gender, religion, occupation, age and so on – and that there was considerable diversity of regional and urban-based identities within the categories of 'Scottish' and 'English'. The modern business ethos in which people are expected to fare according to individual merit, not social status, and my primary location in the HR division where there was a heightened discourse about the value of staff diversity, no doubt conditioned some of these responses. Having said this, I did encounter notions of typical differences between the Scots and the English, both in more casual everyday conversations, and from some staff directly engaging with my queries on the subject. In one sense these are just particular examples of a much wider pattern of expression found in Britain. But what I focus on here is the way these characterisations gained specific salience in the context of the merger.

A recurring theme in the fieldwork when I inquired about Scottish–English differences was that Scots were described as parochial, conservative and insular. As one Scottish BoS staff member from the corporate division put it rather bluntly: 'Scottish people are broadly nationalistic tending towards parochial-narrow minded. English are more open minded and prepared for change'. Another male BoS staff member in the Business division, this time English, wrote:

> I think Scots tend to be more parochial and inward looking than English, although this is obviously a generalism. Many of the Scots I have worked with in England have been loathe to 'migrate' south of the border, but once here are often reluctant to return.

This perception of Scottish parochialism and insularity is bound up with a rather entrenched attitude of antagonism towards the English often conveyed by Scots (especially around matters of football). A relatively new staff member, English by upbringing though with one Scottish parent, had moved to Scotland to work for BoS and expressed her discomfort in this way:

> Yes they are different. My Mum is a Scot and I would not have recognised differences before living here. Since then however, the differences are clear. English people as a whole see themselves as part of Great Britain, whereas the Scots see themselves on the whole as Scottish. The 'Scottish' identity is emphasised continually and I've encountered hostility and feel intimidated sometimes. You don't hear English people saying that they don't like Scots, but I hear Scottish people saying that they don't like the English a lot. The Scots tend to have a narrower outlook on life. The country is not as culturally diverse, particularly in the East and I've heard many racist and bigoted comments said very matter-of-factly, with no shame, which you don't get in England.

I suspect that part of what is happening here is that a fairly middle-class, metropolitan view from the south-east of England is being generalised as 'England'. There is plenty of racism and bigotry to be found in parts of England. Nonetheless, the routinised and somewhat ritualised hostility of Scots towards the English that she refers to, while rarely dangerous, is quite real. Many Scots I spoke to, while expressing resentment towards what they perceived as attitudes of cultural superiority among the English, and an Anglocentric bias in British media and public culture, nonetheless also expressed shame about Scottish hostility towards English persons. As one of my closer informants, a staff trainer, put it in an interview:

> I have had comments like that [in training courses he was leading] and I usually feel embarrassed and it's part of my nature to try and create harmony in any group gathering or team of whatever and I do find some of these things embarrassing. My niece is married to a guy who's English but I did actually ask him the other day, did he really think of himself as English because he's lived for more than half his life in Scotland? But he just ... he has an English accent and people say unkind things, say cruel things, take the Mickey out of him about things like football, which he has no interest in. So I have

found myself interjecting and saying 'look, this is silly. This has gone far enough. This is embarrassing'.

But I think the English staff member quoted previously is conveying more than just her unease with Scottish hostility. While it is not explicitly stated, I think it is reasonable to read her comment as suggesting that Scotland has not kept pace with England in terms of trends towards a more open-minded multicultural view of the world. Scottish informants often accepted this accusation to a degree, and pointed to it as something they disliked about being Scottish. At the same time, they frequently turned the tables, representing the English as insular 'little Englanders', resistant to other cultures, unlike the world-traversing Scots, who are usually more welcomed abroad. According to a fairly recent recruit to BoS's Retail division:

> I think we are much more open and willing to experience new things, embrace cultures and mix with people from other countries. The English tend to be much more xenophobic and insular and almost afraid to acknowledge that there is a world or anything different or better outside their own parameters.

For Scots this question of parochialism sometimes attaches to the perceptions of accents. One questionnaire respondent, as usual qualifying his comments by first noting the shared culture of Scots and English, nonetheless singled out perceptions of accent as crucial to a sense of Scottish difference. An employee in the HR division with many years at BoS, he suggests that Scots often experience

> a sense of social exclusion, based on the perception that Scottish accents are unacceptable and that middle-class jobs and roles are usually filled by people who speak with an English accent (and who may even be English by origin or education). Working class people in England may have a sense of exclusion but will attribute this to class distinction only. I think this concern with accent also makes Scottish people more reserved and less articulate in company.

I had an experience that supported these observations during my fieldwork with one of the groups on a staff-training course on 'Practical Teamwork'. There was a coffee discussion near the end of the second day in which people were comparing their favourite alcoholic drinks and most extreme drinking experiences – the kind of thing a group does when it's letting its hair down and has achieved a certain level of trust. During this, one of the participants said she had been watching a television newscast the night before and had seen some people, who worked in a small Scottish soap factory whose products are apparently favoured by some celebrities, being interviewed. She expressed embarrassment and disapproval at the dialect of the workers who said they could hardly believe that these stars were washing their faces with soap made by 'ma ane hauns'. She also expressed difficulty comprehending what the factory workers were saying. This echoed a conversation from the previous day in which two participants were talking about hearing themselves on recordings (e.g. answering machines) and not recognising their own voices – specifically, not realising they sounded that 'Scottish'. None of these people spoke particularly strong regional/class-based Scottish dialects, but nonetheless these instances suggest a tendency to assess one's own language as somehow deviant in relation to a generic/unmarked norm of English. In recent decades there has been a great deal of celebration of Scottish linguistic and cultural distinctiveness, and revalorisation of vernacular Scots, especially in the fields of fiction, poetry, theatre and popular music. But these vignettes suggest that for many average Scots, perhaps less exposed to some of these trends in the arts, longstanding associations of Scots accents with inferiority and inarticulacy are still in force, and affecting self-perceptions.

This brings me to what is perhaps the bottom line. It is one thing to have the organisation one works for portrayed as encumbered by retrogressive cultural values, but when the problematic traits are ascribed to persons, the charge of obsolescence becomes more acute. More significant than the matter of accents is that of personal character. I repeatedly encountered the claim that Scots and English people differed in ways salient for the new business environment, particularly in terms of a distinction between reticence and assertiveness, which resonates with the ways organisational cultures were contrasted above. When asking about Scottish–English differences I got many responses such as this one from a member of HR:

> Yes, there is a different mentality between the two. Scottish people are less likely to shout about things right away but go and get on with things and sing about things later. In my view the English are far more up front and willing to promote themselves. I would say they have an air of arrogance that the Scots don't have.

A director in staff training described how he taught a course where he would ask 'what is this "culture" thing?' In it he would set a task where people are told to talk about their achievements for two minutes. He found that Scots would normally think that is much too long, but other cultures, such as English and American think it's not enough. When I asked if he found the category of 'Scottishness' important in his work he said:

> There are Scottish traits: being loyal to the institution; we come across as inherently modest; don't like to be publicly recognised; a lack of confidence. I think England has a lot to do with this. People get hung up on the perception of England – as always confident, sure of themselves, aggressive even. When the English win a football match, they're 'world beaters' all of a sudden. Whereas Scots expect to lose at football, and identify with that role ... But Scots could do well to learn from the English. [paraphrased quote from field notes].

I often encountered a 'self-critique' of this Scottish trait, as suggested in the quote above, in which the Scottish lack of confidence was seen as a weakness, and English confidence as something to be emulated. Scottish 'modesty' was not usually viewed as inherently undesirable, and to the contrary, was in fact widely seen as preferable. But – and this is the heart of the matter – it was viewed as a disadvantageous trait in a specific context. This contrast between the Scottish and the English gains specific salience in a competitive business world where confidence and assertiveness are important assets. Anxieties about the ability of Scottish staff to hold their own against more assertive English staff were sometimes voiced. In a changed environment, where staff are in sharper competition with each other, where assertive self-promotion rather than selection from above is expected, where the staff population is more fluid and sustained social ties are less likely to develop within the organisation, and where a general market mentality increasingly permeates all activities, modesty however admirable can be a liability, and confident self-presentation an imperative. That which is generally a virtue in one organisation, becomes a vice in another. A man in Retail who had worked for BoS for over twenty-five years summed up the change to the new environment:

> [BoS used to be] Very close knit, loyal and almost like a 'family culture'. Changing as we move forward – Biggest change – *previously job appointments – you were 'chosen' or selected for a position. Now you have to apply and sell yourself into the job* [emphasis added].

In the context of organisational transformations at BoS, Halifax and HBOS, these conflicts over confidence are matters of consequence for personal fortunes, as people negotiate their identities and careers in an uncertain and competitive world. There was a tendency for HBOS staff, both Scottish and English, but especially the English, to view Scots as culturally parochial or insular within Britain (especially in relation to London), but a reciprocal tendency for Scots to view the English as parochial in relation to Europe and the wider world. Connected to this was a tendency by both Scots and English to construe Scots as characteristically lacking in confidence, and English as characteristically overconfident, stereotypes that may have consequences for how people fare, or at least believe they will fare, within the organisation.

Conclusion: Whither Scotland

The perspective on matters of identity employed in this chapter regards identities not just as ways of symbolically locating ourselves in social landscapes, but also as adaptations to our social environments, adaptations that can become maladaptive if that environment changes, and that may be either easy or difficult to modify. Social identities, national and otherwise, are not static – they evolve in the context of shifting pressures and opportunities.

As I have already suggested, the foregoing account is too temporally limited to track significant trends in social change, but it does perhaps offer a diagnostic moment of a major institution of Scottish society confronting larger processes of social change, and how that encounter was cascading down to the level of personal experiences framed by cultural notions of Scottishness. Let me try to situate this account within the broader historical changes going on in Scotland, before speculating about what it might indicate about those changes. The shift from BoS to HBOS, from staid organisational solidarity to market-responsive individualism, encapsulates a historical shift best described by Paterson, Bechhofer and McCrone in *Living in Scotland: Social and Economic Change since 1980*. The authors observe that 'Scotland has gone through ... profound transformations' (2004: 149) in the last two decades, in line with other Western, post-industrial societies. The population is ageing, having fewer children and living in a more diverse array of household forms. About half the population now participates in a system of mass higher education. Only about 13 per cent still work in manufacturing industry, the major growth in jobs being in the areas of financial intermediation, real estate, renting and business activity (together around 17 per cent). Most individuals and families are able to earn and consume much more than they did two decades ago, and still have some measure of personal security in the form of savings, pensions and insurance. Women have made substantial advances in the spheres of education and employment, particularly women of the middle class. This general picture of rising standards of living and associated aspirations needs to be tempered by the realisation that it is conjoined to increased inequalities in the distribution of wealth across the population, and the shunting of those with less access to educational advancement and heritable wealth into long-term poverty with little means of escape.

The authors conclude by acknowledging a paradox. The egalitarian collectivism that informed Scottish home rule politics in the 1980s and 1990s has lost its original social basis. Contemporary, devolved Scottish politics must now address a changed society, more affluent and individualised, wrought partly by the more intensive market driven economy that its civil society and governing institutions were once so implacably opposed to. While broad public support in Scotland for a government active in public provisioning by means of taxation endures, the widespread predevolution spirit of radicalised discontent has dissipated.

Even with considerable longitudinal data at their disposal these authors are reluctant to speculate too far about where the contemporary political and economic situation in Scotland will lead. The case of the formation of HBOS doesn't hold any answers. But perhaps in its compressed story of organisational transition it epitomises a larger social shift going on in Scotland, with its attendant demands to adjust to a more competitive environment where one's fortune in life is regarded as more of a personal responsibility and less of a collective concern. This in turn suggests a national politics more concerned with creating opportunities for individual advancement, and attending to the demands of business, than that previously fostered by the Labour Party's long-term domination of Scottish politics. The social categories of Scots and Scottishness are well rooted and will not disappear, nor will people's propensity to make sense of themselves through these categories. But some of the conventional content of those categories is less in sync with the structural conditions of Scottish society than they once were, so we should expect the meanings assigned to those categories to adjust, as people try to make realistic and useful sense of their national identities. Scottish identity is on the move.

Note

1. Quotations, other than those from books and articles, come from questionnaire responses. Unless otherwise stated all quotations are taken from different respondents.

Bibliography

Finlay, R. J. (2002) Queen Victoria and the cult of Scottish monarchy. In E. J. Cowan and R. J. Finlay (eds) *Scottish history: The power of the past.* Edinburgh: Edinburgh University Press.

Hearn, J. (2000) *Claiming Scotland: National identity and liberal culture.* Edinburgh: Edinburgh University Press.

Hearn, J. (2007) National identity: Banal, personal and embedded. *Nations and nationalism,* **13**, 657–74.

Leyshon, A. and Thrift, N. (1997) *Money space: Geographies of monetary transformation.* London and New York: Routledge.

McCrone, D. (2001) *Understanding Scotland: The sociology of a nation,* 2nd edn. London: Routledge.

Morton, G. (1999) *Unionist nationalism: Governing urban Scotland, 1830–1860.* East Linton: Tuckwell.

Paterson, L. (1998) *A diverse assembly: The debate on a Scottish Parliament.* Edinburgh: Edinburgh University Press.

Paterson, L., Bechhofer, F. and McCrone, D. (2004) *Living in Scotland: Social and economic change since 1980.* Edinburgh: Edinburgh University Press.

Rosie, Michael (2004) *The sectarian myth in Scotland: Of bitter memory and bigotry.* Basingstoke: Palgrave Macmillan.

Saville, Richard (1996) *Bank of Scotland: A history, 1695–1995.* Edinburgh: Edinburgh University Press.

Therborn, G. (1995) *European modernity and beyond: The trajectory of European societies, 1945–2000.* London: Sage.

Webb, J. (2006) *Organisations, identities and the self.* Basingstoke: Palgrave Macmillan.

8
Universities and Nations in Britain in the Twentieth Century

Lindsay Paterson

Introduction

The role of universities in shaping national identities in Britain does not fit the standard pattern of that relationship elsewhere. Modern projects of nation-building, Gellner argued (1983: 34), have typically required a hierarchically ordered education system with national universities at the top, educating the leadership class and – according to Hroch (1985: 22–3 and 145–9) – defining the nation's culture through scholarship and teaching. Although, as Anderson (2004) notes in his careful comparison of the development of universities throughout Europe in the nineteenth century, no country conforms to Gellner's and Hroch's model exactly, describing it as the standard is not inaccurate. It was most obviously true of the territories ruled by the Habsburgs and by Russia, but was also found in Greece, Norway, Finland and Belgium: the national movements there found their origins in university culture, and new national universities became a source of leading personnel for the states that were eventually formed in the twentieth century. In the words of Cohen (1996: 241), on the Habsburg lands, it was believed that advanced education could aid nation-building by producing 'new professionals, higher officials, and educated employees, but also by shaping students' social and political consciousness'. In different but analogous ways the model can also be applied to the unifying nation-building of Germany, Spain and Italy. For example, the university-educated professionals in Italy 'helped to bind a culturally underdeveloped and divided civil society to [the new] nation state' (Meriggi, 1993: 430–1; Malatesta, 1995). France provided the template, dating from Napoleon's remoulding of higher education to form a new national leadership, the legacy of which persists today.

This doesn't work for Britain. One familiar way of introducing the exception is to point to the overlapping national identities. In Scotland, Wales and England, there was nothing as strong as the cultural and political separatism that grew in the nineteenth century in other parts of Europe to result in national independence, but neither was the unifying Britishness as centralising or homogenising as the analogous movements in Germany, France or even Italy. Although this is true, to understand the universities' role, we need to take a further step, examining the nature of these British identities themselves. On the one hand, university-educated professionals, especially by the twentieth century, could not help being struck by the cultural importance of Britain, which – despite claims by Colley (1992) and others – became much more than a political convenience. Professionals learnt through the ideas and the personal contacts acquired in the classroom that Britain was becoming in the twentieth century a deep, rooted and normative cultural project, expressing principles of universalism, aspirations to detachment from particularistic constraints and respect for difference. At the same time, though, these same professionals had to translate universalist principles into local practice. That was true of professionals everywhere, but, in the peculiar conditions of the multinational British polity, it meant that professionals had to translate British norms to the distinct national traditions of the smaller countries, and to the distinct regional patriotisms of the parts of England.

The argument of this chapter is that the normal professional interpretation of universal concerns for localities came, in Britain, to be mapped onto an older framework, in which the universal was embodied in British culture and the local was defined as Scotland, Wales and the several regional identities of England: this older pattern had emerged first in the late seventeenth century and remained significant until well into the twentieth century. Professionals thus were key agents in maintaining that delicate balance between union and diversity which defined British culture in the twentieth century; and so the universities, educating these people, were among the key institutional supports of this unusual polity.

That experience is perhaps all the more puzzling when we consider that the same state provides an instance of the standard account, in the experience of the southern part of Ireland. At the beginning of the nineteenth century there was a single university, providing no opportunity for the native majority. Trinity College in Dublin had been created in 1592 for the education of the anglicised ruling elites (Anderson, 2006a: 95). As Catholic emancipation came to prominence in British politics after the union of 1801, two concerns raised the question of Catholic educational opportunities. One was a matter of rights. The other, in response, was a sense by the British government that the creation of educated Catholic professionals might build up a class more willing to act as local managers of British policy and of economic development. So the state established in 1845–9 three Queen's Colleges, in Belfast, Cork and Galway. The Belfast institution was successful, fulfilling its function of being the college of a local entrepreneurial middle class, but only because that was Protestant. The Catholic church, especially following the policies of Pope Pius IX, refused to have any dealings with the other two places, which therefore languished. This resistance movement was then a defining moment in the development of Irish nationalism, identifying it with Catholicism as Anderson (2006a: 96) points out. The church sought to establish its own, Catholic, university in Dublin in 1854, employing the Anglican convert John Henry Newman as its first rector (and his inauguration was the occasion for a series of lectures which much later came to define one idea of what a university should stand for: McHugh [1944]). Newman's liberalism did not sit easily with the founders' preferences; he resigned in 1858, and the university struggled to survive, but it was rescued by the Jesuits in the 1880s, renamed University College Dublin, and, in Anderson's words (p. 96), 'besides meeting the demands of the Catholic middle class ... fostered the Gaelic cultural movement, and was the seedbed of a new nationalist intelligentsia'. So this Irish story is an instance of the classic account: it shows higher education forming the nation.

The Irish story can then be taken forward in similar vein beyond 1922. The national university colleges (now including Cork and Galway), and also Trinity, trained a leadership class for the new state. This class was powerfully overshadowed by the Catholic church in the first four decades of independence, but was increasingly secular in the rapid modernisation from the 1960s onwards (Lee, 1989: 581–643). The educational reforms enacted then, mainly at primary and secondary level, first fuelled a wave of emigration of well-educated young people, but also contributed to economic development, and eventually managed to provide employment not only for new generations of graduates but also for many return migrants and new immigrants. So although the beneficial effects of a modernised, indigenous system of university education were delayed, they do, on the whole, add to the standard account of the role of education in helping a new state to emerge from dependency.

This account is not wholly irrelevant to the nations of Britain, especially Wales. But, if Ireland is typical of the rest of Europe, it is not a good guide to its immediate neighbours. It is their story to which this essay is principally devoted. The approach taken here is different from that in most of the other chapters in the book: although reports of surveys and similar research are drawn upon, the argument ranges more widely, seeking to understand the relationship between universities and national identities in Britain over the past century.

Universities and the professional ideal

The argument can be summed up in four propositions. First, British universities have been at the heart of shaping what has been called the professional ideal, the twentieth-century aspiration to take action only on the basis of evidence and rational debate, to select professionals by merit and expertise and to put their capacities at the service of society, superseding partisanship and religious dogma (Perkin, 1989: 4). This ideal, moreover, in contrast to the aristocratic or entrepreneurial ideals, 'could in principle be extended to everyone' (p. 8), because its criteria are intrinsically universal. These criteria also, being universal, 'implied a principle of social justice which extended to the whole population the right to security of income, educational opportunity, decent housing in a clean environment and, some professionals would say, the right and obligation to work' (p. 9). So the ideal was linked to the concept of the moral community of the nation – of which the professionals were the leaders and guarantors.

Second, the quasi autonomy of Scotland and Wales, and the autonomy of cities and counties throughout Britain, depended upon this professional leadership. It was practical and technocratic, the stuff of what Bulpitt (1983) called 'low politics'.

Third, therefore, universities and higher education colleges have been at the heart of the relationship between civil society and the state in twentieth-century Britain, and whatever values and skills their graduates have acquired from their education they have taken into their leading roles there. In sharp contrast to the standard account of the link between universities and state formation, the low politics of this British story might be better described as an instance of what is called 'positivism' in the history of Polish nationalism (in contrast to 'romanticism'): 'foregoing the heroics of soldiers, the positivists extolled the heroism of physicians struggling against sickness or of teachers fighting obscurantism' (Wandycz, 1974: 263).

Finally, then – and this is where the argument becomes general again, going far beyond Britain – democracy itself came to depend on the character of higher education, even when only a small minority of people passed through it. Technocratic democracy has depended on rule by experts. It has attempted to solve the problem of the tension between mass culture and expertise that was adumbrated by Newman in Dublin in 1854, and also by Matthew Arnold, Thomas Carlyle and many others on the threshold of the democratic and professional era: it has adopted a diluted version of Carlyle's idea that democracy could work only if it appointed the wise to govern. So, even when the character of the nation seemed to be set on an unprecedently democratic basis in the twentieth century, the actual formative influence came, through professionals, from the universities.

The chapter elaborates on the specifically educational aspects of these points. Thus not much more is said about the second, the general description of the character of British governance in the twentieth century and the role there of professionals: the main source for that is Bulpitt, 1983; see also, for example, Burgess, 1995; Harvie, 1994; Keating, 1996; Livingston, 1956; McCrone, 2001; and Paterson, 1994. The chapter concludes by considering whether the relationship between university and nation in Britain might be changing under two pressures – the advent of mass participation in higher education, and the partial political self-government which was introduced in Scotland and Wales from 1999.

The role of the professions

Before we get to the specific histories of the universities, however, we have to consider fully how they have contributed to the development of professionalism. The universities had been involved in educating the old professions for many centuries, especially in Scotland, where the church and the legal system depended more thoroughly than they did in England and Wales on the university training which graduates received. But from about the 1890s to the 1970s, their importance greatly increased in providing education to a much wider range of professions (Anderson, 1992; Boyd, 1973; Elliott, 1972: 14–57; Sanderson, 1975: 80–2, 117; and Millerson, 1973): universities and higher education colleges extended their scope into medicine and school teaching to a much greater extent than hitherto, they educated new or modernised professions such as economists, planners, social workers and (after the 1960s) the main financial professions, and they created and sustained the very definition of the scientist in all its multiplying specialist branches. The outcome of these developments by the middle of the twentieth century was measured in a survey of established professions carried out in 1961 for the Robbins Committee on Higher Education. It found that, for scientists and technologists, 'the principal method of entry into professional institutions ... is by means of exempting qualifications gained in universities and in further education', and that paramedical groups and 'works' groups (such as architects) 'draw nearly all their members from universities or further education' (Committee on Higher Education, 1963: 374). Even law became more university-based after the 1960s (as it had always been in Scotland). The senior levels of the professions were more likely to be staffed by graduates than the other levels (Boyd, 1973: 48–58; Rubinstein, 1986). Particularly relevant for our purposes here, the universities became the main source of higher civil servants (Kelsall, 1955: 134–45). One of the few areas of public life which was not dominated by graduates by the middle of the twentieth century – industrialists, only a third of whom were graduates even at senior level immediately after the Second World War – had, like the financial professions, moved firmly in the same direction by the 1970s (Boyd, 1973: 92; Rubinstein, 1986). Part of this expansion of university influence was a shift towards selection by merit into all these careers, whether or not the training was wholly based in universities: in the words of Rubinstein (1986: 192), this 'immensely expanded the universe from which Britain's élites were recruited to virtually the entire middle class and beyond it to the lucky or able from the lower-middle class and, occasionally, the working classes'. The sense of professionals as truly national was strengthened in this sociological sense.

There were several key moments in the process, important in themselves and symbolic of the entire development. The introduction of competitive examinations into recruitment to the civil service and the army was the pioneer. This was the outcome of an official report in 1853 by Sir Stafford Northcote and Sir Charles Trevelyan, and its adoption was encouraged by the administrative disorganisation which surrounded British participation in the Crimean War (1854–6) and by the incompetence of the imperial response to the Indian Uprising of 1857. The full implementation of these changes were not seen immediately, but recruitment based on measured merit came to shape the professions by the beginning of the twentieth century. The standards expected of candidates prompted various reforms to university curricula, and aspiring to a civil service career became a natural choice of able graduates; this ensured that, in the twentieth century, the universities would be, as Perkin (1983: 217) put it, 'at the heart of ... the expanding corporate state'. At this same time – broadly, from the 1840s to the end of the century – the educational basis of the medical professions was made more formal, more legislative regulation was introduced into legal practice, and the first professional bodies emerged governing standards in some financial professions. School teaching aspired to this kind of status, and came closest to achieving it in Scotland, but the main way in which universities became increasingly important in that field was through the growth of secondary education from the 1880s onwards. This new stage of schooling offered unprecedented opportunities for graduate careers, especially for women, whose entry to the older professions remained highly restricted until late in the twentieth century.

This professional class provided a new kind of cultural leadership in the era of the welfare state. Rubinstein (1993) argues that, by the standards of most European states, and of the USA, there was remarkably little alienation of professionals from power during the twentieth century, their normal career taking them into the civil service or into an occupation that led to their working closely with government. Heyck (1998), similarly, proposes that the concept of 'the intellectual' in Britain, far from being absent or despised as is often popularly supposed, acquired a new meaning with the growth of the welfare-state bureaucracy. From older models, it borrowed the normative roles of setting cultural standards and maintaining the criteria for intelligent rigour; but the British intellectual class was not usually political in the sense that was common in, say, France, except on the margins of the professional classes, and, even there, only really during the interwar decades and perhaps the 1960s. It was, in Heyck's words, 'functional', and indeed increasingly 'sociological', the intellectual denoting '"brainworkers" of all sorts, such as professionals, managers, and academics as well as writers'. This usage, he pointed out, was 'no doubt … a reflection of massive social changes – namely the growth of the service sector of the economy, the development of a highly professionalised society, and the expansion of the university system' (p. 213). The social theorist T. H. Marshall argued in 1939 (when he was a lecturer in social work at the London School of Economics) that the important change in the nature of professionalism in the middle of the twentieth century was that the 'state and professions are being assimilated to one another' (p. 334), transcending commerce and politics. Fielding and Portwood (1980) used the term 'bureaucratic professional' to describe this class, meaning those who work closely with the state or are absorbed into it. Johnson (1972) saw this as a stage in the development of most professions, the state coming to mediate between the professional and the client, through regulation, codes of ethics and control of standards of entry and of professional education.

Within all that, a crucial role was played by scientists, a segment of the intellectual class that is often overlooked in certain styles of sociological writing because its cultural and political roles are not perhaps always obvious. Science was highly influential not only in setting the standard of a professional career and in providing an aspiration to an objective style of technocratic government. Science also set the criteria that should govern the very nature of knowledge and, with this, the educational preparation of professionals. The scope and status of science grew in part as a response to fears about British economic performance, and in part also by its own internal dynamic. The intellectual basis of the economy shifted in a firmly scientific direction between the 1870s and the eve of the First World War (Sanderson, 1972: 11). In this process, technological colleges were in some specialist fields as important as the universities, but both mattered, and colleges recurrently were transformed into universities of a standard sort.

The movement was urged forward by the campaigning of prominent scientists such as T. H. Huxley (Desmond, 1998). This led to the modernisation of the curriculum of the Scottish universities and of Oxford and Cambridge (the new intellectual respectability of science symbolised by the opening of the Cavendish laboratories in the 1870s with James Clerk Maxwell as the first occupant of the chair of experimental physics), and the development of the English civic universities (points to which we return below). Huxley's belief that science could offer as intellectually stimulating a university education as the humanities was expressed, for instance, in his address upon being elected Rector of Aberdeen University in 1874, in which he mischievously substituted the word 'science' for 'the ancient languages' in a passage from John Stuart Mill: 'in cultivating ... science as an essential ingredient in education, we are all the while laying an admirable foundation for ethical and philosophical culture'. In his later address (1880) at the opening of Mason's College in Birmingham (the future university), he argued that 'applied science' – of the kind that would be useful to industry – was not a special kind of knowledge, but required the full theoretical preparation of a university education.

Scientific careers in industry and government grew enormously in the twentieth century, a conclusion that is quite contrary to the familiar but dubious thesis made famous by Wiener (1981) and Barnett (1986), who blamed Britain's alleged economic decline on an alleged lack of attention to science and technology. Research by, for example,

Sanderson (1972), Robertson (1984), Edgerton and Horrocks (1994) and Anderson (2006a) has reached the conclusion that scientific research and development came to be at the heart of the growing parts of the British economy. So successful was this technological model set in train by Huxley and his associates that it quite displaced the old idea of the liberal profession as being definitely not scientific, and hence laid the basis for Heyck's functional role of the intellectual. It was widely believed that any tensions between specialisation and general scope could be resolved by requiring entrants to even the most technical of professions to have undergone a prior broad programme of liberal studies (Carr-Saunders and Wilson, 1933: 372–4, 377). Anderson (2006b: 266) observes that the mid-nineteenth-century redefinition of what counted as a university education and hence of 'professional' was, contrary to Wiener etc., 'not at all inspired by reactionary nostalgia or the rejection of modernity'. His comparison of the similarities of France and Britain in this respect led to the conclusions that 'the professional and public-service spirit was a quintessential expression of bourgeois moral and religious seriousness; that the British Empire was a capitalist rather than a neo-feudal enterprise; … [and that] an alternative reading of the history of British education can present it as a triumph of the middle classes' (p. 275). Perkin (1983: 218) summed up the transformation which providing professional education had brought to the universities by the 1920s – 'no longer a finishing school for young gentlemen, [but now] the central power house of modern industry and society'.

Universities and national identity

This brings us to our main point. If the universities and colleges were educating these new professional classes, and if these classes were leading the nation, then what sort of national identity was thereby created? In particular why was this relationship between state and university different from that in Ireland and many other places?

Wales

In some respects the answers are clearest in the one part of Britain, that is Wales, where university politics did share features with these other places. That country had almost no university-type provision even by the middle of the nineteenth century (apart from the small theological college at Lampeter, Anglican in an overwhelmingly Nonconformist culture). The campaign for a Welsh university drew upon the wider movement for greater recognition of Welsh cultural distinctiveness

(Morgan, 1981: 106–11). The complaint was at least as strongly made, however, that the lack of a university prevented Wales from drawing full benefit from a modern economy (Williams, 1993: 28–9), and encouraged too many able young men to enter the church or school teaching rather than the other professions. The first outcome of this campaigning was the creation of a college in Aberystwyth in 1872 and the setting up of an official committee chaired by Lord Aberdare that reported in 1881. This led to the granting of state funds to that institution and to two new colleges, at Cardiff from 1883 and Bangor from 1884. These three were grouped as a federal University of Wales in 1893–6, a fourth college was added in Swansea in 1920, and a medical school was granted a charter in 1931. Underpinning this were the new 'intermediate' schools from 1889 that were also a recommendation of the report, thus creating the first secondary-school system in the UK (Jones and Roderick, 2003: 75–106).

However, as Anderson (1992: 30) notes, the Welsh cultural element in this remained less political than in the analogous developments in Ireland, and was very far from being separatist. The criteria by which the colleges would be judged were instrumental – by how far they had served the needs of the Welsh economy and Welsh society. In that respect, there was disappointment. Industry, increasingly owned outside Wales, provided little support. Sanderson (1972: 121–45) observes that the location of the two northern colleges did not help, in that they established an image of the university as being remote from industry; even slate-mining, a significant northern industry, had little contact with them. A proposed mining department in Cardiff in the first decade of the twentieth century did not come about, the mine owners wanting more control of its activities than the university would allow. Few research services were provided to industry; exceptions in agriculture, forestry and fishing were important in the north but not to the populous south. What was more, especially from the 1920s onward, most scientists graduating from the university entered employment outside Wales. Williams (1997: 349) judges that this was because Welsh industrialists did not appreciate the value of theoretical science for applied work, the myopia against which Huxley had argued in England half a century earlier.

At the same time, though, there was a sense among cultural nationalists that the university was not doing much for Welsh culture. For example, as early as 1895, York Powell, who was professor of history at Oxford, asked 'why have a Welsh university at all if [Welsh language and literature] are thrust into a corner as unimportant subjects'?

(Williams, 1997: 362). Some vociferous student groups in the interwar years felt that the situation had not changed, and their attempts to promote the Welsh language in the universities was part of the same intellectual milieu as led to the founding of Plaid Cymru (Williams, 1997: 295–300). But the view persisted that the purpose of the university was as much to enable Welsh students to compete equally with those from the rest of Britain – which, it was claimed, required that they learn to be fluent in English – as it was to promote the Welsh language. The same was true of religion. Although a respect for learning induced by liberal Nonconformism was a source of the campaigns to have a university established (Morgan, 1981), religion was largely neglected by the new colleges when they were established (Williams, 1997: 363).

These two criticisms of the university point towards its lasting impact in the twentieth century. The university prepared people to be 'educational technocrats', as they were called in 1981 by Ieuan Gwynedd Jones quoted by Williams (1997: 314). It excelled in producing public-service professionals whose credentials could be accepted only if they learnt in English, and engaged with the universalistic concerns that exercised professionals elsewhere. Until the founding of the federal university in 1893, that required also that the colleges use the same system of degrees validated by the University of London as had underpinned the development of the English civic universities: the legacy of this shaped the autonomous degree system which the university then developed. In particular, school teaching became (in the words of Anderson [1992: 33]) 'the great object of ambition for scholars from poor backgrounds'. By the middle of the twentieth century, professional careers in the public service became the main route taken by the university's graduates: around two-thirds of the arts graduates who did not go on to postgraduate studies entered teaching, and the analogous figure for science graduates was around four-fifths (Committee on Higher Education, 1963: 155 and 163). By contrast, only around one in twenty of arts and one in eight of pure science graduates entered industry, and the proportion even for applied science was only just more than for teaching. Moreover, though the university had only weak links with industry, it did engage with problems of social reform, especially from the 1920s onwards.

So the relationship between the University of Wales and the nation in the twentieth century was primarily a matter of its providing professional leadership to social reform. It may have been true that, as Sanderson (1972: 138) says, the colleges were 'taking students from business backgrounds and turning them into young professional people divorced from industry and commerce'; and the force of that might be as strong when we note that they were doing this especially to the upwardly mobile working class students who attended the Welsh colleges until the 1960s in proportions higher than in the rest of Britain (about 33–40 per cent of students compared to no more than about 25–8 per cent: see Anderson [1992: 34 and 63]). But that then led to what Anderson (1992: 33) called 'a nationally minded, Welsh-speaking intelligentsia' (Welsh through upbringing not through the curriculum) that ruled the country locally until after the 1970s, when, in large numbers, students from Wales started attending universities in England (Rees and Istance, 1997: 54 and 62–3).

England

The relationship of universities to nation or state in England could not help being complex because of the complexity of English government and because of the peculiar legacy of Oxford and Cambridge. In any case, in a nation with a long independent history and with a university tradition, in these two places, among the oldest in Europe, the story could certainly not resemble that exemplified in Ireland. Nevertheless, there is a sense here, too, in which university activity between the mid-nineteenth and mid-twentieth centuries may also be described as contributing to building a new nation, once more under the rubric of inventing the idea of the professional.

The role of the two ancient universities has been touched upon already. They responded very efficiently, in the end, to the challenge of having to modernise, aspiring to take on a role loosely analogous to that of the French Grandes Ecoles, the shaping ground of an effectively educated ruling class, and thus 'transformed the idea of a gentleman' into one 'dedicated to the service of his fellows and his country' (Perkin, 1989: 367). Thus, from being resistant to any role in professional training, Oxford and Cambridge became the prime site of its highest expression (Jenkins and Jones, 1950: 99; Rothblatt, 1968: 90–3; Sanderson, 1975: 75–84), imbuing their preparation with the ideas of disinterested professionalism. In the words of Harvie (1976: 14), 'by the end of the [nineteenth] century the two old universities had "nationalised" not only the education of the governing élite, but the content of its instruction'. In the specific field of the study of government and social institutions themselves, the London School of Economics (T. H. Marshall's home) provided similarly definitive leadership, the scientific outcome of that college's Fabian foundation.

But the most innovative part of English developments concerns the new civic universities of the north, and also London University. Their rationale was to provide useful knowledge, and also to inject into the practice of industry and later of civic government a level of theory and rigour without which, as we saw Huxley saying in Birmingham, the application of science could not be achieved.

Sanderson (1972) reviews these developments for the period from 1850 to the aftermath of the Second World War, and he and Armytage (1955) provide numerous instances of the civic universities' working closely with local civil society in these ways. For example, in chemistry, Sir Henry Roscoe in Owens College in Manchester applied research to firms throughout the region; in Bristol, the college worked with the cheese industry; in Birmingham there were contributions to understanding fermentation; and in Leeds there was work on leather, textiles and gas. In mining, the leading centre was Newcastle, having close links with the mines of the north east, but there was also applied research work at Birmingham, Leeds and Nottingham. Birmingham and Sheffield worked with the metals industry. Manchester, Bristol and Southampton had influential schools of engineering, and electrical engineering was a strength at London, Liverpool, Birmingham and Nottingham.

Much of this work was socially reforming by direct intent, not aimed only at local markets (a distinction that is in any case anachronistic). Reading and Bristol led significant developments in agricultural research, aiming at both nutritional standards and the economic well-being of the agricultural industries. Roscoe in Manchester worked with the local board of health to understand chemical pollutants. Throughout England, and as in Wales, careers in secondary-school teaching became important, in the view of Armytage (1955: 256) rescuing many arts and pure science faculties from oblivion. When Mason's College became Birmingham University College in 1898, it inaugurated the study of economics, public finance, accountancy and commercial law, responding to Joseph Chamberlain's hope at the first meeting of the Court that a civic university should inspire the city 'with higher aims and higher intellectual ambitions than would otherwise be possible to people engaged entirely in trading and commercial pursuits' (Armytage, 1955: 243). The future Liberal Cabinet minister R. B. Haldane coined the term 'civic university' in 1902: 'you cannot, without danger of partial starvation, separate science from literature and philosophy' (Armytage: 248; Vincent, 2007). More mystically, but in keeping with the dominant philosophical idealism (as we will see below), Patrick Geddes argued in 1917 that 'now ... is urgent an arousal of the universities to their spiritual responsibilities for the fullness of life in all its phases, individual and social' (Armytage: 261). All these socially reforming activities intensified in importance as the manufacturing economies of northern England went into depression between the wars, and so the universities became the regional intellectual agencies of the ideas that would inform the welfare state. Part of the civic work was preparing students for professional careers of various sorts, in line with the general trends which we noted earlier. That included, by the middle of the twentieth century, entering industry (Sanderson, 1972: 101). In 1962, over two-thirds of the arts and science graduates of the civic universities outside London were entering teaching, public service, commerce or industry, the remainder going to other employment (such as publishing, cultural organisations and the churches) or postgraduate study (Committee on Higher Education, 1963: 155 and 163). The pattern for science graduates from London University was the same, and, although the proportions among arts graduates was lower, it was nevertheless around one half. So, with that partial reservation for London, we can say that the normal career of the graduates of the civic universities in the middle of the twentieth century remained the kind of professional work that would have been recognisable to their nineteenth-century founders.

If the English civic universities had, therefore, reinvented the idea of the university, that was not as fundamentally opposed to the view of Huxley's opponents a hundred years before than is often now supposed. Arnold and Newman did not reject professionalism: their argument was essentially for a period of general cultural preparation before specialist training. Huxley, in turn, was never opposed to literary culture, and made his case on the basis of the unity of human thought. As professionalism rose to its twentieth-century status and influence, the importance of broad educational preparation was repeatedly insisted upon. More practically, it became a requirement of government grants given to these English institutions from 1889, after 1919 through the University Grants Committee (Sanderson, 1972: 104–5). In any case, a broad grounding was, by then, provided in secondary schools.

Scotland

In these respects, England (and Wales) drew inspiration from Scotland. It may seem peculiar to assert this now, but in many important respects the Scottish universities were least changed by the reforms from the mid-nineteenth to the mid-twentieth century, and were most influential on the model that emerged. This seems odd for at least two reasons. One is that an accusation that their essence was destroyed by anglicising reformers from 1889 has formed a premise of Scottish cultural debates since the 1930s, and especially since George Davie revived the argument with his 1961 book *The Democratic Intellect*. The other is that to assert this is to say quite emphatically that Scottish educational nationalism owed almost nothing to the classic model which we summarised at the beginning – nothing to any sense that new universities were needed to forge a new autonomous culture.

Scotland had well-established universities well before the nineteenth century, and these had most recently been one of the core institutions of the Enlightenment. They were, by European standards, quite socially open, partly because they also played something of the role which secondary schools did elsewhere (such as in England, France and Germany). So the question facing them was about reform to meet new needs. Commissions of inquiry took place in 1826 and 1876, and serious changes took place after 1858 and, especially, 1889. The main issue concerned specialisation – how to dispense with elementary teaching that might be better carried out in secondary schools, how to encourage more students to study science, but also how to embed such reforms in the broad, liberal tradition that had been characteristic of the universities in aspiration since their foundation in the fifteenth and sixteenth centuries, and to an extent in reality since the previous wave of modernising reform in the early eighteenth century.

The resulting debates generated much anguishing about the essence of that tradition, a cogent summary of which was given by John Stuart Mill in his rectorial address in Aberdeen in 1867: 'to comment on the course of education at the Scottish Universities is to pass in review every essential department of general culture'. The aspiration to a unity of knowledge was what later was called 'democratic intellectualism' by the Conservative politician Walter Elliot in 1932, and which then provided the ground for Davie's book. It seemed an important tradition, epitomised not only in the scale of the Enlightenment's achievements, but also in the quality of the graduates of the Scottish universities in the nineteenth century, exported all over the Empire to provide trained expertise of a technological as well as administrative sort.

Modernisation did take place. Entrance standards were raised by means of an examination, and by the new leaving certificate of the expanding system of secondary schools. By the first decade of the new century, the normal route of entry was these schools, which had become as successful as their counterparts in Wales (and three to four decades before anything as systematic was in place in England). The old style of arts degree was supplemented by an Honours version, to encourage specialisation. There was less mandatory breadth of study than before, 'the blessed principle of options', complained Herbert Grierson in 1937, offering 'the easiest path towards something that can be called a degree'. Teaching staff were, as elsewhere, expected to specialise, and provision was made for the appointment of ordinary lecturers to supplement the work of the professors.

Nevertheless these changes are best interpreted not as an assault on a tradition of liberal learning but as its adaptation, and again the main purpose was the education of the new professions or of the older ones in modern ways (Anderson, 1983: 252–93; Paterson, 2003a: 73–87). The higher standards that became possible with new routes of entry to degree courses helped to train specialist graduates of the kind that were emerging from the English civic universities: this, and the greater professionalism of university staff themselves, enabled the Scottish universities to develop the same kinds of close links with local industry as were evident in England (Robertson, 1984). By the middle of the twentieth century, as in the English civic universities, over two-thirds of arts and science graduates of the Scottish universities were entering teaching, public service, commerce or industry (Committee on Higher Education, 1963: 155 and 163). The new secondary schools were providing the broad base of liberal culture which used to be one of the outcomes of a university course, and were doing so in a manner that was more socially open (and hence more truly based on merit) than the universities had ever been able to achieve. Science, as in the aspiration by Huxley, took its place alongside the humanities as part of the definition of cultural literacy. The democratic intellect was interpreted as the professional intellect – the characteristic grounding of a new elite.

Ideas of leadership

This reinvention of professionalism, then, provides the common idea that unites the disparate experience of the four or five university systems of Britain – in Wales, in provincial England (which in some ways included London), in Oxford and Cambridge and in Scotland. The tension between science and the humanities that was acutely felt in the nineteenth century – occasioning the great curricular debates around Mill, Huxley, Arnold, Carlyle and Newman – had been resolved into a new synthesis in the service of society. Science became the aspiration of reforming politicians and their civil-service advisers. Social change should be guided by evidence, reason and planning, and the agents of this would be the professions, technically trained but with a grounding in liberal culture. 'The intellectual', opined Bertrand Russell in 1939, 'forms his opinion on evidence', while also reflecting upon 'human life as a whole' (Heyck, 1998: 206). Grierson, for all his nostalgia, had made a similar point in a speech in 1920 to the professional body of school teachers of English literature and language, in which he defined 'professors' as those who (even at risk of unpopularity) 'were troubled with a sense of evidence'. Marshall (1939: 335) argued that the state, in its need for reliable social research, now depended on 'the same professional spirit that inspires the work of the universities'.

Providing further philosophical unity to this was a certain idea of leadership, arriving in Britain from German conceptions of the state, especially Kantian and Hegelian, and promulgated influentially by university teachers such as T. H. Green (1836–82), student of Benjamin Jowett at Balliol College, and later lecturer or professor in history and in moral philosophy there; Sir Henry Jones (1852–1922), student at Glasgow under Edward Caird (who had himself associated closely with Green when at Oxford in the 1860s), and then lecturer or professor in moral philosophy at Aberystwyth, Bangor, St Andrews and Glasgow; and Thomas Jones (1870–1955), student of Henry Jones, lecturer in political economy at Glasgow University and   professor at Queen's University, Belfast, member of the Cabinet Secretariat, 1916–30 and president of the University of Wales at Aberystwyth, 1944–50. Bogdanor (2006) describes the school of thought derived from Green as that of the 'mandarin culture', and traces its influence through several important social reformers in the twentieth century, loosely describable as 'ethical socialists' (although Green himself would not have accepted that label): the role of the state, argued Green, was to free people from constraints, and for this purpose, in Bogdanor's words (p. 149), 'it needed the support of public spirited citizens'. In particular, Green believed in the power of education to create a common culture, and it was this strand in his thinking that was most influential on the development of socialist ideas, although the direct line is from his contemporary F. D. Maurice to R. H. Tawney: the belief here is that professional values had the capacity to civilise the workings of the market.

It was from this milieu that the 'professional ideal' emerged, the universities seeking to fulfil Henry Jones's aspiration that they become the spiritual and intellectual centres of the nation (Gordon and White, 1979: 194). Perkin (1989: 127) sees Green's significance as deriving mainly from his 'clear expression of the professional ideal', and the influence of his and his associates' and students' views on generations of professionals was strong (see also Boucher and Vincent, 2000; Jenks, 1977; Plant, 2006; Watson, 1982). In the words of Harris (1992: 140), tracing its influence on the development of the British welfare state, this current of thought 'by the 1920s was very much the philosophy not of Oxbridge cloisters ... but of slum-clearance and new housing estates, town halls and civic universities'. It ensured that the normative model of the professional in twentieth-century Britain would be that defined by New Liberalism and Fabian socialism, whatever the precise ideology of particular individuals. It sought to draw into professional careers the most able members of all classes, and so was the means by which selection by merit could become meritocracy, government by professionals.

For university culture itself, this combination of social commitment and scientific principles explains the tension which emerged during the twentieth century between their local embeddedness and their aspirations to universalism. As in many other countries, by the last quarter of the century there was a tendency for institutions that had been founded with a local allegiance to detach themselves from that (Paterson, 2001). Specifically, there emerged also a suspicion of Welsh and Scottish nationalism of a political sort. This has frequently been alleged to be due to an inordinate influence by academics of English origin who came to teach at universities in the two smaller countries during the period of post-Robbins expansion (Paterson, 1998). There may be some truth in that, although quite the opposite seems to have been the case in Scotland in the four decades from the 1960s (Paterson and Bond, 2005). But the main comment to make is that the accusation misses the point. The universalism, far from being in tension with the universities' service to local social development, actually came to define it, through their embedding of an ideal of service in professional training and in the provision of professional advice to local and national civil society. That commitment was still strong in both Scotland and England at the end of the century, the main conclusion of the Leverhulme project on academics and national identity (Bond and Paterson, 2005; Paterson and Bond, 2005; Paterson, 2003b): academics continued to be committed to such activities as engaging in public debate, or providing advice to government and commerce, and continued to believe that educating the professions remained an important part of the university's task.

In that combination of universalism and localism lies the universities' unique contribution to the definition of Britishness, and hence their contribution to maintaining the balance between imperial unity and local autonomy. The professional ideal was well suited to this balance. Its injunction to graduates to devote their lives to socially useful pursuits inexorably pulled them into public service (including in commercial arenas), to 'low politics', and hence into the networks of civil society which constituted the very identities of Scotland, Wales and the regions of England. They could thus be committed to local patriotism while pursuing their professional vocation. T. H. Green, pioneering this balance, sought to pursue his commitment to social service on no more exalted a political stage than as an elected member of Oxford Town Council (Gordon and White, 1979: 84–5; Richter, 1964: 347–9). R. B. Haldane saw the main field of universities' civic commitment as being in the cities where they were located (Haldane, 1929: 140). At the same time, the universalism of professional standards gave these workers an allegiance that transcended the local; and that higher allegiance could be readily equated with a Britishness that still aspired to be globally significant. The supreme institutional embodiment of this universal idea was in the National Health Service, but it informed everything that the welfare state sought to do.

This argument does not depend on the resolution of an important question about which not much is known, especially historically (Bond et al., 2006: 6–7) – the extent to which graduates of particular universities stayed in the region of these universities for their employment. The argument does not depend on this because localism is intrinsic to a professional vocation, as are the universal principles by which professional practice is meant to be governed. Nevertheless it does seem likely that these ideological attachments were reinforced by decisions about spatial mobility. Even as late as the 1980s, around one half of graduates of English universities remained in the region of the university for employment for at least about a decade (Belfield and Morris, 1999: 248). Such graduates would have carried the teaching of their universities into professional networks locally.

So the leadership exercised by professionals in the era of the welfare state depended upon an aura of service and an attachment to universal principles. Although this ethos was given its philosophical expression in the older universities, it absorbed the newer very quickly; and, by helping to define what it meant to be a professional, embraced even those professionals who were not graduates, and – by the 1970s – had converted almost all professions to the graduate route. To be British was to be universal and hence was to be able and obliged to serve society in all its local specificity.

Conclusions: Mass higher education, devolution and the professional ideal

That world of ethical professionalism, of the local management of social policy by trusted products of the leading educational institutions of the state, now seems rather distant, although not wholly dead. Its faith in elites, its assumption of a common interpretation of social needs based on a Christian ethic, its restriction of politics to legitimising the rule of technocrats, its persistant understanding of liberal education (including science) as the only secure basis of civilisation: these kinds of professional ideals started to vanish in the 1970s under the onslaught of markets and their associated ideologies of choice and empowerment far more than by the challenge of any kind of reinvented communitarianism. Hayek's critique of the thinking of Green et al. has been far more influential than their direct ideological heirs (Faulks, 1998: 53–73). In Scotland and Wales, a questioning of professional trusteeship has been part of the core nationalist project in the same period, eschewing, with Tom Nairn (1997: 194), Walter Scott's 'silent way to national wealth and consequence', the low politics which had lasted for centuries.

Academics, as we have already noted from the Leverhulme project on academics and national identity, do still firmly believe in service, whether directly in their work with local enterprises or government, or indirectly through the students whom they educate (Bond and Paterson, 2005; Paterson and Bond, 2005; Paterson, 2003b). But they are much more likely to interpret this in merely technical terms than to see it as part of any kind of ethical leadership. This kind of instrumentalism is clamorously promoted also by the people who are in charge of most universities, the principals and vice-chancellors and funding councils. They have used a simplistic version of Britishness as a stick with which to beat alleged parochialism, welcoming the globalisation of funding and students, and forgetting the deeply cultural provenance of the universalism which they rhetorically espouse: T. H. Huxley, with his 1880 belief in Birmingham that 'culture means something quite different from learning or technical skill', is as alien to this world as is Newman. The old Arnoldian sense of liberal education as passing on the best that has been thought and said now tends to be held only by those academics who are resistant to social commitment, doubtful about opening access to wider social groups of students and suspicious of nationalist challenges to the British state (Paterson and Bond, 2005). This disjunction between state identity and social commitment is one reason why the older versions of Britishness have been forgotten: it no longer seems possible to believe, in Wales and Scotland, that professional people might be serving their nation precisely because they were putting into effect British universal values.

Nevertheless, matters are perhaps not so straightforward. The first point is that the context of higher education itself is now so different that we must not be misled into believing that a change in the debate about the institutions that are now called universities signals the end of a whole tradition of thought about the ethical basis of professionalism and public service, or has removed the universities from the debate about national identity. Even at the high point of the histories we have briefly analysed here, at the time of the Robbins Report of 1963, fewer than one in ten young people entered any kind of higher education. The proportion at the end of the century was close to four in ten, and in Scotland had surpassed one half. So universities are no longer preparing a professional élite so much as laying the basis of a whole educated class. The politics of higher education is therefore now part of mainstream debate, as exemplified since the 1990s in the question of student fees and grants. Views on such matters, as on many aspects of social policy, are coloured by national identity: for example, people attached to a Scottish identity in Scotland are generally to the left on educational matters of people who are strongly British, whereas in England a British identity remains somewhat more associated with the welfare state and citizenship (Paterson, 2002). This is still a national role for the universities, but of a quite different sort.

Second, although the ethical principle that is most likely to be found among academics today is a belief in equal opportunities, that in fact underpins a belief that the only acceptably liberal view of the nation is that it is multicultural. Academics in the new, mass higher education then have a continued national role in providing fair opportunities, which extends now to actively striving to overcome obstacles (just as the state was, in Green's philosophy, meant to do) and not merely teaching those who arrive at their doors.

Third, the service role of intellectuals has probably never been so strongly felt, but that is now detached from power. Malcolm Bradbury was prophetic of this as long ago as 1964 (Heyck, 1998: 218): most professionals were being distanced from power because of the rise of mass society (entailing a decline of deference), the growing importance of highly abstruse branches of science and technology, improvements in global communication (spectacularly now compared even to when he wrote) and – especially – the expansion of the universities. Becoming a professional is no longer assumed to be a matter of becoming a social leader. It might not unreasonably be said that the century-long concern of university thinkers with the quality of leadership in a democracy, deriving from Carlyle, has been rendered redundant by history, not because its questions have been answered, but because they are no longer regarded as important. Leslie Stephen's confidence in 1867 (Harvie, 1976: 144) that elected leaders would continue to have 'trained

184 Universities and Nations

intellects' because of the traditional deference of voters has long since ceased to be compelling; whether his faith that losing this would be 'a cheap price to pay for filling up the ... social gulf' between leaders and led is a topic for a different debate, although Stephen would not have supposed that one part of this levelling would be through the opening up of the universities to a majority of the population. For our purposes, the main conclusion is that no longer may the professional ideal be taken to include a leading role in shaping national identity. As with the securing of equal opportunities, the professional contributes to the nation in no more salient a manner than the ordinary active citizen.

Furthermore, finally, there remains, in Scotland and Wales at least, a residual sense of the universities as national property. That is partly because of memory – in Wales of the long campaign for a national university and of the cultural controversies which surrounded the resulting institutions, in Scotland because the rhetoric of a 'democratic intellect' entered public debate at the same time as the movement for political self-government was growing. In Scotland, we know also from the Leverhulme project that academics are more likely to associate their work with promoting the Scottish national interest than academics in England are to make any links with England (Paterson, 2003b). It is likely that Wales would be similar to Scotland in this respect. The promotion of student access, or academics' provision of services to the community, can then take on a dimension of cultural nationalism that is officially absent from their own universities' public pronouncements or from the motives of their colleagues in England (Paterson and Bond, 2005). Debates about the meaning of professionalism can still acquire a sense of the national in these two countries, where a myth of educational openness and respect for knowledge is still held to be constitutive of national identity.

Perhaps, though, Scotland and Wales are not now untypical internationally in having a residual sense of a national role for their universities. Perhaps it is still the absence of that in England that has to be explained. Maybe that country is too heterogeneous for this (but it is not much more so than, say, France or the USA, where a national mission for universities remains a feature of public debate). Maybe there continues to be ambiguity arising from the conflation of 'England' with 'Britain'. Above all – and this affects all three nations – there is still a sense that national allegiance is vaguely improper for the putatively universal claims of scholarship. To the extent that this feeling is more muted in Scotland and Wales, it may be a consequence of that strand of these countries' recent nationalism which seeks to be universal – to assert that self-government would remove their nations from an alleged British parochialism in order to join what is claimed to be the European mainstream. English identity, by contrast, is perceived nowadays to be introverted, just as all three were earlier.

None of these caveats contradicts the main point, that an old ideal of professionalism has died, and with it a particular role for the universities in sustaining a peculiarly British form of complementary national identities. There remains almost nothing in the new debates about professionalism that entails any kind of British identity. Individual professional people might remain attached to Britain, but it could not any longer be said that there was much that is intrinsic to their professionalism which required that. To the extent that it tries to be universal, professional identity is now far more likely to be global in aspiration than it is to be merely British or, if not global, then strongly influenced by the professional cultures of North America or of other parts of the European Union. When, in due course, the instrumental idea of a university decays once again, giving way to a resurgence of interest in cultural purposes, it will be a very different kind of culture from the British one which has now passed.

Bibliography

Anderson, R. D. (1983) *Education and opportunity in Victorian Scotland*. Edinburgh: Edinburgh University Press.

Anderson, R. D. (1992) *Universities and elites in Britain since 1800*. London: Macmillan.

Anderson, R. D. (2004) *European universities from the Enlightenment to 1914*. Oxford: Oxford University Press.

Anderson, R. D. (2006a) *British universities past and present*. London: Hambledon.

Anderson, R. D. (2006b) Aristocratic values and elite education in Britain and France. In D. Lancien and L. de Saint Martin (eds), *Anciennes et nouvelles aristocraties de 1880 à nos jours*. Paris: Editions de la Maison des Sciences de l'Homme, 261–78.

Armytage, W. H. G. (1955) *Civic universities: Aspects of a British tradition*. London: Ernest Benn.

Barnett, C. (1986) *The audit of war: The illusion and reality of Britain as a great nation*. London: Macmillan.

Belfield, C. and Morris, Z. (1999) Regional migration to and from higher education institutions: Scale, determinants and outcomes. *Higher Education Quarterly*, **53**, 240–63.

Bogdanor, V. (2006) Oxford and the mandarin culture: The past that is gone. *Oxford Review of Education*, **32**, 147–65.

Bond, R., Grundy, A. and Charsley, K. (2006) *Scottish graduate migration and retention: Initial research findings from a study co-funded by the ESRC and the Scottish Executive*. Edinburgh: Edinburgh University Press.

Bond, R. and Paterson, L. (2005) Coming down from the ivory tower?: Academics' civic and economic engagement with the community. *Oxford Review of Education*, **31**, 331–51.

Boucher, D. and Vincent, A. (2000) *British idealism and political theory*. Edinburgh: Edinburgh University Press.

Boyd, D. (1973) *Elites and their education*. Windsor: NFER.

Bulpitt, J. (1983) *Territory and power in the United Kingdom*. Manchester: Manchester University Press.

Burgess, M. (1995) *The British tradition of federalism*. London: Leicester University Press.

Carr-Saunders, A. and Wilson, P. (1933) *The professions*. Oxford: Clarendon Press.

Cohen, G. B. (1996) *Education and middle-class society in imperial Austria*. West Lafayette: Purdue University Press.

Colley, L. (1992) *Britons: Forging the nation, 1707–1837*. New Haven: Yale University Press.

Committee on Higher Education (1963) *Higher education: Appendix two (B): Students and their education*, Cmnd. 2154. London: HMSO.

Davie, G. E. (1961) *The democratic intellect*. Edinburgh: Edinburgh University Press.

Desmond, A. (1998) *Huxley: From devil's disciple to evolution's high priest*. Harmondsworth: Penguin.

Edgerton, D. E. H. and Horrocks, S. M. (1994) British industrial research and development before 1945. *Economic History Review*, **47**, 213–38.

Elliot, W. (1932) Scottish heritage in politics. In Atholl et al., *A Scotsman's heritage*. London: Alexander Maclehose and Co., 53–65.

Elliott, P. (1972) *The sociology of the professions*. London: Macmillan.

Engel, A. (1983) The English universities and professional education. In K. H. Jarausch (ed.) *The transformation of higher learning, 1860–1930*.Chicago: University of Chicago Press, 293–305.

Faulks, K. (1998) *Citizenship in modern Britain*. Edinburgh: Edinburgh University Press.

Fielding, A. G. and Portwood, D. (1980) Professions and the state: Towards a typology of bureaucratic professions. *Sociological Review*, **28**, 23–53.

Gellner, E. (1983) *Nations and nationalism*. Oxford: Blackwell.

Gordon, P. and White, J. (1979) *Philosophers as educational reformers*. London: Routledge and Kegan Paul.

Grierson, H. (1920) Speech at Annual General Meeting, reported in *Bulletin of the English Association*, no. 41, September, 28–9.

Grierson, H. (1937) *The university and a liberal education*. Edinburgh: Oliver and Boyd.

Haldane, R. B. (1929) *Richard Burdon Haldane: An autobiography*. London: Hodder and Stoughton.

Harris, J. (1992) Political thought and the welfare state 1870–1940: An intellectual framework for British social policy. *Past and Present*, **135**, 116–41.

Harvie, C. (1976) *The lights of Liberalism: University Liberals and the challenge of democracy*. London: Allen Lane.

Harvie, C. (1994) *The rise of regional Europe*. London: Routledge.

Heyck, T. W. (1998) Myths and meanings of intellectuals in twentieth-century British national identity. *Journal of British Studies*, **37**, 192–221.

Hroch, M. (1985) *Social preconditions of national revival in Europe*. Cambridge: Cambridge University Press.

Huxley, T. H. (1874) Universities: Actual and ideal. In *Collected essays Vol. III*. London: Macmillan, 189–233.

Huxley, T. H. (1880) Science and culture. In *Collected essays Vol. III*. London: Macmillan, 134–59.

Jarausch, K. H. (1983) Higher education and social change: Some comparative perspectives. In K. H. Jarausch (ed.) *The transformation of higher learning, 1860–1930*. Chicago: University of Chicago Press, 9–36.

Jenkins, H. and Jones, D. C. (1950) Social class of Cambridge University alumni of the 18th and 19th centuries. *British Journal of Sociology*, **1**, 93–116.

Jenks, C. (1977) T. H. Green, the Oxford philosophy of duty and the English middle class. *British Journal of Sociology*, **28**, 481–97.

Johnson, T. (1972) *Professions and power*. Macmillan.

Jones, G. E. and Roderick, G. W. (2003) *A history of education in Wales*. Cardiff: University of Wales Press.

Keating, M. (1996) *Nations against the state*. London: Macmillan.

Kelsall, R. K. (1955) *Higher civil servants in Britain*. London: Routledge and Kegan Paul.

Lee, J. J. (1989) *Ireland 1912–1985*. Cambridge: Cambridge University Press.

Livingston, W. S. (1956) *Federalism and constitutional change*. Oxford: Clarendon Press.

Malatesta, M. (1995) Introduction: The Italian professions from a comparative perspective. In M. Malatesta (ed.) *Society and the professions in Italy, 1860–1914*. Cambridge: Cambridge University Press, 1–23.

Marshall, T. H. (1939) The recent history of professionalism in relation to social structure and social policy. *Canadian Journal of Economics and Political Science*, **5**, 325–40.

McCrone, D. (2001) *Understanding Scotland*. 2nd edn. London: Routledge.

McHugh, R. J. (1944) *Newman on university education*. Clonskeagh: Browne and Nolan.

Meriggi, M. (1993) The Italian 'borghesia'. In J. Kocka and A. Mitchell (eds) *Bourgeois society in nineteenth century Europe*. Oxford: Berg, 423–38.

Mill, J. S. (1867) *Inaugural address delivered to the University of St Andrews*. London: Longmans, Green, Reader and Dyer.

Millerson, G. (1973) Education in the professions. In Cook, T. G. (ed.), *Education and the professions*. London: Methuen, 1–18.

Morgan, K. (1981) *Rebirth of a nation: Wales 1880–1980*. Cardiff: University of Wales Press.

Nairn, T. (1997). *Faces of nationalism*. London: Verso.

Paterson, L. (1994) *The autonomy of modern Scotland*. Edinburgh University Press.

Paterson, L. (1998) Scottish higher education and the Scottish parliament: the consequences of mistaken national identity. *European Review*, **6**, 459–74.

Paterson, L. (2001) Higher education and European regionalism. *Pedagogy, Culture and Society*, **9**, 133–60.

Paterson, L. (2002) Governing from the centre: Ideology and public policy. In J., Curtice, D., McCrone, A. Park, and L. Paterson, (eds) *New Scotland: New society?* Edinburgh: Edinburgh University Press, 196–218.

Paterson, L. (2003a) *Scottish education in the twentieth century.* Edinburgh: Edinburgh University Press.

Paterson, L. (2003b) The survival of the democratic intellect: Academic values in Scotland and England. *Higher Education Quarterly,* **57**, 67–93.

Paterson, L. and Bond, R. (2005) Have Scottish academic values been eroded? *Scottish Affairs,* no. 52, summer, 15–44.

Paterson, L. and Bond, R. (2005) Higher education and critical citizenship: a survey of academics' views in Scotland and England. *Pedagogy, Culture and Society,* **13**, 205–31.

Perkin, H. (1983) The pattern of social transformation in England. In Jarausch, K. H. (ed.) *The transformation of higher learning, 1860–1930.* Chicago: University of Chicago Press, 207–18.

Perkin, H. (1989) *The rise of professional society.* London: Routledge.

Plant, R. (2006) T. H. Green: Citizenship, education and the law. *Oxford Review of Education,* **32**, 23–37.

Rees, G. and Istance, D. (1997) Higher education in Wales: The (re-)emergence of a national system? *Higher Education Quarterly,* **51**, 49–67.

Richter, M. (1964) *The politics of conscience: T. H. Green and his age.* London: Weidenfeld and Nicolson.

Robertson, P. (1984) Scottish universities and industry, 1860–1914. *Scottish Economic and Social History,* **4**, 39–54.

Rothblatt, S. (1968) *The revolution of the dons: Cambridge and society in Victorian England.* London: Faber and Faber.

Rubinstein, W. D. (1986) Education and the social origins of British élites, 1880–1970. *Past and Present,* **112**, 163–207.

Rubinstein, W. D. (1993) *Capitalism, culture and decline in Britain, 1750–1990.* London: Routledge.

Sanderson, M. (1972) *The universities and British industry, 1850–1970.* London: Routledge and Kegan Paul.

Sanderson, M. (ed.) (1975) *The universities in the nineteenth century.* London: Routledge and Kegan Paul.

Vincent, A. (2007) German philosophy and British public policy: Richard Burdon Haldane in theory and practice. *Journal of the History of Ideas,* **68**, 157–79.

Wandycz, P. S. (1974) *The lands of partitioned Poland, 1795–1918.* Seattle: University of Washington Press.

Watson, D. (1982) Idealism and education: T. H. Green and the education of the middle class. *British Educational Research Journal,* **8**, 73–83.

Wiener, M. (1981) *English culture and the decline of the industrial spirit, 1850–1980.* Princeton: Princeton University Press.

Williams, J. G. (1993) *The university movement in Wales.* Cardiff: University of Wales Press.

Williams, J. G. (1997) *The University of Wales, 1839–1939.* Cardiff: University of Wales Press.

9
Conclusion: The Politics of Identity

Frank Bechhofer and David McCrone

In this concluding chapter, we shall place national identity in its wider context and discuss its impact, especially its wider political impact on society. The thread running through the chapter can be summarised as, 'does national identity matter?' We start with a brief summary of some of the salient findings discussed in this book, and also describe and discuss our approach to studying and understanding national identity. We hope that this section will help the reader to understand the intellectual background to the research reported in this book and how it is carried out, and thus judge its credibility. We then move on to examine in more general terms what we have called the politics of difference. Drawing upon examples from home and abroad, we argue that seemingly fixed categories of difference are rarely that; much depends on how these are construed and mobilised for political and social purposes. In the penultimate section, we summarise how the peoples of the four countries of the United Kingdom do national identity, and how it might be changing, with implications for the future of the British state itself and the potential for further constitutional change in Britain. Finally, we return to our key question: does national identity matter?

When we applied to The Leverhulme Trust for the grant which made possible our studies of national identity and constitutional change starting in 1999, we wrote:

> Rather than being driven by lawyers, constitutional theorists, or even by politicians, the process of internal constitutional and political change in the UK has been motivated and energised, especially in Scotland, Wales and Northern Ireland, by people's identities, their sense of who they are, how they relate to others, and how this sense of self and other is reflected in their systems of governance.

189

Our previous research, and our reading of the work of others, suggested to us that shifts in national identities were the drivers of constitutional change, rather than the other way round. In other words, we sensed that, over time, there had been a 'cultural' shift among the peoples of these islands which led them to foreground their 'national' identity (English, Scottish, Welsh) over their 'state' (British) identity. This, then, is not a book about 'politics', narrowly defined, although we will have more to say about the relationship, if any, between national identity and constitutional change later in this chapter. In many ways, constitutional issues, and in particular devolution in Scotland and Wales, provided an opportunity to develop our understanding of national identity which, over many years, each and severally, we have built up. What underpins our approach to identity in this book is to see it as providing a vocabulary for making sense of, and talking about, social relationships. Like all vocabularies, identities can take on different meanings and nuances.

Understanding identity

What, then, is distinctive about our approaches?[1] The key, for us, to studying the impact of constitutional change on identities was to find particular research locales, critical cases, where changing identity and its consequences were especially salient, contested or problematic. We took the view that national identity is not an epiphenomenon, interesting only in its own right. It defines who we are, how we want to live and how we relate to others. It affects fundamental political, civic and economic issues such as the legitimacy of official policies, social inclusion and exclusion, prejudice and the mobility of capital and labour. In other words, national and other forms of social identity are not to be thought of purely as 'cultural' matters, on the fringes of social and political life.

We see identity as helping to organise social action in all its manifestations. Thus, the *content* of identity (in this context, for example, what it means to be English or Scottish) affects the types of action seen as legitimate or illegitimate, the types of policies and projects that are endorsed or rejected and the types of goals pursued. The *boundaries* of identity (again, who is seen as English or Scottish) will affect who is accepted as part of the community and who is rejected as 'other'. Finally, the *salience* of identity (for example, whether one sees the division between England and Scotland as relatively important or unimportant) will affect where one feels at home and where is one seen as foreign, and the vigour with which the boundaries of identity are enforced. These aspects of identity, of course, are largely a matter of how identities are carried, altered and used by individuals themselves, and in The Leverhulme Trust funded programme on which this book is based, these issues were pursued at the individual level through large-scale surveys of public opinion, intensive interviews with people and experimental work. This part of the research is reflected here in the chapters by Steve Reicher, Nick Hopkins and Kate Harrison (on the power of national identities), by the editors (on being Scottish), by John Curtice and Anthony Heath (on being English) and by Ross Bond (comparing Scotland and England). We were also interested in the relationship between individual and group identity and larger forms of social organisation, that is, how personal identities and those of social organisations in which people were embedded affect each other, and are articulated and expressed in action. This level of the programme is represented here by Jonathan Hearn's chapter based on his research on the nature, salience and consequences of national identity in a Scottish bank, which, as it turned out,[2] became subject to amalgamation with a more aggressive English former building society. The final strand of the programme focused on the institutional level because institutions themselves are involved in producing and nego-tiating national identity, and refracting it back to people themselves. The chapter by Michael Rosie and Pille Petersoo, discussing how the media in Scotland and England produce and mediate understandings of identities in the context of constitutional change, and the final chapter on the universities by Lindsay Paterson, represent this level of enquiry.

National identity then, as this book has shown, is not simply a matter of individual construction and choice, but is claimed in, and affected by, varying contexts. For example, the media help to frame what it means to be Scottish, English and British by reporting – or not – events in a particular way and using key descriptors as to who 'we' are. National identity is also carried by education systems which mould people in the ways of being 'national', by forging links between identity and culture, and in shaping and translating the relation-ship between universalistic values embedded in education and those deemed specific to a particular nation. One might think that attach-ments to place and to culture are as nothing compared to the over-whelming power of capital. Where 'rationalisation' and amalgamation occur in the banking system, for example, how does the language of nation and locality get used, if at all?

This book, then, aims to show that national identity is at one and the same time a political, sociological and psychological phenomenon. We try to get at issues of national identity by asking individuals whether and how they think of themselves in these terms; we examine how national identity is refracted through institutional arrangements; and we also explore how people react in more experimental situations when confronted by sets of powerful symbols and prompts.

Why should we be interested in identity anyway? For some, the concept is too broad and diffuse to be of much analytical use (Brubaker and Cooper, 2000). For others, it captures the decline of 'traditional' social identities. Zygmunt Bauman has observed:

> If the modern 'problem' of identity was how to construct an identity and keep it solid and stable, the postmodern 'problem of identity' is primarily how to avoid fixation and keep the options open. In the case of identity … the catchword of the modern was creation; the catchword of postmodernity is recycling.
>
> (1996: 18)

Whatever their more general merits, we do not find either of these approaches helpful when it comes to understanding national identity. Our research over many years, using a variety of methods and approaches, suggests that national identity does turn analytical handles, and that it is not an empty category; this postmodern perspective is accordingly one with which we have little sympathy.

Even if one doesn't buy into theories of postmodernity, there is the view that collective social identities have fragmented in the face of processes of individualisation in which, according to Beck 'individuals must produce, stage and cobble together their biographies themselves' (1994: 13). In part, this process of individualisation is deemed driven by commerce, in which 'I buy, therefore I am' is the economic expression of consumer supremacy. In Bauman's words:

> [T]ell me what you buy and in what shops you buy it, and I'll you who you are. It seems that with the help of carefully selected purchases, I can make of myself anything I may wish, anything I believe it is worth becoming. Just as dealing with my personal problems is my duty and my responsibility, so the shaping of my personal identity, my self-assertion, making myself into a concrete someone, is my task and my task alone.
>
> (Bauman, 205)

This assertion of individualism is presumed at the expense of collective social identities such as social class. As Stuart Hall has observed: 'Class cannot serve as a discursive device or mobilising category through which all the diverse social interests and identities of people can be reconciled and represented' (1992: 280). In a test of the view that 'traditional' social identities, notably social class, political party identification, religion and national identity, are no longer important to people, and have in fact declined over time, Anthony Heath and his colleagues analysed survey data from 2005, and where data were available, previous time-points. In fact, they discovered that whereas there had been a considerable decline in religious identification in Britain, and some fall in social class and party identification, national identification had suffered the least decline. On the other hand, a 'sense of belonging to the "imagined community" of Britain does not seem to have any marked effect on social attitudes', in the way, for example, that churches once provided powerful normative reference groups (Heath, Martin and Elgenius, 2007: 28). Further, Scottish and Welsh national identities appear to have much stronger senses of community attached to them than English identity.

Even if one accepts that some forms of social identity have taken precedence over others, there is still a question mark over how identity actually operates. Asserting the primacy of 'agency' over 'structure', of personal choice over social constraint, or indeed the other way round, fails to pinpoint how identification actually operates. Put at its simplest, we take the view that identity is not a thing, a badge, but a process; it is not so much a noun (identity) as a verb (identify with); and that it is less a matter of being than of doing. Identity is the vital link between structure and action, the hinge between the two, just as in terms of social class, 'consciousness' is the hinge element between social structure and social action. The problem of conventional studies of national identity is treating it as a 'thing', an immutable badge affixed to people by virtue of birth or citizenship or ancestry.

The more appropriate metaphor, in our view, is not identity as badge, but identity as prism, a set of criteria for judging the appropriateness or otherwise of claims made by self and others. In some circumstances national identity, however construed, will be salient, and at other times, not. National identity is not an essence, but a framework through which processes and events are refracted. It is a frame of reference which people actively construct, modify and apply for themselves in particular contexts. It is both given to them, and made by them in the course of everyday interactions. It is systematic and ubiquitous, although in most situations it doesn't tell us precisely how to behave. As Steve Reicher, Nick Hopkins and Kate Harrison show, it all depends on what people are trying to say, and who they are comparing themselves with in order to say it. We take the view that national identity is a bit like a playing card in a pack which you use at an opportune moment. What matters is less its face value than how you choose to deploy it in the game. In this respect, national or territorial identity is one of a range of social identities which people adapt or mobilise for different purposes and at different times. The novelist Philip Pullman (2005) has written cogently and forcefully that in conventional usage, '"identity" is a coarse and inaccurate parody encumbered with half-baked baggage and with mis-understanding, resentment and hostility trailing behind it', in large part because it is treated as a noun, rather than a verb, with the effect that people are judged for what they are, and not for what they do. Something similar operates in the distinction between 'prejudice' and 'bigotry', the former being a set of beliefs and attitudes, the latter a set of social actions. One can prosecute the latter in law, but not the former at least while these views remain largely 'internal' to the person. Indeed strictly speaking such beliefs and attitudes are not externally accessible. Even if people make others aware of their views, there is a fine line between expressing a belief (which is admittedly a form of action), and actions based on those beliefs which are subject to the law. In Western societies at least, you cannot prosecute people for their beliefs alone, and once you try to do so there are serious implications for how society operates. Once the law moves off the firmer ground of judging actions into punishing beliefs ('glorifying terrorism', for example, as thought rather than action) then it is on dangerous and illiberal territory. One can, of course, seek to change people's attitudes through education, discussion, persuasion, but only actions are punishable, that is, when thoughts are translated into illegal practices.

How does this apply to our understandings of national identity? The 'being' aspect of national identity is, as we have seen, fairly inactive and implicit (McIlvanney's 'insurance policy' again, or Billig's 'banal' nationalism). It is the raw material of social action, usually necessary but not sufficient, waiting to be shaped and mobilised as and when circumstances permit. In this respect, national identity is a fairly passive thing, not given shape until it is 'done', that is, performed. We can, of course, get some inkling from the way people talk about national iden-tity as to how they might put their attitudes to the test. Thus, when we asked people how they would judge the claims of various others to be 'national', we found that these were systematically structured around key criteria: birthplace, residence, ancestry, accent, 'race' and so on. We cannot say categorically that they would act upon these judgements, because they are usually not called upon to do so, and also few studies are able to observe the process. However, these views provide the raw attitudinal materials which can be mobilised at certain times and in certain situations. Political entrepreneurs, for example, may seek to include or exclude some people from access to social and political goods on the basis of not being 'one of us'. They may try to foreground some criteria and background others. Thus, those on the Right may deem place of birth to be the key discriminator, until it becomes, for their purposes, inoperable: for instance people they deem 'undesirables' may actually be born in the country and have 'national' passports, at which point some other cultural marker such as skin colour or religion or language/accent may become the defining feature which makes the group 'not one of us'.

The politics of difference

In short, identity matters crucially in the politics of difference. Here we pass into radical methodological territory. Even the identity categories cannot be taken for granted. We may imagine, for example, that we are dealing with fixed categories; Scottish, English, British and so on may seem obvious enough, but we cannot make *a priori* assumptions about the content of these categories. *We* may be fairly sure in our own minds, but the person we are talking to may or may not share our understandings.[3] Much of the literature, for example, on ethnic conflict tends to assume the fixity of the social categories: Hutus and Tutsis in Rwanda; Serbs/Croats/Bosnians in the former Yugoslavia. And closer to home: Catholics and Protestants in Northern Ireland. Or should that be Nationalists and Unionists? As soon as we ask that question, we query the basis for the categories themselves. Are we treating 'Catholic' as the proxy for Nationalist, 'Protestant' for Unionist, or is it the other way round? If we use the 'religious' categories, are we assuming that it is a 'religious' conflict at heart? And if we use the 'constitutional' categories, do we take it that in essence it is about whether or not one accepts the partition of Ireland, that it is basically a 'political' conflict and that religion is simply a handy proxy? And does it matter? We may take the view, like Humpty Dumpty in *Alice in Wonderland*: 'When I use a word, it means just what I choose it to mean, neither more or less'. We may have more sympathy with Alice's response: 'The question is whether you can make words mean so many different things'; and even more with Humpty Dumpty's retort: 'The question is, which is to be master, that's all'. In other words, it is a matter of power.

The point is a serious one. The seemingly fixed categories are often ambiguous and tendentious. By all accounts, the divisions between Hutus and Tutsis in Rwanda were created by Belgian imperialists as a way of dividing and ruling in nineteenth century, even though there was little or nothing 'essential' about the difference (Straus, 2006). The social anthropologist, Michael Banton, tells an at first sight amusing tale with serious import. An anthropologist carrying out a study in Ontario, Canada, found residents there referred to (and self-referring) as Ukranians. One man who said that, was asked by the anthropologist which part of Ukraine his family came from. 'They didn't', replied the man. 'They came from Poland. I'm a Polack' (Banton, 1997: 8–9). Banton observed: 'The man was willing to be taken for a Ukrainian because that was the local convention. The local people were not interested in what they saw as the finer details of differentiation in a faraway land. It is in this way that ethnic identities are redefined in new situations' (Banton: 9). There are many examples of such 'refinements'. In nineteenth-century Scotland, for example, migrants from Lithuania became known locally as 'Polish' because that was the more familiar and meaningful category in use among indigenous Scots in the coalfields of the Central Belt[4] (Kay, 1996).

The example we gave earlier of ethnic categories from the former Yugoslavia had deadly consequences. When the state collapsed, historic and ill-remembered rivalries between Serb, Croat and Muslim were activated and amplified, even though objective differences between the groups were minimal, rates of intermarriage very high and co-residence the norm. Thomas Eriksen comments: 'Ethnic boundaries, dormant for decades, were activated; presumed cultural differences which had been irrelevant for two generations were suddenly "remembered" and invoked as proof that it was impossible for the two groups to live side by side. It is only when they *make a difference* (his emphasis) in interaction that cultural differences are important in the creation of ethnic boundaries' (1993: 39). Banton concurs. He cites the work of F. G. Bailey who studied a small Croatian town in 1983 where people lived amicably, while ten years later 'men were away fighting in one or another army; marriages had broken; households had been dispersed as members fled to whatever they claimed to be an ethnic homeland or to refugee camps' (Banton, 2000: 492). Bailey (1996) himself studied castes in Bisipara, India on two occasions. In the first peaceful encounter, he found an awareness of difference, that while racist, people were not obsessed with race; rather, their racism was innocuous because ritualised politeness shaped public discourse. People operated with 'calculated restraint', and what appeared as an ethical rule – moderation in all things – turned out to be a rule based on expediency, the rule regulating conflict. By 1994, Bailey found that things had changed. The media played a key role in amplifying and 'explaining' the conflict which had arisen between Hindus and Muslims around the Ayodhya mosque/ temple site. So too did outside political 'entrepreneurs' and activists. Banton observes in his commentary on Bailey's work: 'The mobilisers' actions stimulate counter-actions from similar persons in opposed groups, and when each side nurses its grievances, conflict escalates, especially if people on one side fail to predict how the others will react. It would appear that sometimes atrocities are perpetuated in order to accelerate processes of escalation' (2000: 495).

What, one might ask, has such violence between ethnic groups to do with national identity in these islands, and in particular, relations between the English, Scots, Welsh and Irish/Northern Irish? It may well seem alarmist to talk about violence and conflict when none such exists, at least on the British mainland. Indeed, some even argue that talking about differences is to talk up differences to the point where they are taken seriously. That is to miss the point. Indeed, there is a tendency in the literature on nationalism to assume that conflict arises because there is a prior and essential difference between social and ethnic groups, whereas, as the examples above illustrate, the truth is probably closer to the view that differences are amplified and made meaningful in the context of conflict. In other words, and to overstate it somewhat: it is not so much that difference generates conflict, as that conflict generates difference. Banton makes three crucial points: firstly, that the key distinction is between classification and nomenclature: 'People give to themselves names which show who they claim to be rather than who they actually are' (1997: 15). Sometimes, rights to names are restricted or have serious political, economic and social implications (like calling yourself 'Kurdish' in Turkey). Secondly, physical differences do not of themselves give rise to cultural differences. It is what people read off signs and markers that matters. The drawing of social boundaries may be influenced by physical characteristics but is not determined by it. 'Phenotypes', outward appearances which are then coupled with genotypes, such as reading skin colour as evidence of the existence of 'race', may operate more exclusively in racially divided societies. Thirdly, it is important to appreciate that the same word may be used with different meanings, and especially that behaviour operates at three levels: people perceive differences (between Americans, Scots, English and so on); they use these perceptions as signs of expected behaviour (Americans are rich; Scots are mean; English are stand-offish), thereby assigning social meaning to categories; and finally, they combine these social meanings to describe who belongs where in classificatory terms, in the extent to which people are 'one of us' or 'unlike us' or even 'hostile to us'.

National identity and the break-up of Britain?

So what can we say about the relationship between national identity and constitutional change in these islands? There is a *prima facie* case for assuming that constitutional change, setting up a parliament in Scotland, and assemblies in Wales and Northern Ireland, is changing people's sense of national identity. After all, as we write, there is a Nationalist government in Edinburgh, albeit a minority one; Plaid Cymru share power with Labour in Wales, and Sinn Féin do likewise with the Democratic Unionists in Northern Ireland. Further, disquiet about how England is governed has arguably grown, especially in the light of the so-called West Lothian question whereby MPs from non-English constituencies at Westminster can vote there on all English matters, but have no control in their own nation over similar issues which are devolved. This leads to a potentially divisive asymmetry as the powers of MPs from English constituencies do not, of course, include devolved legislation.[5] At the time of the 1997 election, devolution was seen by its unionist opponents as 'the thin end of the wedge' leading to the break-up of the United Kingdom, and by its nationalist supporters as the stepping stone to full independence.

In truth, there is no simple answer to these questions. To be sure, the steadily growing pressure for some measure of Scottish devolution dates from before the Second World War, and is clearly fuelled by a sense of Scottish identity. There was, however, no sizeable *change* in that sense of identity which resulted in the devolution settlement. Similarly, thus far, devolution does not seem to have resulted in sizeable changes in national identity. A number of authors in this book make the related point that the relationship between people's national identity and their constitutional preferences is relatively slight. Knowing the first does not allow you to infer the second, or vice versa. Granted, most of this research is focused on Scotland (see, for example, the chapters by Ross Bond and the editors); but in England the relationship is similar if perhaps even more complex (see Curtice and Heath).

What, then, of Wales? We saw in Chapter 4 that the *distribution* of national identity there is somewhere between Scotland's and England's in that the Welsh are more Welsh than the English are English, but not as much as the Scots are Scottish. Is, however, the relationship between national identity and constitutional preferences any closer? It could be, for example, that compared with Scotland, while there may be fewer describing themselves as Welsh, not British, those who do so – what we might call a nationalist core – make a stronger connection between national identity and constitutional preference. In fact, the relationship in Wales is somewhat looser than the one in Scotland. There are indeed fewer describing themselves as Welsh, not British: 21 per cent say this while the equivalent figure is 31 per cent in Scotland (2003 data). Twenty three per cent of these Welsh 'nationals' identify with the nationalist party, Plaid Cymru, compared with 29 per cent of Scottish 'nationals' who identify with the Scottish National Party. Further, only 21 per cent of Welsh 'nationals' want an independent Wales, compared with 47 per cent of Scottish 'nationals' who want an independent Scotland. It seems safe to conclude then that both in Scotland and in Wales there is no close alignment between national identity, constitutional preferences and party identification. As is so often the case with such findings, once we know this we may be tempted to take it as an obvious wisdom. In truth, however, it is somewhat counter-intuitive. Nor are Scotland and Wales exceptional in this regard because in similarly understated nations, such as Catalonia and Quebec, there appears to be a similar lack of alignment (*Scottish Affairs*, 2001).

Let us, however, briefly address the question of national identity in Wales and Northern Ireland, the territories relatively neglected in the chapters of this book. We cannot compare the four countries of the UK systematically because the same questions are not asked consistently in the four countries, nor do surveys occur in identical years. Scotland, England and Wales, for example, were surveyed in 2003 using our preferred Moreno question, while Northern Ireland did not use it. Summarised simply, however, Wales lies somewhere between Scotland and England with 18 per cent declaring themselves 'mainly British' (compared with 8 per cent in Scotland and 23 per cent in England) and 40 per cent claiming a 'mainly national' identity (compared with 69 per cent in Scotland and 40 per cent in England).

The identity preferences in Northern Ireland are in many respects not comparable because of the very different constitutional politics of Northern Ireland, bedevilled as they are by religious difference. Territorial identities in the Province are highly politicised, and they correlate strongly with religion (Protestant or Catholic) and with constitutional preference (Unionist or Nationalist). In 2006, according to the Northern Ireland Life and Times survey, 61 per cent of Catholics said they were Irish, and only 11 per cent British, while 63 per cent of Protestants said they were British, and only 3 per cent Irish. Around a quarter of both Catholics (23 per cent) and Protestants (26 per cent) said they were Northern Irish. In 2007, the Moreno question was asked in Northern Ireland for the first time, and the findings further confirm that no meaningfully straightforward comparison can be made between Northern Ireland and the other countries of the UK. Catholics see themselves overwhelmingly as 'mainly Irish' (75 per cent) with only 5 per cent seeing themselves as mainly British. These proportions are then reversed for Protestants. It is something of an irony that the strongest group of British identifiers do not actually live on the British mainland but in Northern Ireland.

Do we have any sense as to how these distributions may be changing? If there was a steady and sizeable decline in Britishness then that might be thought to threaten the future of the UK. Again, briefly summarising data for 2006, there is a shift in England away from being British, although the movement is into the category 'equally English and British'; there is no shift to speak of towards being mainly or simply English. In Scotland there is no change. The overall trend seems to be that 'British' is ceasing to be a primary identity. England is down to 14 per cent from 25 per cent, Scotland is steady on 8 per cent (possibly a floor effect), and it seems safe to assume that if the question had been asked, the 18 per cent for Wales in 2003 would have been down to or below the English level. Only in Northern Ireland, at least from the 2006 figures, do a majority of the population say they are British if forced to choose, but when given the option, as on multiple identities, this falls to 38 per cent, with the two options 'Irish' (28 per cent), and 'Northern Irish' (26 per cent) making up the majority between them.

Returning to the central issue, does any of this really matter? Could the United Kingdom survive if most people did not actually think of themselves as 'British'? There are a number of caveats to be raised before we conclude that there is something of an identity crisis in the British state. First of all, it is not really a question of being *either* national *or* British, but being *both* national *and* British. After all, it is the case that if people are allowed to choose multiple identities, a clear majority in England (68 per cent), Wales (56 per cent in 2003) and Northern Ireland (56 per cent, where the options are 'British' or 'Irish' or 'British and Irish'), and slightly under a majority in Scotland (43 per cent) say they are British, even though more in Scotland, Wales and Northern Ireland, and virtually the same proportion in England opt for 'national' identities. Only when asked to choose one of these multiple identities do people relegate being British to secondary importance.

In other words, British identity would only become seriously problematic if push came to shove either in changing economic conditions or as a result of political action. If, for example, politicians forced people to choose between national and state identities or insisted on foregrounding citizenship at the expense of national identities, then a political crisis might possibly arise. On the other hand, as long as people are able to mix and match the two, to treat 'British' as some sort of loose set of political, constitutional and cultural commonalities, then it is less problematic. We also know that even those people who do not describe themselves as British are not minded to take a negative view of what British means. In short, while they themselves do not choose to be British, they have little animus towards British iconography and history.

The second caveat relates to what these terms, British, English, Scottish, Welsh and Irish, mean. Simply because to date there has been little connection in England, Scotland and Wales between national identities and people's political and constitutional proclivities (things are again very different in Northern Ireland[6]), it does not mean to say that this will continue in perpetuity. We have described national identities as 'cultural' rather than 'political' because the primary content of these identities is to do with English, Scottish and Welsh culture and they are not infused with political purpose. In other words, just because people deny that they are British, or treat it as secondary to their national identity, most of them are not, at present anyway, wishing away the British state. Paradoxically, the greatest threat to the British state might be if those most anxious to defend it, who seem happy to describe themselves as 'unionists', were to assert its primacy over national identity, and seek to squeeze citizens into a narrow and uniform box. This largely nineteenth-century view of nationality as citizenship seems ill-placed in the multinational and multicultural world of the twenty-first century. Seizing people metaphorically by the throat and insisting that, if you are 'one of us', you must accept a particular understanding of your identity which prioritises a 'state' identity seems neither possible nor desirable. Policing national identity by micromanaging what is included and excluded is not appropriate to modern times, especially in a multinational society like Britain with older and deeply rooted national senses. Certainly, trying to insist on such in

Scotland, Wales and Northern Ireland is unlikely to work. Ironically, it might only stand a chance in England because of the erstwhile conflation, in many English people's minds, of England and Britain, and the fact that England holds 85 per cent of the UK population. Even in England, however, the trends in national identity reported earlier would seem to be running in the opposite direction.

This brings us back to the key point: national identities resemble symbolic containers which contain a jumble of raw materials and historic legacies. If Willie McIlvanney is right, and people are unsure about the precise content of being Scottish or English or Welsh or British, or even Northern Irish, it is because these resemble a dressing-up trunk containing a variety of assemblages to be mixed and matched as required. If politicians and other political entrepreneurs were to insist that there are only limited ways of being a 'national', that only certain people are 'really' nationals, and that everyone has to believe and behave according to fixed rules, then the centre would be unlikely to hold.

Politicians, and for that matter constitutional theorists, should then take note of the research which has been discussed in this book because, if you don't know what you are working with, if you do not understand the social, cultural and political nuances involved, you run the risk of working against rather than with the flow. We have moved beyond the view that constitutional reform is largely a technical matter of ordering and reordering from on high the apparatus of state and its institutions. The skill lies in reading national runes, going with the cultural flow, capturing the sense of national narrative. We can usually tell when a politician, for example, checks the mood and gives it expression, and moves it on; and, of course, and possibly more often, when they can not.

National identity and the potential for change

So, in conclusion, can we answer the question we set ourselves at the beginning of this chapter: does national identity actually matter? One of the key findings of this book is that we can unequivocally say that it does. People use national identity as a key descriptor of themselves; they rate it at least as highly as some of the more taken-for-granted forms of social identity such as being a parent, a partner, a worker, one's gender and social class. It also matters to people because it is an important part of the calculus of social inclusion and exclusion, about who has the right to have access to society's goods and services, and who does not. We have been at pains throughout this book to stress that national identity is 'real'; it is not a figment of politicians' talk (or academics' intellectual fancies, for that matter), nor is it a device of false consciousness to take people's minds off more material forms of social power like social class. We have argued, however, that one should not essentialise national identity, treating it as a taken-for-granted social category, which is the opposite fault. The social world, in other words, is not divided up between 'real' and 'unreal' interests. Talking about national identity is an important way of describing and explaining the world about us. We reach for national descriptors as ways of making sense of things, but not to the exclusion of other descriptors. Social class, gender, ethnicity, national identity and so on are not somehow in competition with each other. There is no one 'right' way of seeing the world, and no one correct language for talking about it.

This does not, of course, explain how and when accounts of social difference are used. Accounting for social difference in terms of social class, gender, ethnicity and national identity may be more meaningful in some situations than in others, for some people more than others. Scots, for example, may make more use of the notion of national iden-tity than English people because it may stand for perceived unequal relationships of power. They may use it to make sense of imbalances, just as we know that women are more likely to use the language of gen-der, and working class people that of social class. In so doing, we can talk about who 'we' are and who we are not, and, crucially, why. Those differences, and how we talk about them, may simply be part of the common currency of everyday life. They are not especially 'political', perhaps even not at all political, most of the time. They do, however, have the potential to be mobilised for political purposes. 'National' cultural differences have the capacity to 'matter' more, to be more significant in people's accounts, as political entrepreneurs attempt to make use of them, although we should never underestimate people's capacity to see through such attempts. In other words, urging people to act 'in the national interest' may simply fall on deaf ears, unless and until they perceive that the social, political and cultural conditions are right. In party politics, there are many attempts at kite-flying, most of which fail, or are closed down by those in higher authority. Issues become more pressing because they are perceived to matter more on the ground. Anomalies like the so-called West Lothian question, which we discussed earlier and which has been around as long as the 300 years in which the British state has been in existence, only matter and lead to demands for their rectification when the wider political climate deems them to be important, and in some sense an affront to the 'proper' way of doing things. In all probability, such an anomaly would never have increased in salience without an amplified sense of Scottish–English differences, just as such differences would not be as important without such anomalies. If this book helps us see that national identity matters, but not necessarily in a predictable and inevitable way, then we will have achieved our task.

Notes

1. We do not wish to imply that everyone contributing to this book buys in to our interpretation. As will be clear from reading the chapters, the authors approach the study of national – and broader social – identities from a variety of perspectives and backgrounds.
2. The research was originally planned to explore national identity in the Scottish bank setting. Shortly after the research began, the amalgamation was proposed and put into operation, thereby providing the opportunity to study national identity under conditions of considerable organisational change. Ironically, as we write this concluding chapter, HBOS itself seems likely to disappear, merging with Lloyds TSB as a result of the banking crisis.
3. In practice of course, this is precisely what most people do assume most of the time, with consequences ranging from the comic to the serious.
4. 'The Lithuanian children suffered the usual playground taunts and the cry of "dirty Poles" appears to have been heard in most Lanarkshire schools at one time or another during this period'. (M. Rodgers, 'The Lanarkshire Lithuanians', in Kay, 1996: 25)
5. This somewhat oversimplifies the situation and the idea of English-only legislation is somewhat misleading. The Barnett formula leads to variations in the funds passed to the devolved territories which depend on the pattern of English spending. Thus any English spending changes on education, health and so on have knock-on effects.
6. Whereas 65 per cent of the 'Irish, not British' want Northern Ireland to reunify with the rest of Ireland, 66 per cent of the 'British, not Irish' want to remain within the UK with a devolved assembly. A further 26 per cent of the 'British, not Irish' want direct rule within the UK (Northern Ireland Life and Times survey, 2007. About 25 per cent of 'Irish, not British' are content to remain within the UK.

Bibliography

Bailey, F. G. (1996) *The civility of indifference: On domesticating ethnicity*. Ithaca, NY: Cornell University Press.
Banton, M. (1997) *Ethnic and racial consciousness*. London: Pearson.
Banton, M. (2000) Ethnic conflict. *Sociology*, **34**, 481–98.
Bauman, Z. (1996) From pilgrim to tourist – or a short history of identity. In S. Hall and P. DuGay (eds) *Questions of cultural identity*. London: Sage.
Beck, U. (1994) The reinvention of politics: Towards a theory of reflexive modernisation. In U. Beck, A. Giddens and S. Lash. *Reflexive modernisation: Politics,*

tradition and aesthetics in the modern social order. Cambridge: Cambridge University Press.

Bond, R., McCrone, D. and Brown, A. (2003) National identity and economic development: Reiteration, recapture, reinterpretation and repudiation. *Nations and Nationalism,* **9**, 371–91.

Brubaker, R. and Cooper, F. (2000) Beyond 'Identity'. *Theory and Society,* **29**, 1–47.

Eriksen, T. H. (1993) *Ethnicity and nationalism.* London: Pluto Press.

Hall, S. (1992) The question of cultural identity. In S. Hall, D. Held and T. McGrew (eds) *Modernity and its futures.* Cambridge: Polity Press.

Heath, A., Martin, J. and Elgenius, G. (2007) Who do we think we are? The decline of traditional social identities. In *British Social Attitudes, The 23rd Report.* London: Sage.

Jenkins, R. (1996) *Social identity.* London: Routledge.

Kay, B. (1996) *The complete Odyssey: Voices from Scotland's recent past.* Edinburgh: Polygon.

Pullman, P. (2005) Identity crisis. *Guardian,* 19 November.

Scottish Affairs (2001) Stateless nations in the 21st century: Scotland, Catalonia and Quebec. Special issue.

Straus, S. (2006) *The order of genocide: Race, power, and war in Rwanda.* Ithaca, NY: Cornell University Press.

Index

Abell, Jackie, 65–6, 89, 94n8
Aberdare, Lord, 172
academics, 182
accents, 6, 28, 80, 86, 147, 157–8
age, 70
aims of book, 15
ancestry, 6, 74, 78, 83, 91
Anderson, Benedict, 2, 4, 122
Anderson, Robert David, 163, 171,
    172, 174
army, 168
Armytage, Walter Harry Green, 175
Arnold, Matthew, 167, 176, 182
arts managers, 5, 8
attitudes, 194
    political, 95–121
authoritarian views, 115–16, 118

Bailey, Frederick George, 196–7
banal nationalism *see under*
    nationalism
Bank of Scotland, 12, 145, 147–8, 191
    see also HBOS
    organisational culture, 148–51, 153,
        159–60
Bannockburn, battle of, 38
Banton, Michael, 196, 197–8
Barnett, Corelli, 170
Barnett formula *see* public spending
Bauman, Zygmunt, 192
BBC
    *BBC Network News and
        Current-Affairs Coverage of the
        Four UK Nations,* 138, 139, 140,
        141, 142
    Radio 4, 123, 132
    Radio Scotland, 123, 132, 136, 137
    Scotland, 136–7
    Six O'Clock News, 128, 140–1
Bechhofer, Frank, 8, 11–12, 97, 160–1,
    191, 198
Beck, Ulrich, 192
Belfast Telegraph, 128

beliefs, 95, 96–7, 194
Bell, Daniel, 4
Berwick-upon-Tweed, 6–7
Billig, Michael, 1, 9, 76, 94n6, 122–3,
    125, 194
Birmingham University College,
    170, 175
birthplace, 5, 74, 78–9, 81, 82, 90, 195
Bisipara, India, 196–7
Bismarck myth, 38
Bogdanor, Vernon, 179
Bond, Ross, 11, 64–5, 73, 191, 198
border areas, 6–7
Bosnians, 195, 196
Bradbury, Malcolm, 183
British National Party (BNP), 90–1
Britishness, 1–2, 42, 44, 45, 61, 91–2,
    98, 133–4, 200–1
    and universities, 164, 180–1, 182,
        184–5
British Social Attitudes surveys,
    10–11, 43, 97, 98
Brubaker, Rogers, 3
Bruce, King Robert the, 38
Bulgaria, 23
Bulpitt, Jim, 166, 167
Burns, Robert, 17, 38

Caird, Edward, 179
Cambridge University, 170, 174
Campaign for an English
    Parliament, 48
capitalism, 144, 145, 146
Carlyle, Thomas, 167, 183
Catalonia, 199
Catholic emancipation, 164–5
Cavendish laboratories, 170
Chamberlain, Joseph, 175
Channel 4 News, 128
churches *see* religion
citizenship, 42, 66
civic universities, 170, 174–5, 176
civil service, 168